History of the Expedition
to Russia, 1812

Volume One

MURAT

History of the Expedition to Russia, 1812

Volume One

General Count Philippe de Ségur

Quamquam animus meminisse horret, luctuque refugit,
Incipiam.— VIRGIL

NONSUCH

First published 1836
Copyright © in this edition 2005
Nonsuch Publishing Ltd

Nonsuch Publishing Limited
The Mill, Brimscombe Port, Stroud, Gloucestershire, GL5 2QG
www.nonsuch-publishing.com

British Library Cataloguing in Publication Data.
A catalogue record for this book is available from the British Library.

ISBN 1-84588-021-8

Typesetting and origination by Nonsuch Publishing Limited
Printed in Great Britain by Oaklands Book Services Limited

CONTENTS

BOOK V

BOOK VI

BOOK VII

INTRODUCTION TO THE
MODERN EDITION

WHEN the remains of Napoleon's *Grande Armée* finally found its way out of Russia and back to France, one of the survivors of the campaign was Philippe Paul, comte de Ségur, a steadfast follower of Napoleon. Born in 1780, he was the son of Louis Philippe, comte de Ségur (who, like his son, was an army officer and a historian), and Antoinette d'Aguesseau. In 1800 de Ségur was inspired to join Napoleon's cavalry as an ordinary recruit after witnessing a parade in Paris and soon afterwards obtained a commission. He served under General Étienne-Jacques-Joseph-Alexandre MacDonald in the Grisons in 1800–01, and his first publication was a record of this campaign, published in 1802.

It was also in 1802 that Colonel Geraud Duroc, later the duc de Frioul, an aide-de-camp to Napoleon Bonaparte, found a position for de Ségur on the personal staff of the *Premier Consul*. In this capacity he witnessed most of the major campaigns of the Consulate and the First Empire and was often employed on diplomatic missions. However, de Ségur saw himself as a soldier rather than a diplomat, and it was a result of his involvement in Napoleon's campaign in Poland (1806-07) that he gained his first experience of Russia. Fighting under the command of General Rapp, commander of the cavalry advance-guard, he was taken prisoner by the Cossacks after leading a charge at the enemy and was kept at Vologda for six months until the French victory at Friedland led to his release.

The following year, his participation in the cavalry action at Sommo-Sierra in Spain during the Peninsular War earned him the rank of colonel, although wounds sustained during the engagement forced him to return to France. He went back to Russia in 1812, this time as a general of brigade in Napoleon's invading army, and in this position he was an eye-witness to the suffering, misery and destruction wreaked upon that force by the Russian army, people and weather. Having survived this disastrous expedition, he went on to fight throughout 1813 and 1814, distinguishing himself at Hanau, near Leipzig, in 1813, when France's ally Bavaria turned against her, and at Reims in 1814. He continued to serve in the army after the restoration of the French monarchy in 1815, but during the so-called 'Hundred Days' he accepted a commission under Napoleon and as a result, after Napoleon's defeat, he was retired from active service. However, in 1831, after the 'July Monarchy' of King Louis Philippe had come to power, he was promoted to lieutenant-general and created a peer, while in 1847 he was awarded the grand cross of the Legion of Honour. He retired permanently after the establishment of the Second Republic in 1848 and died in Paris on 25 February 1873.

In 1824 the first edition of de Ségur's *Histoire de Napoléon et de la grande armée pendant l'année 1812* was published. Surprisingly critical of Napoleon's decision to invade Russia and indeed of the execution of the entire campaign, this account aroused controversy among its survivors and led to a duel between de Ségur and General Gourgaud, who had also been part of the campaign and was incensed at the criticism. In later editions Gourgaud was used as a source to contradict some of de Ségur's more critical points, yet Gourgaud has also been criticised, for refusing to recognise Napoleon's failings. De Ségur provides a personal and vivid account of the destruction of an army, from its glorious and confident entry into Russia to the disintegration of order and the harrowing escape of the remnants from a people and land who remain unconquered to this day.

EDITORIAL NOTE: The footnotes are from the 1836 edition.

TO THE VETERANS
OF THE GRAND ARMY

COMRADES,

I HAVE undertaken the task of tracing the History of the Grand Army and its Leader during the year 1812. I address it to such of you as the frost of the North has disarmed, and who can no longer serve their country, but by the recollection of their misfortunes and their glory. Stopped short in your noble career, you exist much more in the past than in the present; but when the recollections are so grand, it is allowable to live solely on them. I am not afraid, therefore, that by placing before you the most disastrous of your deeds of arms, I shall disturb that repose which you have so dearly purchased. Who is there of us but knows, that from the depth of his obscurity the gaze of the fallen man is involuntarily directed towards the splendour of his past existence—even when its light falls on the shoal on which the bark of his fortune was shattered, and when it displays the fragments of the greatest of shipwrecks?

For myself, I will own, that an irresistible feeling perpetually carries me back to that calamitous epoch of our public and private misfortunes. My memory feels a sort of melancholy pleasure in contemplating and renewing the painful traces which so many horrors have left in it. Is the soul, also, proud of her deep and numerous scars? Does she delight in displaying them? Are they a property of which she has reason to be proud? Or is it rather, that, after the desire of knowing them, her first wish is to impart to others her sensations? To feel, and to excite feeling, are not these the most powerful springs of our souls?

But, in short, whatever may be the cause of the feeling which actuates me, I yield to the desire of retracing the various sensations which I experienced during that fatal war. I have employed my leisure hours in disentangling, arranging, and methodically combining my scattered and confused recollections. Comrades! I also call on you for yours! Suffer not to be lost such great remembrances, which have been so dearly purchased; for us they are the only property which the past leaves to the future. Single, against so many enemies, ye fell with greater glory than they rose. Learn, then, that there was no shame in being vanquished! Raise again those noble fronts, which have been furrowed with all the thunders of Europe! Cast not down those eyes, which have seen so many subjugated capitals, so many vanquished kings! Fortune, doubtless, owed you a more glorious repose; but, such as it is, it depends on yourselves to make a noble use of it. Commit to history your recollections. The solitude and silence of misfortune are propitious to her labours; and let truth, which is always present in the long nights of adversity, at last enlighten labours that may not prove unproductive.

As for me, I will avail myself of the privilege, sometimes painful, sometimes glorious, of telling what I have seen. Perhaps I may be thought to have retraced with too scrupulous care its most minute details; but I felt that nothing was too minute in that prodigious genius and those gigantic feats, without which we should never have known the extent to which human strength, glory, and misfortune, may be carried.

BOOK I

CHAPTER I

RELATIONS OF FRANCE AND RUSSIA SINCE 1807

EVER since 1807, when the space between the Rhine and the Niemen had been passed, the two great empires of which these rivers were the boundaries had become rivals. By his concessions at Tilsit, at the expense of Prussia, Sweden, and Turkey, Napoleon had satisfied only Alexander. That treaty was the result of the defeat of Russia, and the date of her submission to the continental system. It attacked the honour of the Russians, which some of them were capable of comprehending, and their interest, which all could understand.

By the continental system Napoleon had declared an internecive war against the English; to that system he attached his honour, his political existence, and that of the nation under his sway. That system banished from the Continent all merchandise which was English, or had paid duty in any shape to England. It could not be established without the unanimous consent of the continent, and that consent could not be hoped for but under a sole and universal dominion.

France had besides alienated the peoples by her conquests, and the monarchs by her revolution and her new dynasty. Henceforth she could not have either friends or rivals, but merely subjects; for the first would have been false, and the second implacable: it followed that all must be subject to her, or she to all.

From a conviction of this sort, her leader, influenced also by his situation, and urged on by his enterprising character, filled his mind with the vast project of becoming sole master of Europe, by crushing Russia, and wresting Poland from her sway. He had so much difficulty in concealing this project, that indications of it began to escape him in all directions. The immense preparations which so distant an enterprise required, the enormous quantities of provisions and ammunition collecting, the noise of arms, of carriages, and the march of such numbers of soldiers—the universal movement, the majestic and terrible course of all the forces of the West against the East—every thing announced to Europe that her two colossuses were about to measure their strength with each other.

But, to get within reach of Russia, it was necessary to pass beyond Austria, to cross Prussia, and to march between Sweden and Turkey; an offensive alliance, with these four powers was therefore indispensable. Austria was subject to the ascendancy of Napoleon, and Prussia to his arms: to them he had only to declare his intentions; Austria voluntarily and eagerly entered into his plan and Prussia he easily prevailed on to join him.

Austria, however, did not act blindly. Situated between the two colossuses of the North and the West, she was not displeased to see them at war: she looked to their mutually weakening each other, and to the increase of her own strength by their exhaustion. On the 14th of March, 1812, she promised France 30,000 men; but she prepared prudent secret instructions for them. She obtained a vague promise of an increase of territory, as an indemnity for her share of the expenses of the war, and the possession of Gallicia was guaranteed to her. She admitted, however, the future possibility of a cession of part of that province to the kingdom of Poland; but in exchange for that she would have received the Illyrian provinces. The sixth article of the secret treaty establishes that fact.

The success of the war, therefore, in no degree depended on the cession of Gallicia, or the difficulties arising from the Austrian jealousy respecting that possession. Napoleon, consequently, might on his entrance into Wilna have publicly proclaimed the liberation of the whole of Poland, instead of betraying the expectations of her people, astonishing and rendering them indifferent by expressions of doubtful import.

This, however, was one of those prominent points, which in politics as well as in war are decisive, with which every thing is connected, and from which nothing ought to have made him swerve. But whether it was that Napoleon reckoned too much on the ascendancy of his genius, or the strength of his army, and the weakness of Alexander; or that, considering what he left behind him, he felt it too dangerous to carry on so distant a war slowly and methodically; or whether, as we shall presently be told by himself, he had doubts of the success of his undertaking; certain it is, that he either neglected, or could not yet venture, to proclaim the liberation of that country whose freedom he had come to restore.

And yet he had sent an ambassador to her Diet. When this inconsistency was remarked to him, he replied, that "that nomination was an act of war, which only bound him during the war, while by his words he would be bound both in war and peace." Thus it was, that he made no other reply to the enthusiasm of the Lithuanians than evasive expressions, at the very time he was following up his attack on Alexander to the very capital of his empire.

He even neglected to clear the southern Polish provinces of the feeble hostile armies which kept the patriotism of their inhabitants in check, and to secure, by strongly organising their insurrection, a solid basis of operation. Accustomed to short methods, and to rapid attacks, he wished to imitate himself, in spite of the difference of places and circumstances; for such is the weakness of man, that he is always led by imitation, either of others, or of himself, which in the latter case, that of great men, is habit; for habit is nothing more than the imitation of one's self. Accordingly it is by their strongest side that these extraordinary men are undone!

The one in question committed himself to the fortune of battles. Having prepared an army of six hundred and fifty thousand men, he fancied that that had done enough to secure victory, from which he expected every thing. Instead of sacrificing every thing to obtain victory, it was by that he looked to obtain every thing; he made use of it as a *means*, when it ought to have been his end. It was already but too necessary to him. But he confided so much of futurity to it, he overloaded it with so much responsibility, that it became urgent and indispensable to him. Hence his precipitation to get within reach of it, in order to extricate himself from so critical a position.

But we must not be too hasty in condemning so great and universal a genius; we shall shortly hear from himself by what urgent necessity he was hurried on; and, even admitting that the rapidity of his expedition was rash, success would have probably crowned it, if the premature decline of his health had left the physical constitution of this great man all the vigour which his mind still retained.[1]

1. It is positively denied, by General Gourgaud, that Napoleon was at this period in a declining state of health. He states that, on the contrary, the Emperor was able to attend to all his multiplied affairs, to hunt for five or six hours at a stretch, and to pursue many other occupations, which were incompatible with illness.—*Ed.*

CHAPTER II

PRUSSIA

AS to Prussia, of which Napoleon was master, it is not known whether it was from his uncertainty as to the fate which he reserved for her, or as to the period at which he should commence the war, that he refused, in 1811, to contract the alliance which she herself proposed to him, and of which he dictated the conditions in 1812.

His aversion to Frederick William was remarkable. Napoleon had been frequently heard to speak reproachfully of the cabinet of Prussia for its treaties with the French Republic. He said, "It was a desertion of the cause of kings; that the negociations of the court of Berlin with the Directory displayed a timid, selfish, and ignoble policy, which sacrificed its dignity and the general cause of monarchs to petty aggrandisements." Whenever he looked at the outline of the Prussian frontiers upon the map, he seemed to be angry at seeing them still so extensive, and exclaimed, "Is it possible that I have left this man so large a territory?"

This dislike to a mild and pacific monarch was surprising. As there is nothing in the character of Napoleon unworthy of historical remembrance, it is worth while to examine the cause of it. Some persons trace back the origin of it to the rejection which he experienced, when First Consul, from Louis XVIII. of the propositions which he made to him through the medium of the king of Prussia; and they suppose that Napoleon laid the blame of this refusal upon the mediator.

Others attribute it to the seizure of Rumbold, the English agent at Hamburgh, by the orders of Napoleon, and to his being compelled to give him up by Frederick, as protector of the neutrality of the north of Germany.[1] Before that time Frederick and Napoleon had carried on a secret correspondence, which was of so intimate a nature that they used to confide to each other even the details of their family affairs; that circumstance, it is said, put an end to it.

At the beginning of 1805, however, Russia, Austria, and England made ineffectual attempts to engage Frederick in their third coalition against France. The court of Berlin, the queen, the princess, the minister Hardenberg, and all the young Prussian military, excited by the ardour of displaying the inheritance of glory which had been left them by the great Frederick, or by the wish of blotting out the disgrace of the campaign of 1792, entered heartily into the views of the allied powers; but the pacific policy of the king, and of his minister Haugwitz, resisted them, until the violation of the Prussian territory, near Anspach, by the march of a corps of French troops, exasperated the passions of the Prussians to such a degree, that their cry for immediate war prevailed.

Alexander was then in Poland; he was invited to Potsdam, and repaired thither immediately; and on the 3rd of November, 1805, he engaged Frederick in the third coalition. The Prussian army was immediately withdrawn from the Russian frontiers, and M. de Haugwitz repaired to Brünn to threaten Napoleon with it. But the battle of Austerlitz shut his mouth; and within a fortnight after, the wily minister, having quickly turned round to the side of the conqueror, signed with him a participation of the fruits of victory.

Napoleon, meanwhile, dissembled his displeasure; for he had his army to reorganise, to give the grand duchy of Berg to Murat, his brother-in-law, Neufchatel to Berthier, to conquer Naples for his brother Joseph, to mediatise Switzerland, to dissolve the Germanic body, and to create the Rhenish confederation, of which he declared himself protector; to change the republic of Holland into a kingdom, and to give it to his brother Louis. These were the reasons which induced him, on the 15th of December, to cede Hanover to Prussia, in exchange for Anspach, Cleves, and Neufchatel.

The possession of Hanover at first tempted Frederick, but when the treaty was to be signed, he appeared to feel ashamed, and to hesitate; he wished only to accept it by halves, and to retain it merely as a deposit. Napoleon had no idea of such timid policy. "What!" said he, "does this monarch dare neither to make peace nor war? Does he prefer the English to me? Is there another coalition preparing? Does he despise my alliance?" Indignant at the idea, by a fresh treaty, on the 8th of March, 1806, he compelled Frederick to declare war against England, to take possession of Hanover, and to admit French garrisons into Wesel and Hameln.

The king of Prussia alone submitted; his court and his subjects were exasperated; they reproached him with allowing himself to be vanquished without daring to fight; and elevating themselves on the remembrance of their past glory, they fancied that for them alone was reserved the honour of triumphing over the conqueror of Europe. In their impatience they insulted the minister of Napoleon; they sharpened their swords on the threshold of his gate. Napoleon himself they loaded with abuse. Even the queen, so distinguished by her graces and attractions, put on a warlike dress. Their princes, one of them particularly (whose carriage and features, spirit and intrepidity, seemed to promise them a hero) offered to be their leaders. A chivalrous ardour and fury animated the minds of all.

It is asserted, that at the same time there were persons, either treacherous or deceived, who persuaded Frederick that Napoleon was obliged to show himself pacific, that that warrior was averse to war: they added, that he was perfidiously treating for peace with England, on the terms of restoring Hanover, which he was to take back from Prussia. Drawn in at last by the general movement, the king allowed all these passions to burst forth. His army advanced, and threatened Napoleon; fifteen days afterwards he had neither army nor kingdom: he fled alone; and Napoleon dated from Berlin his decrees against England.

Humbled and conquered as Prussia thus was, it was impossible for Napoleon to abandon his hold of her; she would have immediately rallied under the cannon of the Russians. Finding it impossible to gain her to his interests, like Saxony, by a great act of generosity, the next plan was to divide her; and yet, either from compassion or the effect of Alexander's presence, he could not resolve to dismember her. This was a mistaken policy, like most of those where we stop half-way; and Napoleon was not long before he became sensible of it. When he exclaimed, therefore, "Is it possible that I have left this man so large a territory?" it is probable that he did not forgive Prussia the protection of Alexander; he hated her, because he saw that she hated him.

In fact, the sparks of a jealous and impatient hatred escaped from the youth of Prussia, whose ideas were heated by a system of education, national, liberal, and mystical. It was from among them that a formidable power arose in opposition to that of Napoleon. It included all whom his victories had humbled or offended; it had all the strength of the weak and the oppressed, the law of nature, mystery, fanaticism, and revenge! Finding no support on earth, it looked up for aid to heaven, and its moral forces were wholly out of the reach of the material power of Napoleon. Animated by the devoted, ardent, and indefatigable sectarian spirit, it watched all the motions and weakest points of its enemy, insinuated itself into all the interstices of his power, and holding itself ready to seize every opportunity, it waited quietly with the patience and phlegm which are the peculiar characteristics of the Germans, which were the causes of their defeat, and against which our victories wore themselves out.

This vast conspiracy was that of the *Tugendbund*,[2] or *Friends of Virtue*. Its head, in other words, the person who first gave a precise and definite direction to its views, was Stein. Napoleon might perhaps have gained him over to his interests, but he preferred punishing him. His plan happened to be discovered by one of those chances to which the police owes the best part of its miracles; but when conspiracies enter into the interests, passions, and even the consciences of men, it is impossible to seize their ramifications: every one understands without communicating; or rather, all is communication—a general and simultaneous sympathy.

This focus spread its fires and extended more widely every day; it attacked the power of Napoleon in the opinion of all Germany, extended itself into Italy, and threatened its complete overthrow. It was already easy to see that, if circumstances became unfavourable to us, there would be no want of men to take advantage of them. In 1809, even before the disaster of Esslingen, the first who had ventured to raise the standard of independence against Napoleon were Prussians. He sent them to the galleys; so important did he feel it to smother that cry of revolt, which seemed to echo that of the Spaniards, and might become general.

Independently of all these causes of hatred, the position of Prussia, between France and Russia, compelled Napoleon to remain her master; he could not reign there but by force—he could not be strong there but by her weakness.

He ruined the country, although he must have known well that poverty creates audacity; that the hope of gain becomes the moving principle of those who have nothing more to lose; and finally, that in leaving them nothing but the sword, he in a manner obliged them to turn it against himself. In consequence, on the approach of the year 1812, and of the terrible struggle which it was to produce, Frederick, uneasy and tired of his subservient position, was determined to extricate himself from it, either by an alliance or by war. In March, 1811, he offered himself to Napoleon as an auxiliary in the expedition which he was preparing.[3] In the month of May, and again in the month of August, he repeated that offer; and as he received no satisfactory answer, he declared, that as the great military movements which surrounded, traversed, or drained his kingdom, were such as to excite his apprehension that his entire destruction was meditated, "he took up arms, because circumstances imperiously called upon him to do so, deeming it far better to die sword in hand than to fall with disgrace."

It was said at the same time, that Frederick secretly offered to Alexander to give him possession of Graudentz, and his magazines, and put himself at the head of his insurgent subjects, if the Russian army should advance into Silesia. If the same authorities are to be believed, Alexander received this proposition favourably. He immediately sent to Bagration and Wittgenstein sealed marching orders. They were instructed not to open them until they received another letter from their sovereign, which letter he never wrote, having changed his resolution. A variety of causes might have dictated that change; either because he would not dare to be the first to commence so great a war, or the desire to have divine justice and the opinion of mankind on his side, by not appearing the aggressor; or, that Frederick, becoming less uneasy as to the plans of Napoleon, had resolved to follow his fortunes. It is probable, after all, that the noble sentiments which Alexander expressed in his reply to the king were his only motives: we are assured that he wrote to him, "that in a war which might begin by reverses, and in which perseverance was required, he felt courageous only for himself; that the misfortunes of an ally might shake his resolution; that it would grieve him to chain Prussia to his fortune if it was bad; and that if it was good he should always be ready to share it with her, whatever line of conduct necessity might oblige her to pursue."

These details have been certified to us by a witness, although one of subordinate rank. However, whether this counsel proceeded from the generosity or the policy of Alexander, or that Frederick was determined solely by the necessity of the case, it was certain that it was high time for him to come to a decision; for in February, 1812, these communications with Alexander, *if there were such*, or the hope of obtaining better terms from France, having made him hesitate in replying to the definitive propositions of Napoleon, the latter became impatient, reinforced the garrison of Dantzic, and made Davoust enter Pomerania. His orders for this invasion of a Swedish province were repeated and pressing;[4] they were grounded on the illicit commerce carried on by the Pomeranians with the English, and subsequently on the necessity of compelling Prussia to accede to his terms. The Prince of Eckmühl even received orders to hold himself in readiness to take immediate possession of that kingdom, and to seize the person of her sovereign, if within eight days from the date of these orders the latter had not concluded the offensive alliance dictated to him by France; but while the marshal was arranging the few marches necessary for this operation, he received intelligence that the treaty of the 21st of February, 1812, had been ratified.

This submission did not altogether satisfy Napoleon. To his strength he added artifice; his suspicions still led him to covet the occupation of the fortresses, which he was ashamed not to leave in Frederick's hands; he required the king to keep only 50 or 80 invalids in some, and desired that some French officers should be admitted into others; all of whom were to send their reports to him, and to follow his orders. His solicitude extended to everything. "Spandau," said he, in his letters to Davoust, "is the citadel of Berlin, as Pillau is that of Königsberg;" and French troops had orders to be ready to introduce themselves at the first signal: the manner he himself pointed out. At Potsdam, which the king had reserved for himself, and which our troops were interdicted from entering, his orders were, that the French officers should frequently show themselves, in order to observe, and to accustom the people to the sight of them. He recommended every degree of respect to be shown, both to the king and his subjects; but at the same time he required that everything should be taken from the latter, which might be of use to them in an insurrection; he pointed out everything of the kin even to the smallest weapon;[5] and anticipating the possibility of the loss of a battle, and the chances of Prussian *vespers*, he ordered that his troops should be either put into barracks or encampments, with a thousand other precautions of the minutest description. As a final security, in case of the English making a descent between the Elbe and the Vistula—although Victor, and subsequently Augereau, were to occupy Prussia with 50,000 men—he engaged by treaty the assistance of 10,000 Danes.

All these precautions were still insufficient to remove his distrust; when the Prince of Hatzfeld came to require of him a subsidy of 25 millions of francs to meet the expenses of the war which was preparing, his reply to Daru was, "that he would take especial care not to furnish an enemy with arms against himself." In this manner did Frederick, entangled as it were in a net of iron, which surrounded and held him tight in every part, submit to put between 20 and 80,000 of his troops, and his principal fortresses and magazines, at the disposal of Napoleon.[6]

1. "If," says General Gourgaud, we did not know that aversion has no influence in the policy of a man of genius like Napoleon, two much more

efficacious causes of such a feeling might be assigned; namely, the plans and engagements of Prussia previous to the battle of Austerlitz, and the aggression of that power in 1806."—*Ed.*

2. In 1808, several literary men at Königsberg, afflicted with the evils which desolated their country, ascribed it to the general corruption of manners. According to these philosophers, it had stifled true patriotism in the citizens, discipline in the army, and courage in the people. Good men therefore were bound to unite to regenerate the nation, by setting the example of every sacrifice. An association was in consequence formed by them, which took the title of *Moral and Scientific Union.* The government approved of it, merely interdicting it from political discussions. This resolution, noble as it was, would probably have been lost, like many others, in the vagueness of German metaphysics, but about that time William, Duke of Brunswick, who had been stripped of his duchy, had retired to his principality of Oels in Silesia. In the bosom of this retreat he is said to have observed the first progress of the *Moral Union* among the Prussians. He became a member of it; and his heart swelling with hatred and revenge, he formed the idea of another association, which was to consist of men resolved to overthrow the Confederation of the Rhine, and to drive the French entirely out of Germany. This society, whose object was more real and positive than of the first, soon swallowed up the other; and from these two was formed that of the *Tugendbund,* or *Friends of Virtue.*

About the end of May, 1809, three enterprises—those of Katt, Dörnberg, and Schill—had already given proofs of its existence. That of Duke William began on the 14th of May. He was at first supported by the Austrians. After a variety of adventures, this leader, abandoned to his own resources in the midst of subjugated Europe, and left with only 2000 men to combat with the whole power of Napoleon, refused to yield: he stood his ground, and threw himself into Saxony and Hanover; but finding it impossible to raise them into insurrection, he cut his way through several French corps, which he defeated, to Elsfleth, where he found an English vessel waiting to receive and to convey him to England, with the laurels he had acquired.

3. It is denied, by the defenders of Napoleon, that he was then preparing any expedition against Russia; and it is alleged that he rejected the offered Prussian alliance, because his acceptance of it would have seemed a hostile measure against Alexander.—*Ed.*

4. General Gourgaud affirms that the occupation of Pomerania was the unauthorised act of Marshal Davoust.—*Ed.*

5. To this it has been answered, that the event demonstrated Napoleon to have confided too much in Prussia, in leaving to it a numerous army in Silesia; and that a sufficient proof of its not having been deprived of "the smallest weapon," is the fact of the rapidity with which, after the treason of General York, it armed a hundred thousand of the landwehr with reserve muskets, and supplied them with artillery.—*Ed.*

6. By this treaty, Prussia agreed to furnish two hundred thousand quintals of rye, twenty-four thousand of rice, two million bottles of beer, four hundred thousand quintals of wheat, six hundred and fifty thousand of straw, three hundred and fifty thousand of hay, six million bushels of oats, forty-four thousand oxen, fifteen thousand horses, three thousand six hundred waggons, with harness and drivers, each capable of carrying a load of fifteen hundred weight; and finally, hospitals provided with everything necessary for twenty thousand sick. It is true that the value of all these supplies was to be deducted from the arrear of the taxes imposed by the conquest.

CHAPTER III

TURKEY

THESE two treaties opened to Napoleon the road to Russia; but in order to penetrate into the interior of that empire, it was necessary to make sure of Sweden and Turkey.

Military combinations were then on so large a scale, that, in order to sketch a plan of warfare, it was no longer sufficient to study merely the configuration of a province, or of a chain of mountains, or the course of a river. When monarchs, such as Alexander and Napoleon, were contending for the dominion of Europe, it was necessary to regard with an universal *coup d'oeil,* the general and relative position of every state; it was no longer on single maps, but on that of the whole globe, that their policy had to trace its plans of hostility.

Russia is mistress of a commanding position with respect to Europe; her flanks are supported by seas on the north and south. Her government cannot without great difficulty be hemmed in, and forced to submit, in an extent of space almost beyond the imagination to conceive; the conquest of which would require long campaigns, to which her climate is completely opposed. From this, it follows that, without the concurrence of Turkey and Sweden, Russia is less vulnerable. The aid of these two powers was therefore requisite, in order to surprise her, to strive her to the heart in her modern capital, and to turn at a distance, in the rear of its left, her grand army of the Niemen,—and not merely to precipitate attacks on a part of her front, in plains where the extent of space prevented confusion, and left a thousand roads open to the retreat of that army.

The meanest soldier in our ranks, therefore, expected to hear of the combined march of the Grand Vizir towards Kief, and of Bernadotte against Finland. Eight sovereigns were already enlisted under the banners of Napoleon; but the two who had the greatest interest in the quarrel were still deaf to his call. It was an idea worthy of the great emperor, to put all the great governments and all the religions of Europe in motion for the accomplishment of his great designs: their triumph would have been then secured; and if the voice of another Homer had been wanting to this king of so many kings, the voice of the nineteenth century, the great century, would have supplied it; and the cry of astonishment of a whole age, penetrating and piercing through futurity, would have echoed from generation to generation, to the latest posterity!

So much glory was not in reserve for us.

Which of us, in the French army, can ever forget his astonishment, in the midst of the Russian plains, on hearing the news of the fatal treaties of the Turks and Swedes with Alexander; and how anxiously our looks were turned towards our right uncovered, towards our left enfeebled, and upon our retreat menaced? *Then* we only looked at the fatal effects of the peace between our allies and our enemy; *now* we feel desirous of knowing the causes of it.

The treaties concluded about the end of the last century, had subjected the weak sultan of the Turks to Russia; the Egyptian expedition had armed him against us. But ever since Napoleon had assumed the reins of power, a well-understood common interest, and the intimacy of a mysterious correspondence had reconciled Selim with the first consul: a close connexion was established between these two princes, and they had even exchanged portraits with each other. Selim attempted to effect a great revolution in the Turkish customs. Napoleon encouraged him, and was assisting him in introducing the European discipline into the Ottoman army, when the victory of Jena, the war of Poland, and the influence of Sebastiani, determined the sultan to throw off the yoke of Alexander. The English hastened to oppose this, but they were driven from the sea of Constantinople.

Then it was that Napoleon wrote the following letter to Selim:—

"Osterode, April 3, 1807.

"My ambassador informs me of the bravery and good conduct of the Mussulmans against our common enemies. Thou hast shown thyself the worthy descendant of the Selims and the Solimans. Thou hast asked me for some officers; I send them to thee. I regretted that thou hadst not required of me some thousand men,—thou hast only asked for five hundred; I have given orders for their immediate departure. It is my intention that they shall be paid and clothed at my expense, but thou shalt be reimbursed the expenses which they may occasion thee. I have given orders to the commander of my troops in Dalmatia to send thee arms, ammunition, and every thing thou shalt require of me. I have given the same orders at Naples; and artillery has been already placed at the disposal of the pasha of Janina. Generals, officers, arms of every description, even money—I place all at thy disposal. Thou hast only to ask: do so in a precise manner, and all which thou shalt require I will send thee on the instant. Arrange matters with the shah of Persia, who is also the enemy of the Russians; encourage him to stand fast, and to attack vigorously the common enemy. I have beaten the Russians in a great battle; I have taken from them seventy-five pieces of cannon, sixteen standards, and a great number of prisoners. I am at the distance of eighty leagues beyond Warsaw, and am about to take advantage of the fortnight's repose which I have given to my army, to repair thither, and there to receive thy ambassador. I am sensible of the want thou hast of artillerymen and troops; I have offered both to thy ambassador; but he has declined them, from a fear of alarming the delicacy of the Mussulmans. Confide to me all thy wants; I am sufficiently powerful and sufficiently interested in thy prosperity, both from friendship and policy, to have nothing to refuse thee. Peace has been proposed to me here. I have been offered all the advantages which I could desire; but they wished that I should ratify the state of things established between the Porte and Russia by the treaty of Sistowa, and I refused. My answer was, *that it was necessary that the Porte should be secured in complete independence; and that all the treaties extorted from her, during the time that France was asleep, should be revoked.*"

This letter of Napoleon had been preceded and followed by verbal but formal assurances, that he would not sheathe the sword, until the Crimea was restored to the dominion of the crescent. He had even authorised Sebastiani to give the divan a copy of his instructions, which contained these promises.

Such were his words, with which his actions at first corresponded. Sebastiani demanded a passage through Turkey for an army of 25,000 French, which he was to command, and which was to join the Ottoman army. An unforeseen circumstance, it is true, deranged this plan; but Napoleon then made Selim the promise of an auxiliary force of 9000 French, including 5000 artillerymen, who were to be conveyed in eleven vessels of the line to Constantinople. The Turkish ambassador was at the same time treated with the greatest distinction in the French camp; he accompanied Napoleon in all his reviews; the most flattering attentions were paid to him; and the grand-equerry (Caulaincourt,) was already treating with him for an alliance, offensive and defensive, when a sudden attack by the Russians interrupted the negociation.

The ambassador returned to Warsaw, where the same respect continued to be shown him, up to the day of the decisive victory of Friedland. But on the following day his illusion was dissipated; he saw himself neglected; for it was no longer Selim whom he represented. A revolution had just hurled from the throne that monarch, the friend of Napoleon, and with him all hope of giving the Turks a regular army, upon which he could depend. Napoleon, therefore, judging that he could no longer reckon upon the assistance of these barbarians, changed his system. Henceforward it was Alexander whom he wished to gain; and as his was a genius which never hesitated, he was already prepared to abandon the empire of the East to that monarch, in order that he might be left at liberty to possess himself of that of the West.

As his great object was the extension of the continental system, and to make it surround Europe, the co-operation of Russia would complete its development. Alexander would shut out the English from the North, and compel Sweden to go to war with them; the French would expel them from the centre, from the south, and from the west of Europe. Napoleon was already meditating the expedition to Portugal, if that kingdom would not join his coalition. Turkey, therefore, was now become only an accessory in his plans, and he agreed to the armistice, and to the conferences at Tilsit.

A deputation had, meanwhile, arrived from Wilna, soliciting the restoration of their national independence, and professing the same devotion to his cause as had been shown by Warsaw; but Berthier, whose ambition was satisfied, and who began to be tired of war, dismissed these envoys rudely, styling them traitors to their sovereign. The Prince of Eckmühl, on the contrary, favoured their object, and presented them to Napoleon, who was irritated with Berthier for his treatment of these Lithuanians, and received them graciously, without, however, promising them his support. In vain did Davoust represent to him that the opportunity was favourable, owing to the destruction of the Russian army; Napoleon's reply was, "that Sweden had just declared her armistice to him; that Austria offered her mediation between France and Russia, which he looked upon as a hostile step; that the Prussians, seeing him at such a distance from France, might recover from their intimidation; and finally, that Selim, his faithful ally, had just been dethroned; and his place filled by Mustapha IV., of whose dispositions he knew nothing."

The emperor of France continued, therefore, to negociate with Russia; and the Turkish ambassador, neglected and forgotten, wandered about our camp, without being summoned to take any part in the negociations which terminated the war; he returned to Constantinople soon after, in great displeasure. Neither the Crimea, nor even Moldavia and Wallachia, were restored to that barbarous court by the treaty of Tilsit; the restitution of the two latter provinces was only stipulated by an armistice, the conditions of which were never meant to be executed. But as Napoleon professed to be the mediator between Mustapha and Alexander, the ministers of the two powers repaired to Paris. But there, during the long continuance of that feigned mediation, the Turkish plenipotentiaries were never admitted to his presence.

If we must even tell the whole truth, it is asserted, that at the interview at Tilsit, and subsequently, a treaty for the partition of Turkey was under discussion.[1] It was proposed to Russia to take possession of Wallachia, Moldavia, Bulgaria, and a part of Mount

Hemus. Austria was to have Servia and a part of Bosnia; France the other part of that province, Albania, Macedonia, and all Greece as far as Thessalonica; Constantinople, Adrianople, and Thrace, were to be left to the Turks.

Whether the conferences respecting this partition were really of a serious nature, or merely the communication of a great idea, is uncertain; so much is certain, that shortly after the interview at Tilsit, Alexander's ambition was very sensibly moderated. The suggestions of prudence had shown him the danger of substituting for the ignorant, infatuated, and feeble Turkey, an active, powerful, and troublesome neighbour. In his conversations on the subject at that time, he remarked, "that he had already too much desert country; that he knew too well, by the occupation of the Crimea, which was still depopulated, the value of conquest over foreign and hostile religions and manners; that, besides, France and Russia were too strong to become such near neighbours: that two such powerful bodies coming into immediate contact would be sure to jostle; and that it was much better to leave intermediate powers between them."

On the other side, the French emperor urged the matter no further; the Spanish insurrection diverted his attention, and imperiously required his presence, with all his forces. Even previous to the interview at Erfurt, after Sebastiani's return from Constantinople, although Napoleon still seemed to adhere to the idea of dismembering Turkey in Europe, he had admitted the correctness of his ambassador's reasoning: "That in this partition, the advantages would be all against him: that Russia and Austria would acquire contiguous provinces, which would round their dominions, while we should be obliged to keep 80,000 men continually in Greece to retain it in subjection; that such an army, from the distance and losses it would sustain from long marches, and the novelty and unhealthiness of the climate, would require 30,000 recruits annually, which would drain France; that a line of operation extending from Athens to Paris, was out of all proportion; that, besides, it became contracted in its passage at Trieste, at which point only two marches would enable the Austrians to place themselves across it, and thereby cut off our army of observation in Greece from all communication with Italy and France."

Here, Napoleon exclaimed, "that Austria certainly complicated every thing; that she was there like a dead weight; that she must be got rid of; as Europe must be divided into two empires: that the Danube, from the Black Sea to Passau, the mountains of Bohemia to Königsgratz, and the Elbe to the Baltic, should be their lines of demarcation. Alexander should become the emperor of the north, and he of the south of Europe." Abandoning, subsequently, these lofty ideas, and reverting to Sebastiani's observations on the partition of European Turkey, he terminated the conferences, which had lasted three days, with these words:

"You are right, and no answer can be given to that! I give it up. Besides, that accords with my views on Spain, which I am going to unite to France."—"What do I hear?" exclaimed Sebastiani, astonished, "unite it! And your brother!"—"What signifies my brother?" retorted Napoleon; "does one give away a kingdom like Spain? I am determined to unite it to France. I will give that nation a great national representation. I will induce the emperor Alexander to consent to it, by allowing him to take possession of Turkey to the Danube, and by evacuating Berlin. As to Joseph, I will indemnify him."

The congress at Erfurt took place just after this. He could have no motive at that time for supporting the rights of the Turks. The French army, which had advanced imprudently into the very heart of Spain, had met with reverses. The presence of its leader, and that of his armies of the Rhine and the Elbe, became there every day more and more necessary, and Austria had availed herself of the opportunity to take up arms. Uneasy respecting the state of Germany, Napoleon was therefore anxious to make sure of the dispositions of Alexander, to conclude an alliance offensive and defensive with him, and even to engage him in a war. Such were the reasons which induced him to abandon Turkey as far as the Danube to that emperor.

The Porte therefore soon believed that it had reason to reproach us for the war which was renewed between it and Russia. Notwithstanding, in July, 1808, when Mustapha was dethroned, and succeeded by Mahmoud, the latter announced his accession to the French emperor; but Napoleon had then to keep upon terms with Alexander, and felt too much regret at the death of Selim, detestation of the barbarity of the Mussulmans and contempt for their unstable government, to allow him to notice the communication. For three years he returned no reply to the sultan, and his silence might be interpreted into a refusal to acknowledge him.

He was in this ambiguous position with the Turks, when all of a sudden, on the 21st of March, 1812, only six weeks before the war with Russia commenced, he solicited an alliance with Mahmoud; he demanded that, within five days from the period of the communication, all negociation between the Turks and Russians should be broken off; and that an army of 100,000 men, commanded by the sultan himself, should march to the Danube within nine days. The return which he proposed to make for this assistance was, to put the Porte in possession of the very same Moldavia and Wallachia, which, under the circumstances, the Russians were but too happy to restore as the price of a speedy peace; the promise of procuring the restoration of the Crimea, which he had made six years before to Selim, was also renewed.

We know not whether the time which this despatch would take to arrive at Constantinople had been badly calculated, whether Napoleon believed the Turkish army to be stronger than it really was, or whether he had flattered himself with surprising and captivating the determination of the divan by so sudden and advantageous a proposition. It can hardly be supposed that he was ignorant of the long invariable custom of the Mussulmans, which prevented the grand signior from ever commanding his army in person.[2]

It appears as if the genius of Napoleon could not stoop so low as to impute to the divan the brutish ignorance which it exhibited of its real interests. After the manner in which he had abandoned the interests of Turkey in 1807, perhaps he did not make sufficient allowance for the distrust which the Mussulmans were likely to entertain of his new promises; he forgot that they were too ignorant to appreciate the change which recent circumstances had effected in his political views; and that barbarians like them could still less comprehend the feelings of dislike with which they had inspired him, by their deposition and murder of Selim, to whom he was attached, and in conjunction with whom he had hoped to make European Turkey a military power capable of coping with Russia.

Perhaps he might still have gained over Mahmoud to his cause, if he had sooner made use of more potent arguments; but, as he has since expressed himself, it shocked his pride to make use of corruption. We shall besides shortly see him hesitating about beginning a war with Alexander, or laying too much stress on the alarm with which his immense preparations would inspire that monarch. It is also possible, that the last propositions which he made to the Turks, being tantamount to a declaration of war against the Russians, were delayed for the express purpose of deceiving the Czar as to the period of his invasion. Finally, whether it was from all these causes, from a confidence founded on the mutual hatred of the two nations, and on his treaty of alliance with Austria, which had just guaranteed Moldavia and Wallachia to the Turks, he detained the ambassador whom he sent to them on his road, and waited, as we have just seen, to the very last moment.

But the divan was surrounded by the Russian, English, Austrian, and Swedish envoys, who with one voice represented to it, "that the Turks were indebted for their existence in Europe solely to the divisions which existed among the Christian monarchs; that the moment these were united under one influence the Mahometans in Europe would be overwhelmed; and that as the French emperor was advancing rapidly to the attainment of universal empire, it was him whom the Turks had most reason to dread."

To these representations were added the intrigues of the two Greek princes Morozi. They were of the same religion with Alexander, and they looked to him for the possession of Moldavia and Wallachia. Grown rich by his favours and by the gold of England, these dragomans enlightened the unsuspecting ignorance of the Turks, as to the occupation and military surveys of the Ottoman frontiers by the French. They did a great deal more; the first of them influenced the dispositions of the divan and the capital, and the second those of the grand vizir and the army; and as the proud Mahmoud resisted, and would only accept an honourable peace; these treacherous Greeks contrived to disband his army, and compelled him, by insurrections, to sign the degrading treaty of Bucharest with the Russians.

Such is the power of intrigue in the seraglio; two Greeks, whom the Turks despised, there decided the fate of Turkey, in spite of the sultan himself. As the latter depended for his existence on the intrigues of his palace, he, like all despots who shut themselves up in them, was obliged to yield: the Morozi carried the day; but afterwards he had them both beheaded.

1. This assertion is said to be unfounded.—*Ed.*

2. Between the years 1299 and 1695, fourteen sultans took the field at the head of their armies. It was not till the Turkish power began to decline that the Grand Signior ceased to command in person.—*Ed.*

CHAPTER IV

SWEDEN

IN this manner did we lose the support of Turkey; but Sweden still remained to us; her monarch had sprung from our ranks; a soldier of our army, it was to that he owed his glory and his throne: would he desert our cause on the first opportunity he had of showing his gratitude? It was impossible to anticipate such ingratitude; still less, that he would sacrifice the real and permanent interests of Sweden to his former jealousy of Napoleon, and perhaps to a weakness too common among the upstart favourites of fortune; unless it be that the submission of men who have newly attained to greatness to those who enjoy a transmitted rank, is a necessity of their position rather than an error of their self-love.

In this great contest between aristocracy and democracy, the ranks of the former had been joined by one of its most determined enemies. Bernadotte being thrown almost singly among the ancient courts and nobility, did every thing to merit his adoption by them, and succeeded. But his success must have cost him dear, as in order to obtain it he was first obliged to abandon his old companions and the authors of his glory, in the hour of peril. At a later period he did more; he was seen marching over their bleeding corses, joining with all their, and his former, enemies, to overwhelm the country of his birth, and thereby lay that of his adoption at the mercy of the first czar who should be ambitious of reigning over the Baltic.

On the other hand it would appear, that the character of Bernadotte, and the importance of Sweden in the decisive struggle which was about to commence, were not sufficiently weighed in the political balance of Napoleon. His ardent and exclusive genius hazarded too much; he overloaded a solid foundation so much that he made the fabric fall. Thus it was that, after justly appreciating the Swedish interests as naturally bound up with his, the moment he wished to weaken the power of Russia, he fancied that he could exact every thing from the Swedes without promising them enough return; his pride did not make any allowance for theirs, judging that they were too much interested in the success of his cause, for them ever to think of separating themselves from it.

We must, however, take up the history a little earlier; facts will prove that the defection of Sweden was as much attributable to the jealous ambition of Bernadotte as to the unbending pride of Napoleon. It will be seen that her new monarch assumed to himself a great part of the responsibility of the rupture by offering his alliance at the price of an act of treachery.

When Napoleon returned from Egypt, he did not become the chief of his equals with the concurrence of them all. Such of them as were already jealous of his glory, then became still more envious of his power. As they could not dispute the first, they determined to emancipate themselves from the second. Moreau, and several other generals, either by persuasion or surprise, had co-operated in the revolution of the 18th Brumaire; they afterwards repented having done so. Bernadotte had refused all participation in it. Alone, during the night, in Napoleon's own residence, amidst a thousand devoted officers, waiting only for the conqueror's orders, Bernadotte, then a republican, was daring enough to oppose his arguments, to refuse the second place in the republic, and to retort upon his anger by threats. Napoleon saw him depart, bearing himself proudly, and pass through the midst of his partisans, carrying with him his secrets, and declaring himself his enemy, and even his denouncer. Nevertheless, either from respect to his brother, to whom Bernadotte was allied by marriage, from moderation, the usual companion of strength, or from astonishment, he suffered him to depart quietly.

In the course of the same night a conventicle, consisting of ten deputies of the Council of Five Hundred, met at the house of S——; thither Bernadotte repaired. They settled, that at nine o'clock next morning the Council should hold a sitting, to which those only should be invited who were of the same way of thinking; that there a decree should be passed, that in imitation of the Council of Ancients, which had prudently named Bonaparte general of its guard, the Council of Five Hundred had appointed Bernadotte to command theirs;[1] and that the latter, properly armed, should be in readiness to be summoned to it. It was at S——'s house that this plan was formed; it was S—— himself who immediately afterwards hurried to Napoleon and disclosed the whole. A threat from the latter was quite sufficient to keep the conspirators in order; not one of them dared to show his face at the Council, and the next day the revolution of the 18th Brumaire was accomplished.

Bernadotte was prudent enough afterwards to feign submission, but Napoleon had not forgotten his opposition. He kept a watchful eye over all his movements. Not long after, he suspected his being at the head of a republican conspiracy which had been forming against him in the west. A premature proclamation discovered it; an officer who had been arrested for other causes, and an accomplice of Bernadotte, denounced the authors. On that occasion Bernadotte's ruin would have been sealed if Napoleon had been able to convict him of it.[2]

He was satisfied with banishing him to America, under the title of minister of the Republic. But fortune favoured Bernadotte, who was already at Rochefort, by delaying his embarkation until the war with England was renewed. He then refused to go, and Napoleon could no longer compel him.

All the relations between them had thus been those of hatred; and his check only served to aggravate it. Not long after, Napoleon had to reproach Bernadotte with his envious and treacherous inaction during the battle of Auerstadt, and his order of the day at Wagram, in which he had assumed the honour of that victory. He also censured his character, as being much more ambitious than patriotic; and perhaps apprehended the fascination of his manners,—all of them things considered dangerous to a recently established government; and yet he had lavished rank, titles, and distinctions upon him, while Bernadotte, always ungrateful, seemed to accept them merely as the just rewards of his merit, or as an admission of the want which was felt of his services. The dissatisfaction of Napoleon was not unfounded.

Bernadotte, on his side, misusing the emperor's moderation and desire to keep on terms with him, gradually incurred an increase of his displeasnre, which his ambition was pleased to call enmity. He demanded why Napoleon had placed him in such a dangerous and false position at Wagram? Why the report of that victory had been so unfavourable to him? To what was he to attribute the jealous anxiety to weaken his eulogium in the journals by insidious notes? Up to that time, however, the obscure and underhand opposition of this general to his emperor had been of no importance; but a much wider field was then opened to their misunderstanding.

By the treaty of Tilsit, Sweden, as well as Turkey, had been sacrificed to Russia and the continental system. The mistaken or insane politics of Gustavus IV. had been the cause of this. Ever since 1804 that monarch appeared to have enlisted himself in the pay of England; it was he also who had been the first to break the ancient alliance between France and Sweden. He had obstinately persevered in that erroneous policy to such a extent at first, as to contend against France when she was victorious over Russia, and afterwards with Russia and France united. The loss of Pomerania in 1807, and even that of Finland and the islands of Aland, which were united to Russia in 1808, were not sufficient to shake his obstinacy.

It was then that his irritated subjects resumed that power which had been wrested from them, in 1772, and 1788, by Gustavus III., and of which his successor had made so bad a use. Gustavus Adolphus IV. was imprisoned and dethroned; his lineal descendants were excluded from the throne; his uncle was put in his place, and the prince of Holstein-Augustenburg elected hereditary prince of Sweden. The war had been the cause of this revolution, peace was the result of it; it was concluded with Russia in 1809; but the newly-elected hereditary prince then died suddenly.

In the beginning of 1810, France restored Pomerania and the Island of Rugen to Sweden, as the price of her accession to the continental system. The Swedes, worn out, impoverished, and become almost islanders, in consequence of the loss of Finland, were very loth to break with England, and yet they had no remedy; on the other side, they stood in awe of the neighbouring and powerful government of Russia. Finding themselves weak and insulated, they looked round for support.

Bernadotte had recently held the command of the French army which took possession of Pomerania; his military reputation, and still more that of his nation and its sovereign, his fascinating manners, his generosity, and his flattering attentions to the Swedes with whom he had to treat, induced several of them to cast their eyes upon him. They appeared to know nothing of the misunderstanding between this marshal and the emperor; they fancied that by electing him for their prince, they should not only obtain an able and experienced general, but also a powerful mediator between France and Sweden, and a certain protector in the emperor: it happened quite the contrary.

During the intrigues to which this circumstance gave rise, Bernadotte fancied that to his previous complaints against Napoleon he had to add others. When, in opposition to the king, and the majority of the members of the diet, he was proposed as successor to the crown of Sweden; when his pretensions were supported by Charles's prime minister, (a man of no family, who owed, like him, all his illustration to himself,) and the count de Wrede, the only member of the diet who had reserved his vote for him; when he came to solicit Napoleon's interference, why did he, when Charles XIII. desired to know his wishes, exhibit so much indifference? Why did he prefer the union of the three northern crowns on the head of a prince of Denmark? If he, Bernadotte, succeeded in the enterprise, he was not at all indebted for it to the emperor of the French; he owed it to the pretensions of the king of Denmark, which counteracted those of the duke of Augustenburg,[3] his most dangerous rival; to the daring gratitude of the baron de Mœrner, who was the first to come to him and offer to put him on the lists, and to the aversion of the Swedes to the Danes; above all he owed it to a passport which had been adroitly obtained by his agent from Napoleon's minister. It was said that this document was audaciously produced by Bernadotte's secret emissary, as a proof of an autograph mission with which he pretended to be charged, and of the formal desire of the French emperor to see one of his lieutenants, and the relation of his brother, placed upon the throne of Sweden.

Bernadotte also felt that he owed his crown to chance, which brought him in communication with the Swedes, and made them acquainted with his characteristic qualities; to the birth of his son, which secured the hereditary succession; to the address of his agents, who, either with or without his authority, dazzled the poverty of the Scandinavians with the promise of fourteen millions with which his election was to enrich their treasury; and finally to his flattering attentions, which had gained him the voices of several Swedish officers who had been his prisoners. But as to Napoleon, what did he owe to him? What was his reply to the news of the offer made to him by some of the Swedes, when he himself waited upon him to inform him of it? "I am at too great a distance from Sweden, to mix myself up in her affairs. You must not reckon upon my support." At the same time it is true, that either from necessity, from his dreading the election of the duke of Oldenburg, or finally from respect for the wishes of fortune, Napoleon declared that he would leave it to her to decide: and Bernadotte was in consequence elected crown prince of Sweden.

The newly-elected prince immediately paid his respects to the emperor, who received him frankly. "As you are offered the crown of Sweden, I permit you to accept it. I had another wish, as you know; but, in short, it is your sword which has made you a king, and you are sensible that it is not for me to stand in the way of your good fortune." He then entered very fully with him into the whole plan of his policy, in which Bernadotte appeared entirely to concur; every day he attended the emperor's levee together with his son, mixing with the other courtiers. By such marks of deference, he completely gained the heart of Napoleon. He was about to depart, poor. Unwilling that Bernadotte should present himself to the Swedish throne in that necessitous state, like a mere adventurer, the emperor generously presented him with two millions out of his own treasury; he even granted to his family the endowments which, as a foreign prince, Bernadotte could no longer retain himself; and they finally parted on apparent terms of mutual satisfaction.

It was natural that the expectations of Napoleon as to the alliance with Sweden should be heightened by this election, and by the favours which he had bestowed. At first Bernadotte's correspondence with him was that of a grateful inferior, but the very moment he was fairly out of France, feeling himself as it were relieved from a state of long and painful constraint, it is said that his hatred to Napoleon vented itself in threatening expressions, which, whether true or false, were reported to the emperor.

On his side, that monarch, who was compelled to be absolute in his continental system, cramped the commerce of Sweden; he wished her even to exclude American vessels from her ports; and at last he declared that he would only regard as friends the enemies of Great Britain. Bernadotte was obliged to make his election; the winter and the sea separated him equally from the assistance and the attacks of the English; the French were close to his ports; a war with France therefore would be real and effective; a war with England would be merely on paper. The prince of Sweden adopted the latter alternative.

Napoleon, however, being as much a conqueror in peace as in war, and suspecting the intentions of Bernadotte, had demanded from Sweden a sufficient number of sailors to man several ships of his Brest fleet, and the despatch of a body of troops, which were to be in his pay; in this manner weakening his allies to subdue his enemies, so as to allow him to be the master of both. He also required that colonial produce should be subjected in Sweden, the same as in France, to a duty of five per cent. It is even affirmed that he applied to Bernadotte to allow French custom-house officers to be placed at Gottenburg. These demands were evaded.

Soon after, Napoleon proposed an alliance between Sweden, Denmark, and the grand duchy of Warsaw; a northern confederation, of which he would have declared himself the head, like that of the Rhine. The answer of Bernadotte, without being absolutely negative, had the same effect; it was the same with respect to the offensive and defensive treaty which Napoleon again proposed to him. Bernadotte has since declared, that in four successive letters written with his own hand, he had frankly stated the impossibility he was under of complying with his wishes, and repeated his protestations of attachment to his former sovereign, but that the latter never deigned to give him any reply. This impolitic silence (if the fact be true), can only be attributed to the pride of Napoleon, which was piqued at Bernadotte's refusals. No doubt he considered his protestations as too false to deserve any answer.

The irritation increased; the communications became disagreeable; they were interrupted by the recall of Alquier, the French minister in Sweden. As the pretended declaration of war by Bernadotte against England remained a dead letter, Napoleon, who was not to be refused or deceived with impunity, carried on a sharp war against the Swedish commerce by his privateers. By means of them, and the invasion of Swedish Pomerania on the 27th of January, 1812, he punished Bernadotte for his deviations from the continental system, and obtained as prisoners several thousand Swedish soldiers and sailors, whom he had in vain demanded as auxiliaries.

Then also our connection with Russia was broken off. Napoleon immediately addressed himself to the prince of Sweden; his notes were couched in the style of a lord paramount who fancies he speaks in the interest of his vassal, who feels the claims he has upon his gratitude or submission, and who calculates upon his obedience. He demanded that Bernadotte should declare a real war against England, exclude her from the Baltic, and send an army of 40,000 Swedes against Russia. In return for this, he promised him his protection, the restoration of Finland, and twenty millions, in return for an equal amount of colonial produce, which the Swedes were first to deliver. Austria undertook to support this proposition; but Bernadotte, already fashioned to a throne, answered like an independent prince. Ostensibly he declared himself neutral, opened his ports to all nations, proclaimed his rights and his grievances, appealed to humanity, recommended peace, and offered himself as a mediator; secretly he offered himself to Napoleon at the price of Norway, Finland, and a subsidy.[4]

At the reading of a letter conceived in this new and unexpected style, Bonaparte was seized with rage and astonishment. He saw in it, and not without reason, a premeditated defection on the part of Bernadotte, a secret agreement with his enemies! He was filled with indignation; he exclaimed, striking violently on the letter, and the table on which it lay open: "He! the rascal! he presume to give me advice! to dictate the law to me! to dare propose such an infamous act[5] to me! And this from a man who owes every thing to my bounty! What ingratitude!" Then, pacing the room with rapid strides, at intervals he gave vent to such expressions as these: "I ought to have expected it! he has always sacrificed every thing to his interests! This is the same man, who, during his short ministry, attempted the resurrection of the infamous Jacobins! When he had no hope but in confusion, he opposed the 18th of Brumaire! He it was who conspired in the west against the establishment of law and religion! Did not his envious and perfidious inaction betray the French army at Auerstadt? How many times, from regard to Joseph, have I pardoned his intrigues and concealed his faults! And yet I have made him general-in-chief, marshal, duke, prince, and finally king! but see how all these favours, and the pardon of so many injuries are thrown away on a man like this! If Sweden, half devoured by Russia, for a century past, has retained her independence, she owes it to the support of France. But it matters not; Bernadotte requires the baptism of ancient aristocracy! a baptism of blood, and of French blood! and you will soon see, that to satisfy his envy and ambition, he will betray both his native and adopted country."

All attempts to calm him were fruitless. In vain was it represented to him, that Bernadotte's new situation imposed other duties on that prince; that the cession of Finland to Russia had separated Sweden from the continent, almost made an island of that country, and thereby enlisted her in the English system.—In such critical circumstances, all the need which he had of this ally was unable to vanquish his pride, which revolted at a proposition which he regarded as insulting: perhaps also in the new prince of Sweden he still saw the same Bernadotte who was lately his subject, and his military inferior, and who at last affected to have carved for himself a destiny independent of his. From that moment his instructions to his minister bore the impress of that disposition; the latter, it is true, softened the bitterness of them, but a rupture became inevitable.

It is uncertain which contributed most to it, the pride of Napoleon; or the ancient jealousy of Bernadotte; it is certain that on the part of the former the motives of it were honourable. "Denmark," he said, "was his most faithful ally; her attachment to France had cost her the loss of her fleet and the burning of her capital. Must he repay a fidelity which had been so cruelly tried, by an act of treachery such as that of taking Norway from her to give to Sweden?"

As to the subsidy which Sweden required of him, he answered, as he had done to Turkey, "that if the war was to be carried on with money, England would be always sure to outbid him;" and above all, "that there was weakness and disgrace in triumphing by corruption." Reverting by this to his wounded pride, he terminated the conference by exclaiming, "Bernadotte impose conditions on me! Does he fancy then that I stand in need of him? I will soon bind him to my victorious career, and compel him to follow my sovereign impulse."

Meanwhile the active and speculative English, who were out of his reach, made a judicious estimate of the weak points of his system, and found the Russians ready to act upon their suggestions. They it was who had been endeavouring for the three years to draw the forces of Napoleon into the defiles of Spain, and to exhaust them; it was they also who were on the watch to take advantage of the vindictive enmity of the prince of Sweden.

Knowing that the active and restless vanity of men newly risen from obscurity is always uneasy and susceptible in the presence of ancient upstarts, George and Alexander were lavish of their promises and flattery, in order to cajole Bernadotte. It was thus that they caressed him, at the time that the irritated Napoleon was threatening him; they promised him Norway and a subsidy, when the other, forced to refuse him that province of a faithful ally, took possession of Pomerania. While Napoleon, a monarch deriving his elevation from himself, relying on the faith of treaties, on the remembrance of past benefits, and on the real interests of Sweden, required succours from Bernadotte, the hereditary monarchs of London and Petersburgh requested his opinion with deference, and submitted themselves by anticipation to the counsels of his experience. Finally, while the genius of Napoleon, the grandeur of his elevation, the importance of his enterprise, and the habit of their former connections, still classed Bernadotte as his lieutenant, these monarchs appeared already to treat him as their general. How was it possible for him not to seek to escape on the one hand from his sense of inferiority, and on the other hand to resist a mode of treatment and promises so seductive? Thus the future prospects of Sweden were sacrificed, and her independence for ever laid at the mercy of Russian faith, by the treaty of Petersburgh, which Bernadotte signed on the 24th of March, 1812. That of Bucharest, between Alexander and Mahmoud, was concluded on the 28th of May.—Thus did we lose support for our two wings.

Nevertheless, the emperor of the French, at the head of more than six hundred thousand men, and already too far advanced to think of receding, flattered himself that his strength would decide every thing; that a victory on the Niemen would cut the knot of all these diplomatic difficulties, which he probably too much despised; and that then all the monarchs of Europe, compelled to acknowledge his ascendancy, would be eager to return into his system, and that all those satellites would be drawn into its vortex.

1. The Council of Five Hundred had no separate guards. The guard of the whole legislative body was intrusted to the troops of the First Military Division.—*Ed.*

2. Napoleon is said to have had sufficient evidence; but to have yielded to the entreaties of Joseph and his wife in behalf of Bernadotte.—*Ed.*

3. Brother of the deceased prince of that name.

4. It is stated, by General Gourgaud, that Bernadotte's demand of Norway was made at a much later period than is here assigned to it; that Napoleon did not break out into a fit of passion on receiving it; and that he merely said, "I will not buy a doubtful ally at the expense of a faithful friend."—*Ed.*

5. Napoleon no doubt alluded to the proposal which Bernadotte made to him to take Norway from Denmark, his faithful ally, in order by this act of treachery to purchase the assistance of Sweden.

BOOK II

CHAPTER I

THE APPROACHING STRUGGLE

NAPOLEON meanwhile was still at Paris, in the midst of his great officers, who were alarmed by the terrible encounter which was preparing. The latter had nothing more to acquire, but much to preserve; their personal interest, therefore, was united with the general desire of nations, which were tired of war; and without disputing the utility of this expedition, they dreaded its approach. But they only confessed this to each other in secret, either from fear of giving umbrage, of impairing the confidence of nations, or of being proved wrong by the result; for these reasons in Napoleon's presence they were silent, and even appeared to be uninformed as to a war, which for a considerable time had furnished a subject of conversation to the whole of Europe.

But at length this respectful taciturnity, which he himself he had taken pains to impose, became disagreeable to him; he suspected that it proceeded more from disapprobation than reserve. Obedience was not sufficient for him; it was his wish to combine it with conviction: that was like another conquest. Besides, no one so well as himself could estimate the power of public opinion, which, according to him, *creates or destroys sovereigns*. In short, whether through policy or self-love, it was his desire to persuade.

Such were the dispositions of Napoleon and of grandees who surrounded him, when the veil being about to be rent, and war evident, it was obvious that their silence towards him would be a worse indiscretion than hazarding a few timely words. Some of them, therefore, commenced the discussion, and the emperor anticipated the others.

A show was made[1] at first of comprehending all the emergencies of his position. "It was necessary to complete what had been begun; it was impossible to stop short on so rapid an acclivity, and so near the summit. The empire of Europe was adapted to his genius; France would become its centre and its base; great and entire, she would perceive around her none but states so feeble and so divided, that all coalition among them would be contemptible or impossible; but, with such object, why did he not commence the task by subjecting and partitioning the states immediately around him?"

To this objection Napoleon replied, "That such had been his project in 1809, in the war with Austria, but that the reverse he had met with at Esslingen had deranged his plan; that that event, and the doubtful dispositions which Russia had since exhibited, had led him to marry an Austrian princess, and strengthen himself by an alliance with the Austrian against the Russian emperor.

"That he did not create circumstances, but that he would not allow them to escape him; that he comprehended them all, and held himself in as much readiness as possible for their appearance; that in order to accomplish his designs, he was fully aware that twelve years were necessary, but that he could not afford to wait so long.

"That, besides, he had not provoked this war; that he had been faithful to his engagements with Alexander; proofs of which were to be found in the coldness of his relations with Turkey and Sweden, which had been delivered up to Russia, one almost entirely, the other shorn of Finland, and even of the Isles of Aland, which were so near Stockholm. That he had replied to the distressed appeal of the Swedes, only by advising them to make the cession.

"That, nevertheless, as far back as 1809, the Russian army destined to act in concert with Poniatowski in Austrian Gallicia had come forward too late, was too weak, and had acted perfidiously; that since that time, Alexander, by his ukase of the 31st of December, 1810, had abandoned the continental system, and by his prohibitions declared an actual war against French commerce; that he was quite aware that the interest and national spirit of the Russians might have compelled him to do so; but that he had then communicated to the emperor that he was aware of his position, and would enter into every kind of arrangement which his repose required; notwithstanding which, Alexander, instead of modifying his ukase, had assembled 80,000 men, under pretence of supporting his custom-house officers; that he had suffered himself to be seduced by England; and that, lastly, he even now refused to recognise the thirty-second military division, and demanded the evacuation of Prussia by the French; which was equivalent to a declaration of war."

Amidst all these complaints, some persons thought they perceived that the pride of Napoleon was wounded by the independent attitude which Russia was daily re-assuming. The dispossession of the Russian Princes of Oldenburg of her duchy, led to other conjectures; it was said that hints had been given, both at Tilsit and Erfurt, about a divorce,[2] after which a closer alliance might be contracted with Russia; that these hints had not been taken, that Napoleon retained a resentful remembrance of it. This fact is affirmed by some, and denied by others.

But all those passions which so despotically govern other men, possessed but a feeble influence over a genius so firm and vast as his: at the utmost, they may have imparted the first momentum which impelled him into action earlier than he would have wished: but without penetrating too deeply into the recesses of this great mind, a single idea, an obvious fact, was enough to hurry him, sooner or later, into that decisive struggle,—that was, the existence of an empire, which rivalled his own in greatness, which was still young, like its prince, and growing every day; while the French empire, already mature, like its emperor, could scarcely anticipate anything but a decrease.

However great might be the height to which Napoleon had elevated the throne of the south and west of Europe, he perceived the northern throne of Alexander ever ready to overshadow him by its eternally menacing position. On those icy summits of Europe, whence, in ancient times, so many floods of barbarians had rushed forth he saw forming all the elements of a new inundation. Hitherto Austria and Prussia had opposed sufficient barriers to it; but these he had himself humbled and over-thrown; he remained, therefore, single in the field, and the sole champion of the civilization, the wealth, and the enjoyments of the nations of the south, against the rude ignorance, and fierce cupidity, of the poor nations of the north, and against the ambition of their emperor and his nobility.

It was obvious that war alone could decide this grand arbitrament—this great and eternal struggle between the poor and the rich; and, nevertheless, this war, with reference to us, was neither European, nor even national. Europe entered into it against her inclination, because its object was to add to the strength of her conqueror. France was exhausted, and anxious for her repose; her grandees, who formed the court of Napoleon, were alarmed at the double-headed character of the war, at the dispersion of our armies from Cadiz to Moscow; and even when admitting the *eventual* necessity of the struggle, its *immediate* urgency did not appear to them so legitimately proved.

They knew that it was more especially by an appeal to his political interest that they had any chance of shaking the resolution of a prince, whose principle was, "that there are individuals whose conduct can but rarely be regulated by their feelings, but always by circumstances." In this persuasion, one of his ministers[3] said to him, "that his finances required peace;" but he replied, "On the contrary, they are embarrassed, and require war." Another[4] added, "that his revenues had never, in fact, been in a more satisfactory state; that, according to the statement he had furnished, of from three to four thousand millions of francs, it was really wonderful to find France unencumbered with any demandable debts; but that this prosperous condition was approaching its termination, since it appeared that with the year 1812 a ruinous campaign was to commence; that, hitherto, war had supported the expense of war; that we had every where found the table laid out; but that, in future, we could no longer live at the expense of Germany, since she had become our ally; but, on the contrary, it would be necessary for us to support her contingents, and that without any hope of remuneration, whatever might be the result; that we should have to pay at Paris for every ration of bread which would be consumed at Moscow, as the new scenes of action offered us no harvest to reap after victory, but hemp, pitch, and tar, and masting, which would certainly go but a small way towards the discharge of the expenses of a Continental war. That France was not in a condition to subsidise all Europe in this manner, especially at a moment when her resources were drained by the war in Spain; that it was like lighting a fire at both ends at once, which, gaining ground upon the centre, exhausted by so many efforts, would probably end in our own destruction."

This minister was listened to; the emperor surveyed him with a smiling air, accompanied with one of his familiar caresses. He imagined that he had secured conviction, but Napoleon said to him,—"So you think that I shall not be able to find any one to pay the expenses of the war?" The duke was endeavouring to discover on whom the burden was to fall, when the emperor, by a single word, disclosing all the grandeur of his designs, closed the lips of his astonished minister.

He estimated, however, but too accurately all the difficulties of his enterprise. It was, perhaps, owing to these, that he incurred the reproach of availing himself of a method which he had rejected in the Austrian war, and of which the celebrated Pitt had set the example in 1793.[5]

Towards the end of 1811, the prefect of police at Paris learnt, it was said, that a printer was secretly counterfeiting Russian bank-notes; he ordered him to be arrested: the printer resisted; but in the end his house was broken open, and himself taken before the magistrate, whom he astonished by his assurance, and still more by his appeal to the minister of police. This printer was instantly released: it was even added, that he continued his forging occupation; and that, from the moment of our first advance into Lithuania, we propagated the report that we had found several millions of Russian bank-notes at Wilna in the military chests of the hostile army.

Whatever may have been the origin of this counterfeit money, Napoleon contemplated it with extreme repugance; it is even unknown whether he resolved on making any use of it; at least, it is certain that during the period of our retreat, and when we abandoned

Wilna, the greater part of these bills were found there untouched, and burnt by his orders.

1. The arch-chancellor (Cambacères).

2. The plan of divorcing Josephine was not formed till a much later period. The Russian princess, whom Napoleon wished to obtain in 1810, was the grand duchess Anne.—*Ed.*

3. Count Mollien.

4. The Duke of Gaeta (Gaudin).

5. This is erroneous. The forged assignats were not fabricated by the English government, but by some of the French royalist chiefs.—*Ed.*

CHAPTER II

ARGUMENTS AGAINST
THE WAR

PRINCE PONIATOWSKI, nevertheless, to whom this expedition appeared to hold out the prospect of a throne, generously united his exertions with those of the emperor's ministers in the attempt to demonstrate its danger. Love of country was in this Polish prince a great and noble passion; his life and death have proved it; but it never infatuated him. He depicted Lithuania as an impracticable desert; its nobility as already become half Russian; the character of its inhabitants as cold and backward:[1] but the impatient emperor interrupted him; he required information for the sake of conducting the enterprise, and not be to deterred from it.

It is true that the greater part of these objections were but a feeble repetition of all those which, for a long time past, had presented themselves to his own mind. People were not aware of the extent to which he had appreciated the danger; of his multiplied exertions, from the 30th of December, 1810, to ascertain the nature of the territory which, sooner or later, was destined to become the theatre of a decisive war; how many emissaries he had despatched for the purpose of survey; the numerous reports which he caused to be prepared for him respecting the roads to Petersburgh and Moscow, and the dispositions of the inhabitants, especially of the mercantile class; and, finally, the resources of every kind which the country was capable of supplying. If he persevered, it was because, far from deceiving himself as to his own strength, he did not share that confidence in it which, perhaps, prevented others from perceiving of how much consequence the crippling the power of Russia was to the future existence of the great French empire.

In this spirit, he once more addressed himself to three[2] of his great officers, whose well-known services and attachment authorised a tone of frankness. All three, in the capacity of ministers, envoys, and ambassadors, had become acquainted with Russia at different epochs .He endeavoured to convince them of the utility, the justness, and the necessity of this war but one[3] of them, in particular, often interrupted him with impatience; for when a discussion had once commenced, Napoleon submitted to all its little breaches of decorum.

This great officer, yielding to the inflexible and impetuous frankness which he derived from his character, from his military education, and, perhaps, from the province which gave him birth, exclaimed, "That it was useless for Napoleon to deceive himself, or pretend to deceive others; that after possessing himself of the Continent, and even of the states belonging to the family of his ally, that ally could not be accused of abandoning the continental system. While the French armies covered all Europe, how could the Russians be reproached for increasing their army? Did it become the ambition of Napoleon to denounce the ambition of Alexander?

"That, in addition to this, the determination of that prince was made up; that, Russia once invaded, no peace could be expected, while a single Frenchman remained upon her soil; that, in that respect, the national and obstinate pride of the Russians was in perfect harmony with that of their emperor.

"That, it was true, Alexander's subjects accused him of weakness, but very erroneously; that he was not to be judged of by the complacency of which, at Tilsit and at Erfurt, his admiration, his inexperience, and a tincture of ambition, had rendered him capable. That this prince loved justice; that he was anxious to have right on his side, and he might, indeed, hesitate till he thought it was so, but then he became inflexible; that, finally, looking to his position with reference to his subjects, he incurred more danger by making a disgraceful peace, than by sustaining an unfortunate war.

"How was it possible, moreover, to avoid seeing that in this war every thing was to be feared, even our allies? Did not Napoleon hear their discontented kings murmuring that they were only his prefects? When they, all of them, only waited a suitable occasion in order to turn against him, why run the risk of giving that occasion birth?"

At the same time, supported by his two colleagues, the duke added, "that since 1805 a system of war which compelled the most disciplined soldier to plunder, had sown the seeds of hatred to us throughout the whole of that Germany which the emperor now designed to traverse. Was he then going to precipitate himself and his army beyond all those nations whose wounds, for which they were indebted to us, were not yet healed? What an accumulation of enmity and revenge would he not, by so doing, interpose between himself and France!

"And upon whom did he call, to be his *points d'appui*?—on Prussia, whom for five years we had been devouring, and whose alliance was hollow and compulsory! He was about, therefore, to trace the longest line of military operations ever drawn, through countries whose fear was taciturn, supple, and treacherous, and which, like the ashes of volcanoes, concealed terrific flames, the eruption of which might be provoked by the smallest collision.[4]

"To sum up all,[5] what would be the result of so many conquests? To substitute lieutenants for kings, who, more ambitious than those of Alexander, would, perhaps, imitate their example, without, like them, waiting for the death of their sovereign,—a death, moreover, which he would inevitably meet among so many fields of battle, and that, too, before the consolidation of his labours; while each war revived in the interior of France the hopes of all kinds of parties, and rekindled discussions which had been regarded as at an end.

"Did he wish to know the opinion of the army? That opinion pronounced that his best soldiers were then in Spain: that the regiments, being too often recruited, wanted unity; that they were not reciprocally acquainted; that each was uncertain whether in case of danger, it could depend upon the other; that the front rank vainly concealed the weakness of the two others; that already, from youth and weakness, many of them sunk in their first march beneath the mere burden of their knapsackss and their arms.

"And, nevertheless, in this expedition, it was not so much the war which was disliked, as the country where it was to be carried on.[6] The Lithuanians, it was said, desired our presence; but on what a soil? in what a climate? in the midst of what peculiar manners? The campaign of 1806 had made all those points, but too well known! Where could they ever halt, in the midst of these level plains, devoid of every species of position fortified by nature or by art?

"Was it not notorious, that all the elements protected these countries from the first of October to the first of June? that, at any other time than the short interval comprised between these two epochs, an army engaged in those deserts of mud or ice might perish there entirely, and ingloriously?" And, they added, "that Lithuania was more Asiatic than Spain was African; and that the French army, already all but banished from France by a perpetual war, wished at least to preserve its European character.

"Finally, when face to face with the enemy in these deserts, what different motives must actuate the different armies! On the side of the Russians were country, independence, every description of interest, private and public, even to the secret good wishes of our allies! On our side, and in the teeth of so many obstacles, glory alone, unassociated even with the desire of gain, to which the frightful poverty of those countries offered no attraction.

"And what is the end of so many exertions? The French already no longer recognised each other, in the midst of a country now uncircumscribed by any natural frontier, and in which the diversity was so great in manners, persons, and languages." On this particular point, the eldest[7] of these great officers added, "That such an extension was never made without proportionate exhaustion; that it was blotting out France to merge it in Europe; for, in fact, when France should become Europe, she would be France no longer. Would not the meditated departure leave her solitary, deserted, without a ruler, without an army, accessible to every diversion? Who, then, would there be to defend her?" "*My renown!*" exclaimed the emperor: "*I leave my name behind me, and the fear inspired by a nation in arms.*"

And, without appearing in the least shaken by so many objections, he declared, "that he was about to organise the empire into cohorts of

Ban and *Arriere Ban*: and without mistrust to leave to Frenchmen the protection of France, of his crown and of his glory.

"That, as to Prussia, he had secured her tranquillity by the impossibility in which he had placed her of moving, even in case of his defeat, or of a descent of the English on the coasts of the North Sea, and in our rear; that he held in his hands the civil and military police of that kingdom; that he was master of Stettin, Custrin, Glogau, Torgau, Spandau, and Magdeburg; that he would post some clear-sighted officers at Colberg, and an army at Berlin; and that with these means, and supported by the fidelity of Saxony, he had nothing to fear from Prussian enmity.

"That as for the rest of Germany, an ancient system of policy, as well as the recent intermarriages with Baden, Bavaria, and Austria, attached her to the interests of France; that he made sure of such of her kings as were indebted to him for their new titles: that after having enchained anarchy, and ranged himself on the side of kings, strong as he was, the latter could not attack him without inciting their people by the principles of democracy, but that sovereigns would doubtless not ally themselves with that natural enemy of thrones—an enemy which, had it not been for him, would have overthrown them, and against which he alone was capable of defending them.

"That, besides, the Germans were a tardy and methodical people, and that in dealing with them, he should always have time on his side; that he commanded all the fortresses of Prussia; that Dantzic was a second Gibraltar." This was incorrect, especially in winter. "That Russia ought to excite the apprehension of all Europe, by her military and conquering government, as well as by her savage population, already so numerous, and which augmented annually in the proportion of half a million. Had not her armies been seen in all parts of Italy, in Germany, and even on the Rhine? That by demanding the evacuation of Prussia, she required an impossible concession; since to abandon Prussia, morally ulcerated as she was, was to surrender her into the hands of Russia, in order to be turned against ourselves."

Proceeding afterwards with more animation, he exclaimed, "Why do you menace my absence with the different parties still alleged to exist in the interior of the empire? Where are they? I see but a single one against me; that of a few royalists, the principal part of whom are of the ancient *noblesse,* old and inexperienced. But they dread my downfall more than they desire it. This is what I told them in Normandy: 'I am cried up as a great captain, as an able politician, but I am scarcely mentioned as an administrator: that which I have, however, accomplished, of the most beneficial description, is the stemming of the revolutionary torrent; it would have swallowed up every thing, Europe and yourselves! I have united the most opposite parties, amalgamated rival classes, and yet there exist among you some obstinate nobles who resist; they refuse my places! Very well! what is that to me? It is for your advantage, for your security, that I offer them to you. What would you do singly by yourselves, and without me? You are a mere handful opposed to masses. Do you not see that it is necessary to put an end to this struggle between the *commons*, and the *nobility*, by a complete fusion of all that is most worthy of preservation in the two classes? I offer you the hand of amity, and you reject it! But what need have I of you? While I support you, I do myself an injury in the eyes of the people; for what am I but the king of the *commons*: is not that sufficient?"

Passing more calmly to another question: "He was quite aware," he said, "of the ambition of his generals; but it was diverted by war, and would never be sanctioned in its excesses by French soldiers, who were too proud, and too much attached to their country. That if war was dangerous, peace had also its dangers: that in bringing back his armies into the interior, it would enclose and concentrate there too many interests and daring passions, which repose and their association would tend to set in a ferment, and which he should no longer be able to keep within bounds: that it was necessary to give free vent to all such aspirations: and that, after all, he dreaded the less without the empire than within it."

He concluded thus: "Do you dread the war, as endangering my life? It was thus that, in the times of conspiracy, attempts were made to frighten me about Georges; he was said to be every where upon my track: that wretched being was to fire at me. Well! suppose he had! He would at the utmost have killed my *aide-de-camp*: but to kill me was impossible! Had I at that time accomplished the decrees of fate? I feel myself impelled towards a goal of which I am ignorant. The moment I have reached it, as soon as I am no longer of service,—an atom will then suffice to put me down; but till then, all human efforts can avail nothing against me. Whether I am in Paris, or with the army, is, therefore, quite indifferent. When my hour comes, a fever, or a fall from my horse in hunting, will kill me as effectually as bullet: our days are numbered."

This opinion, useful as it may be in the moment of danger, is too apt to blind conquerors to the price at which the great results which they obtain are purchased. They indulge a belief in predestination, either because they have experienced, more than other men, whatever is most unexpected in human destiny, or because it relieves their consciences of too heavy a load of responsibility. It was like a return to the times of the crusades, when these words, *it is the will of God*, were considered a sufficient answer to all the objections of a prudent and pacific policy.

In fact, the expedition of Napoleon into Russia bears a mournful resemblance to that of St. Louis into Egypt and Africa! These invasions, the one undertaken for the interests of Heaven, the other for those of the earth, had both a similar termination; and these two great catastrophes afford a lesson to the world, that the vast and profound calculations of this age of intelligence may be followed by the same results as the irregular bursts of religious frenzy in ages of ignorance and superstition.

In these two enterprises, however, there can be no comparison between their opportunities or their chances of success. The last was indispensable to the completion of a great design which was almost accomplished; its object was not out of reach; the means for effecting it were adequate. It may be, that the moment for its execution was ill-chosen; that the progress of it might be sometimes too precipitate, at other times unsteady; but on these points facts will speak sufficiently: it is for them to decide.

1. It is asserted, and with much appearance of truth, that no such opinion was ever given by Prince Poniatowski; that his opinion was, in fact, of a diametrically opposite kind—*Ed.*

2. The Duke of Frioul (Duroc), the Count de Segur (the author's father), the Duke of Vicenza (Caulaincourt).

3. The Duke of Vicenza.

4. The Duke of Vicenza, the Count de Segur.

5. The Count de Segur.

6. The Duke of Frioul, the Count de Segur, the Duke of Vicenza.

7. M. de Segur.

CHAPTER III

NAPOLEON'S ARGUMENTS

IN this manner did Napoleon reply to all objections. His skilful hand was able to comprehend and turn to his purpose every disposition; and, in fact, when he wished to persuade, there was a kind of charm in his deportment which it was impossible to resist. One felt overpowered by his superior strength, and compelled, as it were, to submit to his influence. It was, if it may be so expressed, a kind of magnetic influence; for his ardent and variable genius infused itself entirely into all his desires, the least as well as the greatest: whatever he willed, all his energies and all his faculties united to accomplish: they appeared at his beck; they hastened forward; and obedient to his dictation, simultaneously assumed the forms which he desired.

It was thus that the greater part of those whom he wished to gain over found themselves, as it were, completely carried away. Who could help feeling flattered at seeing the master of Europe appearing to have no other ambition, no other desire than that of convincing you? to behold those features, so formidable to multitudes, expressing towards you no other feeling but a mild and affecting benevolence; to hear that mysterious man, whose every word was historical, yielding, as if for your sake alone, to the irresistible impulse of the most frank and confiding disclosure; and that voice, so caressing while it addressed you, was it not the same, whose lowest whisper rang throughout all Europe, announced wars, decided battles, settled the fate of empires,

raised or destroyed reputations? What vanity could resist a charm of
so great potency? Any defensive position was forced on all points; his
eloquence was so much more persuasive, as he himself seemed to speak
the language of conviction.

On this occasion, there was no variety of tints with which his
brilliant and fertile imagination did not adorn his project, in order
to convince and allure. The same text supplied him with a thousand
different commentaries, with which the character and position of each
of his interlocutors inspired him; he enlisted each in his undertaking,
by presenting it to him under the form and colour, and point of view
most likely to gratify him.

We have just seen in what way he silenced the one who felt alarmed
at the expenses of the conquest of Russia, which he wished him to
approve, by holding out the perspective, that another would be made
to defray them.

He told the military man, who was astonished by the hazard of
the expedition, but likely to be easily seduced by the grandeur of
ambitious ideas, that peace was to be conquered at Constantinople;
that is to say, at the extremity of Europe; the individual was thus led
to anticipate, that it was not merely to a marshal's staff, but to a royal
sceptre, that he might then elevate his pretensions.

To a minister[i] of high rank under the ancient *régime*, whom the idea
of shedding so much blood, to gratify ambition, filled with dismay, he
declared "that it was a war of policy exclusively; that it was the English
alone whom he meant to attack through Russia; that the campaign
would be short; that afterwards France would be at rest; that it was
the fifth act—the *dénouement* of the drama."

To others, he pleaded the ambition of Russia, and the force of
circumstances, which dragged him into the war spite of himself.
With superficial and inexperienced individuals, to whom he neither
wished to explain nor dissemble, he cut matters short, by saying, "you
understand nothing of all this; you are ignorant of its antecedents and
its consequents."

But to the princes of his own family he had long revealed the state
of his thoughts; he complained that they did not properly understand
his position. "Can you not see," said he to them, "that as I was not

born upon a throne, I must support myself on it, as I ascended it, by my renown? that it is necessary for that to go on increasing; that a private individual, become a sovereign like myself, can no longer stop; that he must be continually ascending, and that to remain stationary will be his ruin!"

He then depicted to them all the ancient dynasties armed against his, devising plots, preparing wars, and seeking to destroy, in his person, the dangerous example of a self-created monarch. It was on that account that every peace appeared in his eyes a conspiracy of the weak against the strong, of the vanquished against the victor; and especially of the great by birth against the great by their own exertions. So many successive coalitions had confirmed him in that apprehension! Indeed, he often thought of no longer tolerating an ancient government in Europe, of constituting himself into an epoch, of becoming a new era for thrones; in short, of making every thing take its date from him.

It was in this manner that he disclosed his inmost thoughts to his family, by those vivid pictures of his political position, which, at the present day, will probably appear neither false nor over-coloured: and yet the gentle Josephine, always occupied with the task of restraining and calming him, often gave him to understand "that, along with the consciousness of his superior genius, he never seemed to possess sufficient consciousness of his own power; that, like all jealous characters, he incessantly required fresh proofs of its existence. How came it, amidst the noisy acclamations of Europe, that his anxious ear could hear the few solitary voices which disputed his legitimacy? that in this manner his troubled spirit was always seeking agitation as its element: that strong as he was to desire, but feeble to enjoy, he himself, therefore, would be the only one whom he could never conquer."

But in 1811 Josephine was separated from Napoleon, and although he still continued to visit her in her seclusion, the voice of that empress had lost the influence which continual intercourse, habits of affectionate familiarity, and mutual confidence, impart.

Meanwhile fresh disagreements with the pope complicated the relations of France. Napoleon then addressed himself to cardinal Fesch. Fesch was a zealous churchman, and overflowing with Italian vivacity: he defended the papal pretensions with obstinate ardour; and such was the warmth of his discussions with the emperor, on a former occasion, that the latter got into a passion, and told him "that he would compel him to obey." "And who contests your power?" returned the cardinal: "but force is not argument; for if I am right, not all your power can make me wrong. Besides your majesty knows that I do not fear martyrdom."—"Martyrdom!" replied Napoleon, with a transition from violence to laughter, "do not reckon on that, I beseech you, M. le Cardinal: martyrdom is an affair in which there must be two persons concerned; and as to myself I have no desire to make a martyr of any individual."

It is said that these discussions assumed a more serious character towards the end of 1811. An eye-witness asserts that the cardinal, till that time a stranger to politics, then began to mix them up with his religious controversies; that he conjured Napoleon not thus to fly in the face of men, the elements, religion, earth, and heaven, at the same time; and that, at last, he expressed his apprehension of seeing him sink under such a weight of enmity.

The only reply which the emperor made to this vehement attack was to take him by the hand, and leading him to the window, to open it, and inquire, "Do you see that star above us?"—"No, sire."—"Look again?"—"Sire, I do not see it."—"Very well! *I* see it!" replied Napoleon. The cardinal, seized with astonishment, was silent, concluding that there was no human voice sufficiently loud to make itself heard by an ambition so gigantic, that it already reached the heavens.

As to the witness of this singular scene, he understood in quite a different sense these words of his sovereign. They did not appear to him like the expression of an overweening confidence in his destiny, but rather of the great distinction which Napoleon meant to infer as existing between the grasp of his genius and that of the cardinal's policy.

But granting that even Napoleon's soul was not altogether exempt from a tendency to superstition, his intellect was both too strong and too enlightened to permit such vast events to depend upon a weakness. One great inquietude possessed him; it was the idea of that same death, which he appeared so much to brave. He felt his strength decaying; and he dreaded that when he should be no more, the French empire, that sublime trophy of so many labours and victories, would fall a prey to dismemberment.

"The Russian emperor," he said, "was the only sovereign who pressed upon the summit of that colossal edifice. Replete with youth and animation, the strength of his rival was constantly augmenting, while his was already on the decline." It seemed to him that Alexander, on the banks of the Niemen, only waited the intelligence of his death, to possess himself of the sceptre of Europe, and wrest it from the hands of his feeble successor. "While all Italy, Switzerland, Austria, Prussia, and the whole of Germany, were marching under his banners, why should he delay to anticipate the danger, and consolidate the fabric of the great empire, by driving back Alexander and the Russian power, enfeebled as they would be by the loss of all Poland, beyond the Borysthenes?"

Such were his expressions, pronounced in the closeness of intimacy; they, doubtless, comprised the real motives of that terrible war. As to his precipitation in commencing it, it would seem that he was hurried on by the instinct of his approaching death. An acrid humour diffused through his blood, and to which he imputed his irascibility, ("but without which," added he, "battles are not to be gained,") undermined his constitution.

It would require a more profound knowledge of the organisation of the human frame than we possess, to enable us to decide whether this concealed malady was not one of the causes of that restless activity which hurried on the course of events, and originated both his elevation and his fall.

This internal enemy testified its presence, more and more, by a secret pain, and by the violent spasms of the stomach which it inflicted. As early as 1806, at Warsaw, during one of its agonising crises, Napoleon was[2] heard to exclaim, "that he carried within him the germ of premature dissolution; and that he should die of the same malady as his father."

Short rides in hunting, even the most gentle gallop of his horse, already began to fatigue him: how then was he to support the long journeys, and the rapid and violent movements preparatory to battles? Thus it was, that while the greater part of those who surrounded him concluded him to be impelled into Russia by his vast ambition, by his restless spirit, and his love of war, he in solitude, and almost unobserved, was poising the fearful responsibilities of the enterprise, and urged by necessity, he only made up his mind to it after a course of painful hesitation.

At length, on the 3d of August, 1811, at an audience in the midst of the ambassadors of all Europe, he declared himself; but this burst of anger, which was the presage of war, was an additional proof of his repugnance to commence it. It might be that the defeat which the Russians had just sustained at Rudschuk, had inflated his hopes; perhaps he imagined that he might, by menace, arrest the preparations of Alexander.

It was to Prince Kourakin, the Russian ambassador, that he addressed himself. That ambassador having replied by protestations of the pacific intentions of his master, Napoleon interrupted him: "No," exclaimed he, "your master desires war; I know, through my generals, that the Russian army is hurrying towards the Niemen! The emperor Alexander deludes, and gains over all my envoys!" Then, perceiving Caulaincourt, he rapidly traversed the hall, and accosting him, said: "Yes, and you too have become a Russian: you have been seduced by the emperor Alexander." The duke firmly replied, "Yes, sire; because, in this question, I consider him to be a Frenchman." Napoleon was silent; but from that moment he treated that great dignitary coldly, without, however, absolutely repelling him: several times he even essayed, by fresh arguments, intermixed with familiar caresses, to win him over to his opinion, but ineffectually; he always found him inflexible; ready to serve him, but without approving the nature of the service.

1. Count Molé.
2. By the Count Lobau.

CHAPTER IV

PROPOSALS TO ENGLAND AND RUSSIA

WHILE Napoleon, prompted by his natural character, by his position, and by circumstances, thus appeared to wish for, and to accelerate the period of conflict, he preserved the secret of his embarrassment. The year 1811 was wasted in parleys about peace, and preparations for war. 1812 had just begun, and already the horizon was become obscured. Our armies in Spain had given way; Ciudad Rodrigo was taken by the English (on the 19th of January, 1812); the discussions of Napoleon with the Pope increased in bitterness; Kutusof had destroyed the Turkish army on the Danube (on the 8th of December, 1811); France even became alarmed about her means of subsistence; every thing, in short, appeared to divert the attention of Napoleon from Russia; to recall it to France, and fix it there; while he, far from blinding his judgment, recognised in these contrarieties the admonitions of his ever-faithful fortune.

It was, especially, in the midst of those long winter nights, when individuals are left more than usually to their own reflections, that his star seemed to enlighten him with its most brilliant illumination: it exhibited to him the different ruling genii of the vanquished nations, in silence awaiting the moment for avenging their wrongs; the dangers which he was about to confront, those which he left behind him, even in his own family: it showed him that, like the returns of his army, the census of the population of his empire was delusive, not so much in respect to its numerical as to its real strength; scarcely any men were included in it but such as were old in years, or worn out in the service, and children—few men in the prime of life. Where were they? The tears of wives, the cries of mothers answered! bowed in sadness to the earth, which but for them, would remain uncultivated, they cursed the scourge of war as identified in his person.[1]

Nevertheless, he was about to attack Russia, without having subjected Spain; forgetting the principle of which he himself so often supplied both the precept and example, "never to strike at two points at once: but at one only, and always in mass." Wherefore, then, should he abandon a brilliant, though uncertain position, in order to throw himself into a situation so critical, that the slightest check might ruin every thing; and where every reverse would be decisive?

At such moments, no necessity of position, no sentiment of self-love, could prompt Napoleon to combat his own arguments, and prevent him from listening to himself. Hence he became thoughtful and agitated. He collected accounts of the actual condition of the different powers of Europe; he ordered an exact and complete summary of them to be made; he became absorbed in its perusal; his anxiety increased; to him, of all men, irresolution was a punishment.

Frequently was he discovered half reclined on a sofa, where he remained for hours plunged in profound meditation; then he would start up, convulsively, and with an ejaculation, fancying he heard his name, he would exclaim, "Who calls me?" Then rising, and walking about with hurried steps, he at length added, "No! beyond a doubt, nothing is yet sufficiently matured round me, even in my own family, to admit of so distant a war. It must be delayed for three years!" And he gave orders that the summary which reminded him of the dangers of his position should be constantly left on his table. It was his frequent subject of consultation, and every time he did so, he approved and repeated his first conclusions.

It is not known what dictated so salutary a measure; but it is certain, that about that epoch (the 25th of March, 1812), Czernicheff was the bearer of new proposals to his sovereign. Napoleon offered to make a declaration that he would not contribute, either directly or indirectly, to the re-establishment of the kingdom of Poland; and to come to an understanding about the other subjects in dispute.[2]

At a later period, (on the 17th of April,) the Duke of Bassano proposed to Lord Castlereagh an arrangement relative to the Peninsula, and the kingdom of the Two Sicilies; and in other respects offered to negociate on the basis, that each of the two powers should keep all that war could not wrest from it. But Castlereagh replied, that the engagements of good faith would not permit England to treat, without making the recognition of Ferdinand VII. as king of Spain, a preliminary of the negociation.

On the 25th of April, Maret, in apprising Count Romanzoff of this communication, recapitulated a portion of the complaints which Napoleon made against Russia;—firstly, the ukase of the 31st of December, 1810, which prohibited the entry into Russia of the greater part of French productions, and destroyed the continental system; secondly, the protest of Alexander against the union of the duchy of Oldenburgh; and thirdly, the armaments of Russia.

This minister referred to the fact of Napoleon having offered to grant an indemnity to the duke of Oldenburgh, and to enter into a formal engagement not to concur in any undertaking for the re-establishment of Poland; that in 1811, he had proposed to Alexander to give Prince Kourakin the requisite powers to treat with the duke of Bassano respecting all matters in dispute; but that the Russian emperor had eluded the overture, by promising to send Nesse to Paris; a promise which was never fulfilled.

The Russian ambassador, almost at the same time, transmitted the emperor Alexander's ultimatum. It required the entire evacuation of Prussia; that of Swedish Pomerania; and a reduction of the garrison of Dantzic. On the other hand, he offered to accept an indemnity for the duchy of Oldenburgh; he was willing to enter into commercial arrangements with France; and finally promised empty modifications of the ukase of the 31st December, 1810.

But it was too late: besides, at the point to which both parties were now arrived, that ultimatum necessarily led to war. Napoleon was too proud, both of himself and of France, he was too much overruled by his position, to yield to a menacing negociator, to leave Prussia at liberty to throw herself into the open arms of Russia, and thus to abandon Poland. He was too far advanced; he would be obliged to retrograde, in order to find a resting point; and in his situation, Napoleon considered every retrograde step as the incipient point of a complete downfall.

1. To this it has been replied, that a census, taken after the fall of Napoleon, proved the population of France to have received an increase of five millions.

2. This declaration was made twelve months previously—*Ed.*

CHAPTER V

PREPARATIONS AND DELAYS

His wishes for delay being thus frustrated, he surveyed the enormous volume of his military strength; the recollections of Tilsit and Erfurt were revived; he received with complacency delusive information respecting the character of his rival. At one time, he hoped that Alexander would give way at the approach of so menacing an invasion; at another, he gave the reins to his conquering imagination; he indulgently allowed it to deploy its masses from Cadiz to Casan, and to cover the whole of Europe. In the next moment his fancy rioted in the pleasure of being at Moscow. That city was eight hundred leagues from him, and already he was collecting information with respect to it, as if he was on the eve of occupying it. A French physician having recently arrived from that capital, he questioned him as to the diseases there prevalent; he even went back to the plague which had formerly desolated it; he was desirous to learn its origin, progress, and termination. The answers of this physician were so satisfactory, that he immediately attached him to his service.

Fully impressed, however, with a sense of the peril in which he was about to embark, he sought to surround himself with all his friends. Even Talleyrand was recalled; he was to have been sent to Warsaw, but the jealousy of a rival[1] and an intrigue again involved him in disgrace; Napoleon, deluded by a calumny, adroitly circulated, believed that he had been betrayed by him. His anger was extreme; its expression terrible. Savary made vain efforts to undeceive him, which were prolonged up to the epoch of our entry into Wilna; there that minister again sent a letter of Talleyrand to the minister; it depicted the influence of Turkey and Sweden on the Russian war, and made an offer of employing his most zealous efforts in negociating with those two powers.

But Napoleon only replied to it by an exclamation of contempt: "Does that man believe himself to be so necessary? Does he expect to teach me?" He then compelled his secretary to send that letter to the very minister who stood most in dread of Talleyrand's influence.

It would not be correct to say, that all those about Napoleon beheld the war with an anxious eye. Inside the palace, as well as without it, many military men were found who entered with ardour into the policy of their chief. The greater part agreed as to the possibility of the conquest of Russia, either because their hopes discerned in it a means of acquiring something, according to their position, from the lowest distinction up to a throne; or that they suffered themselves to participate in the enthusiasm of the Poles; or that the expedition, if conducted with prudence, might fairly look to success; or to sum up all, because they conceived everything possible to Napoleon.

Among the ministers of the empire, several disapproved it; the greater number preserved silence; one alone has been accused of flattery, and that without the least foundation. It is true he was heard to repeat, "that the emperor was not sufficiently great; that it was necessary for him to become greater still, in order to be able to stop." But that minister was, in reality, what so many courtiers wished to appear; he had a real and absolute faith in the genius and fortune of his sovereign.

In other respects, it is wrong to impute to his counsels a large portion of our misfortunes. Napoleon was not a man to be influenced. As soon as his object was marked out, and he had taken steps towards its attainment, he admitted of no farther contradiction. He then appeared as if he would hear nothing but what flattered his determination; he repelled with ill-humour, and even with apparent incredulity, all disagreeable intelligence, as if he feared to be shaken by it. This mode of acting changed its name according to its fortune; when fortunate it was called force of character; when unfortunate, it was designated as infatuation.

The knowledge of such a disposition induced sore subalterns to make false reports to him. Even a minister himself felt occasionally compelled to maintain a dangerous silence. The former inflated his hopes of success, in order to imitate the proud confidence of their leader, and that their countenance might stamp upon his mind the impression of a happy omen; the second sometimes declined communicating bad news, in order, as he said, to avoid the harsh rebuffs which he had then to encounter.

But this fear, which did not restrain Caulaincourt and several others, had as little influence upon Duroc, Daru, Lobau, Rapp, Lauristou, and sometimes even Berthier. These ministers and generals, each in his sphere, did not spare the emperor when the truth was to be told. If it so happened that he was enraged by it, Duroc, without yielding, assumed an air of indifference; Lobau resisted with roughness; Berthier sighed, and retired with tears in his eyes; Caulaincourt and Daru, the one turning pale, the other reddening with anger, repelled the vehement contradictions of the emperor; the first with impetuous obstinacy, and the second with short and dry determination.

It should, however, be added here, that these warm discussions were never productive of bad consequences; good temper was restored immediately after, apparently without leaving any other impression than redoubled esteem on the part of Napoleon, for the noble frankness which they had just displayed.

I have entered into these details, because they are either not known, or imperfectly known; because Napoleon in his closet was quite different from the emperor in public; and because this part of the palace has hitherto remained secret. For, in this new and serious court, there was little conversation; all were rigorously classed, so that one *salon* knew not what passed in another. Finally, because it is difficult to comprehend the great events of history, without a perfect knowledge of the character and manners of its principal personages.

Meantime a famine threatened France. The universal panic quickly aggravated the evil, by the precautions which it suggested. Avarice, always prompt in seizing the means of enriching itself, monopolised the corn while at a low price, and waited till hunger should repurchase it at its weight in gold. The alarm then became general. Napoleon was compelled to suspend his departure; he impatiently urged his council; but the steps to be taken were important, his presence necessary; and that war, in which the loss of every hour was irreparable, was delayed for two months.[2]

The emperor did not give way to this obstacle; the delay, besides, gave the new harvests of the Russians time to grow. These would supply his cavalry; his army would require fewer means of transport in its train; its march, being lighter, would be more rapid; he would sooner reach the enemy: and this great expedition, like so many others, would be terminated by a battle.

Such were his hopes; for, without deceiving himself as to his good fortune, he reckoned on its influence upon others; it entered into his estimate of his forces. It was for this reason that he always pushed it forward where other things failed, making up by it whatever was deficient in his means, without fearing to wear it out by constant use, in the conviction that both his allies and enemies would place even more faith in it than himself. However, it will be seen in the sequel of this expedition, that he placed too much reliance on its power, and that Alexander contrived to escape from it.

Such was Napoleon! Superior to the passions of men by his native greatness, and also by the circumstance of being controlled by a still greater passion! for when, indeed, are these masters of the world ever entirely masters of themselves? Meantime blood was again about to flow; and thus, in their great career, the founders of empires press forward to their object, like Fate, whose ministers they seem, (and whose march neither wars nor earthquakes, nor all the scourges which Providence permits, ever arrest,) without deigning to make the utility of their purposes comprehensible to their victims.

1. The rival, here alluded to, was Maret, duke of Bassano, and the charge against him appears to be unjust —*Ed*.

2. All the necessary measures, to avert the threatened evil of a famine, had been taken by Napoleon before the end of the year 1811.—*Ed*.

BOOK III

CHAPTER I

THE START OF THE CAMPAIGN

THE time for deliberation had passed, and that for action at length arrived. On the 9th of May, 1812, Napoleon, hitherto always triumphant, quitted a palace which he was destined never again to enter victorious.

From Paris to Dresden his march was a continued triumph. The east of France, which he first traversed, was a part of the empire entirely devoted to him; very different from the west and the south, it was only acquainted with him by means of benefits and victories. Numerous and brilliant armies, attracted by the fertility of Germany, and which imagined themselves marching to a prompt and certain glory, proudly traversed those countries, scattering their money among them and consuming their productions. War, in that quarter, always bore the semblance of justice.

At a later period, when our victorious bulletins reached them, the imagination, astonished to see itself surpassed by the reality, caught fire; enthusiasm possessed these people, as in the times of Austerlitz and Jena; numerous groups collected round the couriers, whose tidings were listened to with avidity; and the inhabitants, in a transport of joy, never separated without exclamations of "Long live the emperor! Long live our brave army!"

It is, besides, well known that this portion of France has at all times been warlike. It is frontier ground; its inhabitants are nursed amidst the din of arms; and arms are, consequently, held there in honour. It was the common conversation in that quarter, that this war would liberate Poland, so much attached to France; that the barbarians of Asia, with whom Europe was threatened, would be driven back into their native deserts; that Napoleon would once more return, loaded with all the fruits of victory. Would not the eastern departments profit most by that event? Up to that time, were they not indebted for their wealth to war, which caused all the commerce of France with Europe to pass through their hands? Blockaded, in fact, in every other quarter, the empire only breathed and received its supplies through its eastern provinces.

For ten years their roads had been covered with travellers of all ranks, hastening to admire the great nation, its daily embellished metropolis, the masterpieces of all the arts, and of all ages, which victory had there assembled; and especially that extraordinary man who seemed destined to carry the national glory beyond every degree of glory hitherto known. Gratified in their interests, flattered in their vanity, the people of the east of France owed every thing to victory. Neither were they ungrateful; they followed the emperor with their warmest wishes: on all sides were acclamations and triumphal arches: on all sides the same intensity of devotion.

In Germany there was less affection, but, perhaps, more homage. Conquered and subjected, the Germans, either as soothing to their vanity, or from habitual inclination for the marvellous, were tempted to consider Napoleon as a supernatural being. Astonished, transported, and carried along by the universal impulse, these worthy people exerted themselves to *be*, sincerely, all that it was requisite to *seem*.

They hurried forward to line both sides of the long road by which the emperor passed. Their princes quitted their capitals and thronged the towns where the great arbiter of their destiny was to pass a few short moments of his journey. The empress and a numerous court followed Napoleon; he proceeded to confront the terrible risks of a distant and perilous war, as if he were returning victorious and triumphant. It was not thus that he was formerly accustomed to march to combat.

He had expressed a wish that the emperor of Austria, several kings, and a crowd of princes, should meet him at Dresden on his way: his desire was fulfilled; all thronged to him—some led by hope, others prompted by fear: for himself, his motives were to make sure of his power, to exhibit and to enjoy it.

In this approximation with the ancient house of Austria, his ambition delighted in exhibiting to Germany a family meeting. He imagined that so brilliant an assemblage of sovereigns would advantageously contrast with the insulated state of the Russian monarch, who would probably be alarmed by so general a desertion. Besides, this assembly of coalesced monarchs seemed to announce that this war with Russia was European.

There he was in the centre of Germany, exhibiting to it his consort, the daughter of its emperors, sitting by his side. Whole nations had quitted their homes to throng his path; rich and poor, nobles and plebeians, friends and enemies, all hurried to the scene. Their curious and anxious groups were seen crowding together in the streets, the roads, and the public places; they passed whole days and nights with their eyes fixed on the gate and windows of his palace. It was not his crown, his rank, the splendour of his court, but him only, on whom they desired to feast their eyes; it was a memento of his features which they were anxious to obtain; they wished to he able to tell their less fortunate countrymen and posterity that they had seen Napoleon.

On the stage, poets so far degraded themselves as to make him a divinity. It was in this manner that whole nations became his flatterers.

There was, in fact, little difference between kings and people in the homage of admiration; no one waited for the example of imitation; the agreement was unanimous. Nevertheless, the inward sentiments were very different.

At this important interview, we were attentive in observing the different degrees of zeal which these princes exhibited, and the various shades of our chieftain's pride. We had hoped that his prudence, or the worn-out feeling of displaying his power, would prevent him from abusing it; but was it to be expected that he, who, while yet an inferior, never spoke, even to his superiors, but the language of command, now that he was the conqueror and master of them all, could submit to tedious and minute details of ceremony? He, however, displayed moderation; and even tried to make himself agreeable; but it was obviously an effort, and not without allowing the fatigue it gave him to be perceived. Among these princes, he had rather the air of receiving them, than of being by them received.

As to them, it might be said, that, knowing his pride, and become hopeless of subduing him, except by means of himself, these monarchs and their people only humbled themselves before him, in order to aggravate the disproportion of his elevation, and by so doing, to dazzle his moral vision. In their assemblies, their attitude, their words, even the tone of their voice, attested his ascendency over them. All were there for his sake alone! They scarcely hazarded an objection, so impressed were they with the full conviction of that superiority, of which he was himself too well aware. A feudal lord could not have exacted more of his vassal chiefs.

His levee presented a still more remarkable spectacle! Sovereign princes came to it in order to obtain an audience of the conqueror of Europe. They were so intermingled with his officers, that the latter were frequently warning each other to take care, and not to crowd upon these new courtiers, who were confounded with them. It was that the presence of Napoleon made distinctions disappear; he was as much their chief as ours. This common dependency appeared to put him on a level. It is probable that, even then, the ill-disguised military pride of several French generals gave offence to these princes, with whom they conceived themselves raised to an equality; and, in fact, whatever may be the noble blood and rank of the vanquished, his victor becomes his equal.

The more prudent among us, however, began to be alarmed; they said, but in an under-tone, that a man must fancy himself more than human to denaturalise and displace every thing in this manner, without fearing to involve himself in the universal confusion. They saw these monarchs quitting the palace of Napoleon with their eyes inflamed, and their bosoms swoln with the most poignant resentment. They pictured them, during the night, when alone with their ministers, giving vent to the heart-felt chagrin by which they were devoured. Every thing was calculated to render their suffering more acute! How importunate was the crowd which it was necessary to pass through, in order to reach the gate of their proud master, while their own remained deserted! for every thing, even their own people, appeared to betray them! When he was boasting of his good fortune, was it not evident that he was insulting their misfortunes? They had, therefore, come to Dresden in order to swell the pomp of Napoleon's triumph—for it was over them that he thus triumphed: each cry of admiration offered to him was a cry of reproach to them; his grandeur was their humiliation, his victory their defeat.

Doubtless they, in this manner, gave vent to their bitter feelings; and hatred, day after day, sank more deeply into their hearts. One prince was observed to withdraw precipitately from this painful position. The empress of Austria, whose ancestors General Bonaparte had dispossessed in Italy, made herself remarked by her aversion, which she vainly endeavoured to disguise; it escaped from her in her first movements, which Napoleon instantly detected, and subdued by a smile: but she used her spirit and attractions in gently winning hearts, in order to sow them afterwards with the seeds of her hatred.

The Empress of France unintentionally aggravated this fatal disposition. She was observed to eclipse her mother-in-law by the superior magnificence of her dress: if Napoleon required more reserve, she resisted, and even wept, till the emperor, either, through affection, fatigue, or absence of mind, was induced to give way. It is also asserted that, notwithstanding her origin, remarks calculated to wound the German vanity escaped that princess, in extravagant comparisons between her native and her adopted country. Napoleon rebuked her for this, but gently; he was pleased with a patriotism which he had himself inspired; and he fancied he repaired her imprudent language by the munificence of his presents.

This assemblage, therefore, could not fail of irritating a variety of feelings: the vanity of many was wounded by the collision. Napoleon, however, having exerted himself to please, thought that he had given general satisfaction: while waiting at Dresden the result of the marches of his army, the numerous columns of which were still traversing the territories of his allies, he more especially occupied himself with his political arrangements.

General Lauriston, ambassador from France at Petersburgh, received orders to apply for the Russian emperor's permission to repair to Wilna, in order to communicate definitive proposals to him. General Narbonne, aide-de-camp of Napoleon, set off for the imperial head-quarters of Alexander, in order to assure that prince of the pacific intentions of France, and to invite him to Dresden. The archbishop of Malines was despatched in order to direct the impulses of Polish patriotism. The king of Saxony made up his mind to the loss of the grand duchy; but he was flattered with the hope of a more substantial indemnity.

Meantime, ever since the first days of meeting, surprise was expressed at the absence of the king of Prussia from the imperial court;[1] but it was soon understood that he was prohibited from coming. This prince was the more alarmed in proportion as he had less deserved such treatment. His presence would have been embarrassing. Nevertheless, encouraged by Narbonne, he resolved on making his appearance. When his arrival was announced to the emperor, the latter grew angry, and at first refused to see him:— "What did this prince want of him? Was not the constant importunity of his letters, and his continual solicitations sufficient? Why did he come again to persecute him with his presence? What need had he of him?" But Duroc insisted; he reminded Napoleon of the want that he would experience of Prussia, in a war with Russia; and the doors of the emperor were opened to the monarch. He was received with the respect due to his superior rank. His renewed assurances of fidelity, of which he gave numerous proofs, were accepted.

It is said that the Prussian monarch was at that time led to expect the possession of the Russo-German provinces, which his troops were to be commissioned to invade. It is even affirmed that, after their conquest, he demanded their investiture from Napoleon. It has been added, but in vague terms, that Napoleon allowed the Prince-Royal of Prussia to aspire to the hand of one of his nieces. This was to be the remuneration for the services which Prussia was to render him in this new war. He promised, so he expressed himself, that he would go and sound her. It was thus that Frederick, by becoming the relation of Napoleon, would be able to preserve his diminished power; but proofs are wanting, to show that the idea of this marriage seduced the King of Prussia, in the way that the hope of a similar alliance had seduced the Prince of Spain.

Such at that time was the submission of sovereigns to the power of Napoleon. It offers a striking example of the empire of necessity over all persons, and shows to what length the prospect of gain and the fear of loss will lead princes as well as private persons.

Napoleon, meanwhile, still waited the result of the negociations of Lauriston and of Narbonne. He hoped to vanquish Alexander by the mere aspect of his united army, and, above all, by the menacing splendour of his residence at Dresden. He himself expressed this opinion when, some days after, at Posen, he said to General Dessolles, "the assemblage at Dresden not having persuaded Alexander to make peace, we must now look for it only from war."

On that day he talked of nothing but his former victories. It seemed as if, doubtful of the future, he recurred to the past, and that he found it necessary to arm himself with all his most glorious recollections, in order to confront a peril of so great a magnitude. In fact, then, as well as subsequently, he felt the necessity of deluding himself with the alleged weakness of his rival's character. As the period of so great an invasion approached, he hesitated in considering it as certain; for he no longer possessed the consciousness of his infallibility, nor that warlike assurance which the fire and energy of youth impart, nor that confidence of victory which makes it certain.

In other respects, these parleys were not only attempts to preserve peace, but an additional *ruse de guerre*. By them he hoped to render the Russians either sufficiently negligent to let themselves be surprised when dispersed, or, if united, sufficiently presumptuous to venture to wait its approach. In either case, the war would be finished by a coup-de-main, or by a victory. But Lauriston was not received. Narbonne, when he returned, stated, "that he had found the Russians in a state of mind as remote from dejection as from boasting. From their emperor's reply to him, it appeared that they preferred war to a dishonourable peace; that they would take care not to expose themselves to the hazards of a battle against too formidable an enemy; and that, in short, they were resolved on making every sacrifice, in order to spin out the war, and to baffle Napoleon."

This answer, which reached the emperor in the midst of the greatest display of his glory, was treated with contempt. To say the truth, I must add, that a great Russian nobleman had contributed to deceive him: either from mistaken views, or from artifice, this Muscovite had persuaded him, that his own sovereign would recede at the sight of difficulties, and be easily discouraged by reverses. Unfortunately, the remembrance of Alexander's obsequiousness to him at Tilsit and at Erfurt confirmed the French emperor in that fallacious opinion.

He remained till the 29th of May at Dresden, proud of the homage which he knew how to appreciate, exhibiting to Europe the princes and kings, sprung from the most ancient families of Germany, forming a numerous court round a prince deriving all distinction from himself. He appeared to take a pleasure in multiplying the effects of the great games of fortune, as if to encircle with them, and render less extraordinary, that which had placed him on the throne, and thus to accustom others as well as himself to them.

---

1. It appears that the circumstance of the king of Prussia being absent from Dresden was occasioned by his expecting Napoleon at Berlin. When the emperor found that he could not visit Berlin, he invited the king of Prussia to Dresden, and the invitation was immediately accepted.—*Ed.*

CHAPTER II

ARRIVAL IN POLAND

AT length, impatient to conquer the Russians, and escape from the homage of the Germans, Napoleon quitted Dresden. He only remained at Posen long enough to satisfy the Poles. He neglected Warsaw, whither the war did not imperiously call him, and where he would again have been involved in politics. He stopped at Thorn, in order to inspect his fortifications, his magazines, and his troops. There the complaints of the Poles, whom our allies were pillaging without mercy, and insulting, reached him. Napoleon addressed severe reproaches, and even threats, to the king of Westphalia; but it is well known that these were thrown away; that their effect was lost in the midst of too rapid a movement; that, besides, his fits of anger, like all other fits, were followed by exhaustion that then, with the return of his natural good humour, he regretted, and frequently tried to soften the pain he had occasioned; that, finally, he might reproach himself as the cause of the disorders which provoked him; for, from the Oder to the Vistula, and even to the Niemen, if provisions were abundant and properly stationed, the less portable foraging supplies were deficient. Our cavalry were already forced to cut the green rye, and to strip the houses of the thatch, in order to feed their horses. It is true, that all did not stop at that; for when one disorder is authorised, how can others be forbidden?

The evil augmented on the other side of the Niemen. The emperor had calculated upon a multitude of light cars and heavy wagons, each destined to carry several thousand pounds weight, through a sandy region, which carts, with no greater weight than some quintals, found difficulty in traversing. These conveyances were organised in battalions and squadrons. Each battalion of light cars, called *comtoises*, consisted of six hundred, and might carry six thousand quintals of flour. The battalion of heavy vehicles, drawn by oxen, carried four thousand eight hundred quintals. There were besides twenty-six squadrons of wagons, loaded with military equipages; a great quantity of wagons with tools of all kinds, as well as thousands of artillery and hospital wagons, one siege and six bridge equipages.

The provision-wagons were to take in their loading from the magazines established on the Vistula. When the army passed that river, it was ordered to provide itself, without halting, with provisions for twenty-five days, but not to use them till it was beyond the Niemen. In conclusion, the greater part of these means of transport failed, either because the organisation of soldiers, to act as conductors of military convoys, was essentially vicious, honour and ambition not lending their support to discipline; or chiefly because these vehicles were too heavy for the soil, the distances too considerable, and the privations and fatigues too great; certain it is that the greater number of them scarcely reached the Vistula.

The army, therefore, provisioned itself on its march. The country being fertile, horses, wagons, cattle, and provisions of all kinds, were swept off; every thing was taken, even to such of the inhabitants as were necessary to conduct these convoys. Some days after, at the Niemen, the embarrassment of the passage, and celerity of the first hostile marches, caused all the fruits of these requisitions to be abandoned with an indifference only equalled by the violence with which they had been seized.

The importance of the object, however, was such as might excuse the irregularity of these proceedings. That object was to surprise the Russian army, either collected or dispersed; in short, to make a *coup-de-main* with 400,000 men. War, the worst of all scourges, would thus have been shortened in its duration. Our long and heavy baggage-wagons would have encumbered our march. It was much more convenient to live on the supplies of the country, as we should be able to indemnify the loss afterwards. But superfluous wrong was committed as well as necessary wrong, for who can stop midway in the commission of evil? What chief could be responsible for the crowd of officers and soldiers who were scattered through the country in order to collect its resources? To whom were complaints to be addressed? Who was to punish? All was done in the course of a rapid march; there was neither time to try, nor even to find out the guilty. Between the affair of the day before, and that of the following day, how many others had sprung up! for at that time the business of a month was crowded into a single day.

Moreover, some of the leaders set the example; there was a positive emulation in evil. In that respect many of our allies surpassed the French. We were their teachers in every thing; but in copying our qualities, they caricatured our defects. Their gross and brutal plunder was perfectly revolting.

But the emperor was desirous to have order kept in the middle of disorder. Pressed by the accusing reproaches of two allied nations, two names were more especially distinguished by his indignation. In his letters are found these words: "I have suspended generals —— and ——. I have suppressed the brigade ——; I have cashiered it in the face of the army, that is to say, of Europe.—I have written to ——, informing him that he runs great risks of being broken, if he does not take care." Some days after he met this ——, at the head of his troops, and still indignant, he called to him, "You disgrace yourself; you set the example of plunder. Be silent, or go back to your father; I do not want your services."

From Thorn, Napoleon descended the Vistula. Graudentz belonged to Prussia; he avoided passing it; but as that fortress was important to the safety of the army, an officer of artillery and some fire-workers were sent thither, with the ostensible motive of making cartridges; the real motive remained a secret; the Prussian garrison, however, was numerous, and stood on its guard, and the emperor, who had proceeded onward, thought no more of it.

It was at Marienburg that the emperor again met Davoust. That marshal, whether through pride, natural or acquired, was not well pleased to recognise as his leader any other individual than the master of

Europe. His character besides is obstinate, despotic, and tenacious; and as little inclined to yield to circumstances as to men. In 1809, Berthier was his commander for some days, during which Davoust gained a battle, and saved the army, by disobeying him.[1] Hence arose a terrible hatred between them: during the peace it augmented, but secretly; for they lived at a wide distance from each other, Berthier at Paris, Davoust at Hamburgh; but this Russian war brought them together.

Berthier was getting enfeebled. Ever since 1805, war had become completely odious to him. His talent especially lay in his activity and his memory. He could receive and transmit, at all hours of the day and night, the most multiplied intelligence and orders; but on this occasion he had conceived that he was entitled to give orders himself. These orders displeased Davoust. Their first interview was a scene of violent altercation; it occurred at Marienburg, where the emperor had just arrived, and in his presence.

Davoust expressed himself harshly, and even went so far as to accuse Berthier of incapacity or treachery. They both threatened each other, and when Berthier was gone, Napoleon, influenced by the naturally suspicious character of the marshal, exclaimed, "It sometimes happens that I entertain doubts of the fidelity of my oldest companions in arms; but at such times my head turns round with chagrin, and I do my utmost to banish so heart-rending a suspicion."

While Davoust was probably enjoying the dangerous pleasure of having humbled his enemy, the emperor proceeded to Dantzic, and Berthier, stung by resentment, followed him there. From that time, the zeal, the glory of Davoust, the exertions he had made for this new expedition, all that ought to have availed him, began to be looked upon unfavourably. The emperor had written to him "that as the war was about to be carried into a barren territory, where the enemy would destroy every thing, it was requisite to prepare for such a state of things, by providing every thing within ourselves:" Davoust had replied to this by enumerating his preparations—"He had 70,000 men, who were completely organised; they carried with them twenty-five days' provisions. Each company comprised swimmers, masons, bakers, tailors, shoemakers, armourers, and workmen of every class. They carried every thing they required with them; his army was like a colony; hand-mills followed. He had anticipated every want; all means of supplying them were ready."

Such great exertions ought to have pleased; they, however, displeased; they were misrepresented. Insidious observations were made in the hearing of the emperor. "This marshal," said they to him, "wishes to have it thought that he has foreseen, arranged, and executed every thing. Is the emperor, then, to be no more than a spectator of this expedition? Must the glory of it devolve on Davoust?"—"In fact," exclaimed the emperor, "one would think it was he that commanded the army."[2]

They even went further, and awakened some of his dormant fears: "Was it not Davoust who, after the victory of Jena, drew the emperor into Poland? Is it not he who is now anxious for this new Polish war?—he who already possesses such large property in that country, whose accurate and severe probity has won over the Poles, and who is suspected of aspiring to their throne?"

It is not easy to say whether the pride of Napoleon was shocked by seeing that of his lieutenants encroaching so much on his own; or whether, in the course of this irregular war, he felt himself thwarted more and more by the methodical genius of Davoust; certain it is, the unfavourable impression against him struck deeper; it was productive of fatal consequences; it removed from his confidence a bold, persevering, and prudent warrior, and favoured his predilection for Murat whose rashness was much more flattering to his hopes. In other respects, these dissensions between his great officers did not displease Napoleon; they gave him information; their harmony would have made him uneasy.

From Dantzic the emperor proceeded, on the 12th of June, to Königsberg. At that place ended the inspection of his immense magazines, and of the second resting point and pivot of his line of operations. Immense quantities of provisions, adequate to the immensity of the undertaking, were there accumulated. No detail had been neglected. The active and impassioned genius of Napoleon was then entirely directed towards that most important and difficult department of his expedition. In that he was profuse of exhortations, orders, and even money, of which his letters are a proof. His days were occupied in dictating instructions on that subject; at night he frequently rose to repeat them again. One general received, on a single day, six despatches from him, all distinguished by the same solicitude.

In one, these words were remarked: "For masses like these, if precaution be not taken, the grain of no country can suffice." In another: "It will be requisite for all the provision-wagons to be loaded with flour, bread, rice, pulse, and brandy, besides what is necessary for the hospital service. The result of all my movements will assemble 400,000 men on a single point. There will be nothing then to expect from the country, and it will be necessary to have every thing within ourselves." But, on the one hand, the means of transport were badly calculated; and, on the other, he allowed himself to be hurried on as soon as he was put in motion.

1. No such battle was fought by Davoust. That the movements of Berthier were absurd and dangerous is, however, a fact.—*Ed.*

2. The emperor, on the contrary, is said to have been much gratified by the exertions of Davoust, and to have held him up as a model to his generals, with respect to arrangements for the wants and comforts of the troops.—*Ed.*

CHAPTER III

THE MARCH TO THE NIEMEN

IN his route from Königsberg to Gumbinnen, Napoleon reviewed several of his armies; conversing with the soldiers in a gay, frank, and often abrupt style; well aware that, with such unsophisticated and hardy characters, abruptness is looked upon as frankness, rudeness as force, haughtiness as true nobility; and that the delicacy and graces which some officers bring with them from drawing-rooms are in their eyes no better than weakness and pusillanimity; that these appear to them like a foreign language, which they do not understand, and the accents of which strike them as ridiculous.

According to his usual custom, he promenaded before the ranks. Knowing in which of his wars each regiment had been with him, at the sight of the oldest soldiers he occasionally halted; to one he recalled the battle of the Pyramids; another he reminded of Marengo, Austerlitz, Jena, or Friedland, and always by a single word, accompanied by a familiar caress. The veteran, who believed himself personally recognised by his emperor, rose in consequence in the estimation of his junior companions, who regarded him as an object of envy.

Napoleon, in this manner, continued his inspection; he overlooked not even the youngest soldiers: it seemed as if every thing which concerned them was to him matter of deep interest; their least wants seemed known to him. He interrogated them: Did their captains take care of them? had they received their pay? were they in want of any requisite? he wished to see their knapsacks.

At length he stopped at the centre of the regiment; there being apprised of the places that were vacant, he required aloud the names of the most meritorious in the ranks; he called those who were so designated before him, and questioned them. How many years' service? how many campaigns? what wounds? what exploits? He then appointed them officers, and caused them to be immediately installed, himself prescribing the forms;—all these were particularities which delighted the soldier! They told each other how this great emperor, the judge of nations in the mass, occupied himself with them in their minutest details; that they composed his oldest and his real family! Thus it was that he instilled into them the love of war, of glory and himself.

The army, meantime, marched from the Vistula to the Niemen. This last river, from Grodno as far as Kowno, runs parallel with the Vistula. The river Pregel, which forms a link between them, was loaded with provisions: 220,000 men repaired thither from four different points; there they found bread and some foraging provisions. These provisions ascended that river with them, as far as its direction would allow.

When the army was obliged to quit the flotilla, its select corps took with them sufficient provisions to reach and cross the Niemen, to prepare for a victory, and to arrive at Wilna. There the emperor calculated on the magazines of the inhabitants, on those of the enemy, and on his own, which he had ordered to be brought from Dantzic, by the Frischhaff, the Pregel, the Deine, the Frederic canal, and the Vilia.

We were now upon the verge of the Russian frontier; from right to left, or from south to north, the army was disposed in the following manner, in front of the Niemen. In the first place, on the extreme right, and issuing from Gallicia, on Drogiczin, Prince Schwartzenberg and 34,000 Austrians; on their left, coming from Warsaw, and marching on Bialystock and Grodno, the king of Westphalia, at the head of 79,200 Westphalians, Saxons, and Poles; by the side of them was the Viceroy of Italy, who had just effected the junction, near Marienpol and Pilony, of 79,500 Bavarians, Italians, and French;

next, the Emperor, with 220,000 men, commanded by the king of Naples, the Prince of Eckmühl, the Dukes of Dantzic, Istria, Reggio, and Elchingen. They advanced from Thorn, Marienwerder, and Elbing, and, on the 23rd of June, had assembled in a single mass near Nogarisky, a league above Kowno. Finally, in front of Tilsit was Macdonald, and 32,500 Prussians, Bavarians, and Poles, composing the extreme left of the grand army.

Every thing was now ready. From the banks of the Guadalquivir, and the shores of the Calabrian Sea, to the Vistula, were assembled 617,000 men, of whom 480,000 were already present; one siege and six bridge equipages, thousands of provision-wagons, innumerable herds of oxen, 1372 pieces of cannon, and thousands of artillery and hospital wagons, had been directed, assembled, and stationed at a short distance from the Russian frontier river.[1] The greatest part of the provision-wagons were alone behind.

Sixty thousand Austrians, Prussians, and Spaniards, were preparing to shed their blood for the conqueror of Wagram, of Jena, and of Madrid; for the man who had four times beaten down the power of Austria, who had humbled Prussia, and invaded Spain. And yet all were faithful to him. When it is considered that one-third of the army of Napoleon was either foreign to him or hostile, one hardly knows at which to be most astonished,—the daringness of one party or the resignation of the other. It was in this manner that Rome made her conquests contribute to her future means for conquering.

As to us Frenchmen, he found us all full of ardour. Habit, curiosity, and the pleasure of exhibiting themselves in the character of masters in new countries, actuated the soldiers; vanity was the great stimulant of the younger ones, who thirsted to acquire some glory which they might recount, with the attractive gasconading peculiar to soldiers; these inflated and pompous narratives of their exploits being moreover indispensable to their relaxation when no longer under arms. To this must certainly be added, the prospect of plunder; for the exacting ambition of Napoleon had as often disgusted his soldiers, as the disorders of the latter tarnished his glory. A compromise was necessary: ever since 1805, it had been tacitly understood, that they should bear with his ambition, and he with their plundering.

This plunder, however, or rather this marauding system, was generally confined to provisions, which, in default of supplies, were exacted of the inhabitants, but often too extravagantly. The most culpable plunderers were the stragglers, who are always numerous in frequent forced marches. These disorders, indeed, were never tolerated. In order to repress them, Napoleon left *gendarmes* and flying columns on the track of the army; and when these stragglers subsequently re-joined their corps, their knapsacks were examined by their officers, or, as was the case at Austerlitz, by their comrades, and strict justice was then executed among themselves.

The last levies were certainly too young and too feeble; but the army had still a stock of brave and experienced men, used to critical situations, and whom nothing could intimidate. They were recognisable at the first glance by their martial countenances, and by their conversation; they had no other past nor future but war; and they could talk of nothing else. Their officers were worthy of them, or at least were becoming so; for, in order to preserve the ascendency of his rank over such men, it was necessary that an officer should have wounds to show, and be able to appeal to his own exploits.

Such was, at that period, the life of those men; all was action within its sphere, even to words. They often boasted too much, but even that had its advantage; for as they were incessantly put to the proof, it was then necessary for them to be what they wished to appear. Such especially is the character of the Poles; they boast in the first instance of being more than they have been, but not more than they are capable of being. Poland, in fact, is a nation of heroes! pawning their words for exploits beyond the truth, but subsequently redeeming them with honour, in order to verify what at first was neither true nor even probable.

As to the old generals, some of them were no longer the hardy and simple warriors of the republic; honours, hard service, age, and the emperor particularly, had contributed to soften many of them down. Napoleon compelled them to adopt a luxurious style of living by his example and his orders; according to him, it was a means of influencing the multitude. It might be, also, that such habits prevented them from accumulating property, which might have made them independent: for, being himself the source of riches, he was glad to keep up the necessity of repairing to it, and in this manner to bring them back within his influence. He had, therefore, pushed his generals into a circle from which it was difficult for them to escape; forcing them to pass incessantly from want to prodigality, and from prodigality to want, which he alone was able to relieve.

Several had nothing but their appointments, which accustomed them to an ease of living with which they could no longer dispense. If he made them grants of land, it was out of his conquests, which were exposed to insecurity by war and which war only could preserve.

But in order to retain them in dependence, glory, which with some was a habit, with others a passion, with all a want, was the all-sufficient stimulant; and Napoleon, absolute master as he was of his own century, and even dictating to history, was the distributor of that glory. Though he fixed it at a high price, there was no rejecting his conditions; one would have felt ashamed to confess one's weakness in presence of his strength, and to stop short before a man whose ambition was still mounting, great as was the elevation which he had already attained.

Besides, the renown of so great an expedition was full of attraction; its success seemed certain; it promised to be nothing but a military march to Petersburgh and Moscow. With this last effort his wars would probably be terminated. It was a last opportunity, which one would repent to have let escape; one would be annoyed by the glorious narratives which others would give of it. The victory of to-day would make that of yesterday so old! And who would wish to grow old with it?

And then, when war was kindled in all quarters, how was it possible to avoid it? The scenes of action were not indifferent; here Napoleon would command in person; elsewhere, though the cause might be the same, the contest would be carried on under a different commander. The renown shared with the latter would be foreign to Napoleon, on whom, nevertheless, depended glory, fortune, every thing; and it was well known, whether from preference or policy, that he was only lavish of his favours to those whose glory was identified with his own; and that he rewarded less generously such exploits as he did not share. It was requisite, therefore, to serve in the army which he commanded; hence the eagerness of young and old to fill its ranks. What chief had ever before so many means of power? There was no hope which he could not flatter, excite, or satiate.

Finally, we loved him as the companion of our labours; as the chief who had conducted us to renown. The astonishment and admiration which he inspired flattered our self-love; for all these we shared in common with him.

With respect to that youthful *élite*, which in those times of glory filled our camps, its enthusiasm was natural. Who is there amongst us who, in his early years, has not been fired by the perusal of the warlike exploits of the ancients and of our ancestors? Should we not have all desired, at that time, to be the heroes whose real or fictitious history we were perusing? During that state of enthusiasm, if those recollections had been suddenly realised before us; if our eyes, instead of reading, had witnessed the performance of those wonders; if we had felt their sphere of action within our reach, and if employments had been offered to us by the side of those brave Paladins, whose adventurous lives and brilliant renown our young and vivid imaginations had so much envied; which of us would have hesitated? Who is there that would not have rushed forward, replete with joy and hope, and disdaining an odious and disgraceful repose?

Such were the rising generations of that day. At that period every one was at liberty to be ambitious! a period of intoxication and prosperity, during which the French soldier, lord of all things by victory, considered himself greater than the nobleman, or even the sovereign whose states he traversed! To him it appeared as if the kings of Europe only reigned by permission of his chief and of his arms.

Thus it was that habit attracted some, disgust at camp service others; novelty prompted the greater part, and especially the thirst of glory; but all were stimulated by emulation. In fine, confidence in a chief who had been always fortunate, and the prospect of a speedy victory, which would terminate the war at a blow, and restore us to our firesides; for a war, to the entire army of Napoleon (as it was to some volunteers of the court of Louis XIV.) was often no more than a single battle, or a short and brilliant journey.

We were now about to reach the extremity of Europe, where never European army had been before! We were about to erect new columns of Hercules. The grandeur of the enterprise; the agitation of co-operating Europe; the imposing spectacle of an army of 400,000 foot, and 80,000 horse: so many warlike reports and martial clamours, kindled the minds of veterans themselves. It was impossible for the coldest to remain unmoved amid the general impulse; to escape from the universal attraction.

In conclusion;—independent of all these motives for animation, the composition of the army was good, and every good army is desirous of war.

1. From official documents, containing notes made by the hand of Napoleon, General Gourgaud estimates the French army, when it crossed the Niemen, at 325,900 men, with 984 pieces of cannon. The number of the French troops was 155,400, of the allies 170,500.—*Ed.*

BOOK IV

———•———

CHAPTER I

THE OPPOSING ARMIES

NAPOLEON, satisfied, thus addressed his army. "Soldiers," said he, "the second Polish war is commenced. The first was concluded at Friedland and at Tilsit. At Tilsit, Russia swore eternal alliance with France, and war with England. She now violates her oaths. She will give no explanation of her capricious conduct, until the French eagles have repassed the Rhine; by that means leaving our allies at her mercy. Russia is hurried away by fatality; her destiny must be accomplished. Does she then believe us to be degenerated? Are we not still the soldiers of Austerlitz? She places us between war and dishonour; the choice cannot be doubtful. Let us advance, then; let us cross the Niemen, and carry the war into her territory! The second Polish war will be as glorious for the French arms as the first; but the peace we shall this time conclude will carry with it its own guarantee; it will put an end to the fatal influence which Russia for the last fifty years has exercised over the affairs of Europe."

This tone, which was at that time deemed prophetic, befitted an expedition of an almost fabulous character, it was quite necessary to invoke Destiny and give credit to its empire, when the fate of so many human beings, and so much glory, was about to be consigned to its mercy.

The emperor Alexander also harangued his army, but in a very different manner. The difference between the two nations, the two sovereigns, and their reciprocal position, were conspicuous in these proclamations. In fact, the one, which was defensive, was unadorned and moderate; the other, offensive, was replete with boldness and the confidence of victory. The first appealed to religion, the other to fatality; the one to love of country, the other to love of glory; but neither of them referred to the liberation of Poland, which was the real object of the war.

We marched towards the east, with our left towards the north, and our right towards the south. On our right, the wishes of the people of Volhynia were entirely in our favour; as, in the centre, were those of Wilna, Minsk, and the whole of Lithuania, and Samogitia; in front of our left, Courland and Livonia awaited their fate in silence.

The army of Alexander, 300,000 strong, kept those provinces in awe. From the banks of the Vistula, from Dresden, from Paris itself, Napoleon had critically estimated it. He had ascertained that its centre, commanded by Barclay, extended from Wilna and Kowno to Lida and Grodno, resting its right on the Vilia, and its left on the Niemen.

The latter river protected the Russian front by the deviation which it makes from Grodno to Kowno; for it was only in the interval between these two cities, that the Niemen, running toward the north, intersected the line of our attack, and served as a frontier to Lithuania. Before reaching Grodno, and on quitting Kowno, it flows westward.

To the south of Grodno was Bagration, with 65,000 men, in the direction of Wolkowisk; to the north of Kowno, at Rossiana and Keydani, Wittgenstein, with 26,000 men, formed a substitute for that natural frontier.

At the same time, another army of 50,000 men, called the reserve, was assembled at Lutsk, in Volhynia, in order to keep that province in check, and observe Schwartzenberg; it was confided to Tormasoff, till the treaty about to be signed at Bucharest permitted Tchitchakoff, and the greater part of the army in Moldavia, to unite with it.

Alexander, and, under him, his minister of war, Barclay de Tolly, commanded all these forces. They were divided into three armies, called, the first western army, under Barclay; the second western army, under Bagration; and the army of reserve, under Tormasoff. Two other corps were forming; one at Mozyr, in the environs of Bobruisk;

and the other at Riga and Dünabourg. The reserves were at Wilna and Swentziany. Finally, a vast entrenched camp was erecting before Drissa, within an elbow of the Dwina.

The French emperor's opinion was, that this position behind the Niemen was neither offensive nor defensive, and that the Russian army was no better off for the purpose of effecting a retreat; that this army, being so much scattered over a line of sixty leagues, might be surprised and dispersed, as actually happened to it; that, with still more certainty, the left of Barclay, and the entire army of Bagration, being stationed at Lida and at Wolkowisk, in front of the marshes of the Berezina, which they covered, instead of being covered by them, might be thrown back on them and taken; or, at least, that a sudden and immediate attack on Kowno and Wilna would cut them off from their line of operation, indicated by Swentziany and the entrenched camp at Drissa.

In fact, Doctoroff and Bagration were already separated from that line; for, instead of remaining in mass with Alexander, in front of the roads leading to the Dwina, to defend them and profit by them, they were stationed forty leagues to the right.

For this reason it was that Napoleon separated his forces into five armies. While Schwartzenberg advanced from Gallicia with his 30,000 Austrians, (whose numbers he had orders to exaggerate,) to keep Tormasoff in check, and draw the attention of Bagration towards the south; while the King of Westphalia, with his 80,000 men, would employ that general in front, towards Grodno, without pressing him too vehemently at first; and while the Viceroy of Italy, in the direction of Pilony, would be in readiness to interpose between the same Bagration and Barclay; in fine, while at the extreme left, Macdonald, debouching from Tilsit, would invade the north of Lithuania, and fall on the right of Wittgenstein, Napoleon himself, with his 200,000 men, would precipitate himself on Kowno, on Wilna, and on his rival, and destroy him in the first onset.

Should the emperor of Russia give way, he would press him hard, and throw him back upon Drissa, and as far as the commencement of his line of operations; then, all at once, propelling his detachments to the right, he would surround Bagration and the whole of the corps of the Russian left, which, by this rapid irruption, would be separated from their right.

I will shortly sketch a brief and rapid summary of the history of our two wings, being anxious to return to the centre, and to be enabled uninterruptedly to exhibit the great scenes which were passing there. Macdonald commanded the left wing; his invasion, supported by the Baltic, drove the right wing of the Russians before him; it threatened Revel first, next Riga, and even Petersburgh. He soon reached Riga. The war became stationary under its walls; although of little importance it was conducted by Macdonald with prudence, science, and glory, even in his retreat, to which he was neither compelled by the winter nor by the enemy, but solely by Napoleon's orders.

With regard to his right wing, the emperor had counted on the support of Turkey, which failed him. He had inferred that the Russian army of Volhynia would follow the general movement of Alexander's retreat; but, on the contrary, Tormasoff advanced upon our rear. The French army was thus uncovered, and menaced with being turned on those vast plains. Nature not supplying it in that quarter with any support, as she did on the left wing, it was necessarily compelled to rely entirely on itself. Forty thousand Saxons, Austrians, and Poles, remained there in observation.

Tormasoff was beaten; but another army, rendered available by the treaty of Bucharest, arrived and formed a junction with the remnant of the first. From that moment, the war upon that point became defensive. It was carried on feebly, as was to be expected, notwithstanding some Polish troops and a French general were left with the Austrian army. That general had been long and strenuously cried up for ability, although he had met with reverses, and his reputation was not undeserved.

No decisive advantage was gained on either side. But the position of this corps, almost entirely Austrian, became more and more important, as the grand army retreated upon it. It will be seen whether Schwartzenberg deceived its confidence,—whether he left us to be surrounded on the Berezina,—and whether it be true, that he seemed on that occasion to aspire to no other character than that of an armed witness to the great dispute.

CHAPTER II

FROM THE NIEMEN
TO WILMA

BETWEEN these two wings, the grand army marched to the Niemen, in three separate masses. The King of Westphalia, with 80,000 men, moved upon Grodno; the Viceroy of Italy, with 75,000 men, upon Pilony; Napoleon, with 220,000 men, upon Nogaraiski, a farm situated three leagues beyond Kowno. The 23rd of June, before daylight, the imperial column reached the Niemen, but without seeing it. The borders of the great Prussian forest of Pilwisky, and the hills which line the river, concealed the great army, which was about to cross it.

Napoleon, who had travelled in a carriage as far as that, mounted his horse at two o'clock in the morning. He reconnoitred the Russian river, without disguising himself, as has been falsely asserted, but under cover of the night crossing this frontier, which five months afterwards he was only enabled to repass under cover of the same obscurity.[1] When he came up to the bank, his horse suddenly fell, and threw him on the sand. A voice exclaimed, "This is a bad omen; a Roman would recoil!" It is not known whether it was himself, or one of his retinue, who pronounced these words.

His task of reconnoitring concluded, he gave orders that, at the close of the following day, three bridges should be thrown over the river, near the village of Poniémen: he then retired to his head-quarters where he passed the whole day, sometimes in his tent, sometimes in a Polish house, listlessly reclined, in the midst of a breathless atmosphere, and a suffocating heat, vainly courting repose.

On the return of night he drew nigh again to the river. The first who crossed it were a few sappers in a small boat. To their astonishment they approached the Russian bank, and landed, without encountering any obstacle. There they found peace; the war was entirely on their own side; all was tranquil on this foreign soil, which had been described to them as so menacing. A subaltern officer of Cossacks, however, commanding a patrole, presented himself to their view. He was alone, and appeared to consider himself in full peace, and to be ignorant that the whole of Europe in arms was at hand. He inquired of the strangers who they were?—"Frenchmen!" they replied.—"What do you want?" rejoined the officer; "and wherefore do you come into Russia?"—A sapper briskly replied, "To make war upon you; to take Wilna; to deliver Poland."—The Cossack then withdrew; he disappeared in the woods, into which three of our soldiers, giving vent to their ardour, and with a view to sound the forest, discharged their fire-arms.

Thus it was, that the feeble report of three muskets, to which there was no reply, apprised us of the opening of a new campaign, and the commencement of a great invasion.

Either from a feeling of prudence, or from presentiment, this first signal of war threw the emperor into a state of violent irritation. Three hundred voltigeurs immediately passed the river, in order to cover the erection of the bridges.

The whole of the French columns then began to issue from the valleys and the forest. They advanced in silence to the river, under cover of thick darkness. It was necessary to touch them in order to recognise their presence. Fires, even to sparks, were forbidden; they slept with arms in their hands, as if in the presence of an enemy. The crops of green rye, moistened with a profuse dew, served as beds for the men, and provender to the horses.

The night, its coolness preventing sleep, its obscurity prolonging the hours, and augmenting wants; finally, the dangers of the following day, every thing combined to give solemnity to this position. But the expectation of a great battle supported our spirits. The proclamation of Napoleon had just been read; the most remarkable passages of it were repeated in a whisper, and the genius of conquest kindled our imaginations.

Before us was the Russian frontier. Our ardent gaze already sought to invade the promised land of our glory athwart the shades of night. We seemed to hear the joyful acclamations of the Lithuanians, at the approach of their deliverers. We pictured to ourselves the banks of the rivers lined with their supplicating hands. Here, we were in want of every thing; there, every thing would be lavished upon us! The Lithuanians would hasten to supply our wants; we were about to be encircled by love and gratitude. What signified one unpleasant night? The day would shortly appear, and with it its warmth and all its illusions. The day did appear! and it revealed to us dry and desert sands, and dark and gloomy forests! Our eyes then reverted sadly upon ourselves, and we were again inspired by pride and hope, on observing the imposing spectacle of our united army.

Three hundred yards from the river, on the most elevated height, the tent of the emperor was conspicuous. Around it the hills, their slopes, and the subjacent valleys, were covered with men and horses. As soon as the earth exhibited to the sun those moving masses, clothed with glittering arms, the signal was given, and instantly the multitudes began to file off in three columns, towards the three bridges. They were observed to take a winding direction, as they descended the narrow plain which separated them from the Niemen, to approach it, to reach the three passages, to compress and prolong their columns, in order to traverse them, and at last reach that foreign soil, which they were about to devastate, and which they were soon destined to cover with their own enormous wrecks.

So great was their ardour, that two divisions of the advanced guard disputed for the honour of being the first to pass, and were near coming to blows; and some exertions were necessary to quiet them. Napoleon hastened to plant his foot on the Russian territory. He took this first step towards his ruin without hesitation. At first, he stationed himself near the bridge, encouraging the soldiers with his looks. The latter all saluted him with their accustomed acclamations. They appeared, indeed, more animated than he was; whether it was that he felt oppressed by the weight of so great an aggression, or that his enfeebled frame could not support the effect of the excessive heat, or that he was already astonished by finding nothing to conquer.

At length he became impatient; all at once he dashed across the country into the forest which girt the sides of the river. He put his horse to the extremity of his speed; in his eagerness he seemed desirous to come singly in contact with the enemy.[2] He rode more than a league in the same direction, surrounded throughout by the same solitude; after which he found it necessary to return to the vicinity of the bridges, whence he re-descended the river with his guard towards Kowno.

Some thought they heard the distant report of cannon. As we marched, we listened to distinguish on which side the battle was going on. But, with the exception of some troops of Cossacks on that, as well as the ensuing days, the atmosphere alone displayed itself in the character of an enemy. In fact, the emperor had scarcely passed the river, when a rumbling sound began to agitate the air. In a short time the day became overcast, the wind rose, and brought with it the inauspicious mutterings of a thunder-storm. That menacing sky and shelterless country filled us with melancholy impressions. There were even some amongst us, who, enthusiastic as they had lately been, were terrified at what they conceived to be a fatal presage. To them it appeared that those combustible vapours were collected over our heads, and descended upon the territory we approached, in order to prevent us from entering it.

It is quite certain, that the storm in question was as great as the enterprise in which we were engaged. During several hours, its black and heavy masses accumulated and hung over the whole army: from right to left, over a space of fifty leagues, it was completely threatened by its lightnings, and overwhelmed by its torrents; the roads and fields were inundated; the insupportable heat of the atmosphere was suddenly changed to a disagreeable chilness. Ten thousand horses perished on the march, and more especially in the bivouacs which followed. A large quantity of equipages remained abandoned on the sands; and great numbers of men subsequently died.

A convent served to shelter the emperor against the first fury of the tempest. From hence he shortly departed for Kowno, where the greatest disorder prevailed. The claps of thunder were no longer heard; those menacing reports, which still murmured over our heads, appeared to be forgotten. For, though this common phenomenon of the season might have shaken the firmness of some few minds, with the majority the time of omens had passed away. A scepticism, ingenious in some, thoughtless or coarse in others, earth-born passions and imperious wants, have diverted the souls of men from that heaven whence they are derived, and to which they should return. The army, therefore, recognised nothing but a natural and unseasonable accident in this disaster; and far from interpreting it as the voice of reprobation of this great aggression, for which, moreover, it was not responsible, found in it nothing but a ground of imprecation against fortune or the skies, which whether by chance, or otherwise, offered it so terrible a presage.

That very day, a private calamity was added to is general disaster. At Kowno, Napoleon was exasperated, because the bridge over the Vilia had been thrown down by the Cossacks, and opposed the passage of Oudinot. He affected to despise the obstacle, like every thing else that opposed him, and ordered a squadron of his Polish guard to swim the river. These fine fellows threw themselves into it without hesitation. At first, they proceeded in good order, and when out of their depth redoubled their exertions. They soon reached the middle of the river by swimming. But there, the increased rapidity of the current broke their order. Their horses then became frightened, and were carried away by the violence of the waves. They no longer swam, but floated about in scattered groups. Their riders struggled, and made vain efforts: their strength gave way, and they, at last, resigned themselves to their fate. Their destruction was certain; but it was for their country; it was in her presence, and for the sake of her deliverer, that they had devoted themselves; and, even when on the point of being engulfed for ever, they suspended their unavailing struggles, turned their faces towards Napoleon, and exclaimed, "*Vive l'Empereur!*" Three of them were remarked, who, with their heads still above the billows, repeated this cry and perished instantly. The army was struck with mingled horror and admiration.[3]

As to Napoleon, he prescribed with promptitude and precision the measures necessary to save the greater number, but without appearing affected: either from the habit of subduing his feelings; from considering the ordinary emotions of the heart as weaknesses in time of war, of which it was not for him to set the example, and therefore necessary to suppress; or, finally, that he anticipated much greater misfortunes, compared with which the present was a mere trifle.

A bridge thrown over this river conveyed Marshal Oudinot and the second corps to Keydani. During that time, the rest of the army was still passing the Niemen. The passage took up three entire days. The army of Italy did not pass it till the 29th, in front of Pilony. The army of the King of Westphalia did not enter Grodno till the 30th.

From Kowno Napoleon proceeded in two days as far as the defiles which defend the plain of Wilna. He waited, in order to make his appearance there, for news from his advanced posts. He was in hopes that Alexander would contest with him the possession of that capital. The report, indeed, of some musketry, encouraged him in that hope; when intelligence was brought him that the city was undefended. Thither he advanced, thoughtful and dissatisfied. He accused his generals of the advanced guard of suffering the Russian army to escape. It was the most active of them, Montbrun, whom he reproached, and against whom his anger rose to the point of menace. A menace without effect, a violence without result! and less blameable than remarkable in a warrior, because they contributed to prove all the importance which he attached to an immediate victory.

In the midst of his anger his dispositions for entering Wilna displayed address. He caused himself to be preceded and followed by Polish regiments. But more occupied by the retreat of the Russians than the grateful and admiring acclamations of the Lithuanians, he rapidly passed through the city, and hurried to the advanced posts. Several of the best hussars of the 8th, having ventured themselves in a wood, without proper support, had just perished in an action with the Russian guard; Segur,[4] who commanded them, after a desperate defence, had fallen, covered with wounds.

The enemy had burnt his bridges and his magazines, and was flying by different roads, but all in the direction of Drissa. Napoleon ordered all that the fire had spared to be collected, and restored the communications. He sent forward Murat and his cavalry, to follow the track of Alexander: and after throwing Ney upon his left, in order to support Oudinot, who had that day driven back the lines of Wittgenstein, from Develtowo as far as Wilkomir, he returned to occupy the place of Alexander at Wilna. There, his unfolded maps, military reports, and a crowd of officers requiring his orders, awaited his arrival. He was now on the theatre of war, and at the moment of its most animated operations; he had prompt and urgent decisions to make; orders of march to give; hospitals, magazines, and lines of operation, to establish.

It was necessary to interrogate, to read, and to compare; and at last to discover and grasp the truth, which always appeared to fly and conceal itself in the midst of a thousand contradictory answers and reports.

This was not all: Napoleon, at Wilna, had a new empire to organise: the politics of Europe, the war of Spain, and the government of France, to direct. His political, military, and administrative correspondences which he had suffered to accumulate for several days, imperiously demanded his attention. Such indeed, was his custom, on the eve of a great event, as that would necessarily decide the character of many of his replies, and impart a colouring to all. He therefore established himself at his quarters, and in the first instance threw himself on a bed, less for the sake of sleep than of quiet meditation; whence, abruptly starting up shortly after, he rapidly dictated the orders which he had conceived.

Intelligence was just then brought him from Warsaw and the Austrian army. The discourse at the opening of the Polish diet displeased the emperor; and he exclaimed, as he threw it from him, "This is French! It ought to be Polish!" As to the Austrians, it was never dissembled to him that, in their whole army, there was but one on whom he could depend, and that was its commander. The certainty of that seemed sufficient for him.

1. Napoleon was disguised in the great coat and cap of one of the Polish light-horse of his guard, and it was broad daylight when he reconnoitred the Niemen.—*Ed.*

2. This is incorrect, Napoleon reconnoitred at the head of a strong body of cavalry—*Ed.*

3. Only one person was drowned—*Ed.*

4. Brother of the Author.

CHAPTER III

THE LITHUANIANS

MEANTIME, all circumstances contributed to rekindle in the hearts of the Lithuanians the embers of their almost expiring patriotism. On one side, the precipitate retreat of the Russians, and the presence of Napoleon; on the other, the cry of independence emitted by Warsaw, and more especially the sight of those Polish heroes, who returned with liberty to the soil from which they had been expelled along with her. The first days, therefore, were entirely devoted to joy: the happiness appeared general—the display of feeling universal.

The same sentiments were thought to be traceable everywhere; in the interior of the houses, as well as at the windows, and in the public places. The people congratulated and embraced each other on the high roads; the old men once more resumed their ancient costume, reviving ideas of glory and independence. They wept with joy at the sight of the national banners which had been just re-erected; an immense crowd followed them, rending the air with their acclamations. But this enthusiasm, unreflecting in some, and the mere effect of excitement in others, was but of short duration.

On their side, the Poles of the grand duchy were always animated by the noblest enthusiasm; they were worthy of liberty, and sacrificed to it those advantages for which liberty is sacrificed by the greater part of mankind. Nor did they belie themselves on this occasion: the diet of Warsaw constituted itself into a general confederation, and declared the kingdom of Poland restored; it convened the dietins; invited all Poland to unite; summoned all the Poles in the Russian army to quit Russia: caused itself to be represented by a general council; maintained in other respects the established order; and, finally, sent a deputation to the king of Saxony, and an address to Napoleon.

The senator Wibicki presented this address to him at Wilna. He told him "that the Poles had neither been subjected by peace nor by war, but by treason; that they were therefore free by right, before God and man; that being so now in fact, the assertion of that right became a duty; that they claimed the independence of their brethren, the Lithuanians, who were still slaves; that they offered themselves to the entire Polish nation as the centre of a general union; but that it was for him who dictated his history to the age, in whom resided the force of Providence, to support those efforts which he could not but approve; that on that account they came to solicit Napoleon the Great to pronounce these few words, '*Let the kingdom of Poland exist!*' and that it then would exist; that all the Poles would devote themselves to the orders of the founder of the fourth French dynasty, to whom ages were but as a moment, and space no more than a point."

Napoleon replied: "Gentlemen deputies of the confederation of Poland, I have listened with deep interest to what you have just told me. Were I a Pole, I should think and act like you; I should have voted with you in the assembly of Warsaw: the love of his country is the first duty of civilised man.

"In my position, I have many interests to reconcile, and many duties to fulfil. Had I reigned during the first, second, or third partition of Poland, I would have armed my people in her defence. When victory supplied me with the means of re-establishing your ancient laws in your capital, and in a portion of your provinces, I did so without seeking to prolong a war, which might have continued to waste the blood of my subjects.

"I love your nation! For sixteen years I have found your soldiers by my side, on the plains of Italy and of Spain. I applaud what you have done; I authorise the efforts which you wish to make; I will do all that depends on me to second your resolutions. If your efforts be unanimous, you may cherish the hope of compelling your enemies to recognise your rights; but in countries so distant and so extensive, it can only be in the united efforts of the population which inhabits them, that you can discover just grounds of success.

"From the first moment of my entering Poland, I have used the same language to you. To this it is my duty to add, that I have guaranteed to the emperor of Austria the integrity of his dominions, and that I cannot sanction any manœuvre, or the least movement, tending to disturb his peaceable possession of the Polish provinces which remain to him.

"Only provide that Lithuania, Samogitia, Witepsk, Polotsk, Mohilef, Volhynia, the Ukraine, Podolia, be animated by the same spirit which I have witnessed in the Greater Poland; and Providence will crown your good cause with success. I will recompense that devotion of your provinces which renders you so interesting, and has acquired you so many claims to my esteem and protection, by every means that can, under the circumstances, depend upon me."

The Poles had imagined that they were addressing the sovereign arbiter of the world, whose every word was a law, and whose course no political compromise was capable of arresting. They were unable to comprehend the cause of the circumspection of this reply. They began to doubt the intentions of Napoleon; the zeal of some was cooled; the lukewarmness of others confirmed; all were intimidated. Even those around him asked each other what could be the motives of a prudence which appeared so unseasonable, and with him so unusual. "What, then, was the object of this war? Was he afraid of Austria? Had the retreat of the Russians disconcerted him? Did he doubt his good fortune, or was he unwilling to contract, in the face of Europe, engagements which he was not sure of being able to fulfil?

"Had the coldness of the Lithuanians infected him? or rather, did he dread the explosions of a patriotism which he might be unable to master? Was he still undecided as to the destiny he should bestow upon them?"

Whatever were his motives, it was obviously his wish that the Lithuanians should appear to liberate themselves; but as, at the same time, he created a government for them, and gave a direction to their public feeling, that circumstance placed him, as well as them, in a false position, wherein everything terminated in errors, contradictions, and half measures. There was no reciprocal understanding between the parties; a mutual distrust was the result. The Poles desired some positive guarantees in return for the many sacrifices they were called upon to make. But their union in a single kingdom not having been pronounced, the alarm which is common at the moment of great decisions increased, and the confidence which they had just lost in him, they also lost in themselves. It was then that he nominated seven Lithuanians to form the new government. The choice was unlucky in some points; it displeased the jealous pride of an aristocracy at all times difficult to satisfy.[1]

The four Lithuanian provinces of Wilna, Minsk, Grodno, and Bialystock, had each a government commission and national sub-prefects. Each commune was to have its municipality; but Lithuania was, in reality, governed by an imperial commissioner, and by four French auditors, with the title of intendants.

In short, from these, perhaps inevitable, faults, and from the excesses of an army placed between the alternative of famishing, or plundering its allies, there resulted a universal coolness. The emperor could not remain blind to it; he had calculated on four millions of Lithuanians; a few thousands were all that joined him! Their pospolite, which he had estimated at more than 100,000 men, had decreed him a guard of honour; only three horsemen attended him![2] The populous Volhynia remained immoveable, and Napoleon again appealed from them to victory. When fortunate, this coolness did not disturb him sufficiently; when unfortunate, whether through pride or justice, he did not complain of it.

As for us, ever confident in him and in ourselves, the dispositions of the Lithuanians at first affected us very little; but as our forces diminished, we began to look about us, and with our exigency our attention was awakened. Three Lithuanian generals, distinguished by their names, their property, and their sentiments, followed the emperor. The French generals at last reproached them with the coolness of their countrymen. The ardour of the people of Warsaw, in 1806, was held out to them as an example. The warm discussion which arose, passed, as well as several others similar, (which it is necessary to bring into one view,) at Napoleon's quarters, near the spot where he was employed; and as there was truth on both sides, as, in these conversations, the opposite allegations combated without destroying each other, and as the first and last causes of the coolness of the Lithuanians were therein revealed, it is impossible to omit them.

These generals then replied, "That they considered they had received with becoming sentiments the liberty which we had brought them; that, moreover, every one expressed regard according to his habitual character; that the Lithuanians were colder in their manner than the Poles, and, consequently, less communicative; that, after all, the feeling might be the same, though the expression was different.

"That, besides, there was no similarity in the cases; that in 1806, it was after having conquered the Prussians, that the French had delivered Poland, but that now, on the contrary, if they delivered Lithuania from the Russian yoke, it was before they had subjugated Russia. That, consequently, it was natural for the first to receive a victorious and certain freedom with transport; and equally natural for the last to receive an uncertain and dangerous liberty with gravity; that a property was not purchased with the same air as if it were received gratuitously; that six years back, at Warsaw, there was nothing to be done but prepare for festivals; while, at the present moment, at Wilna, where the whole power of Russia had just been exhibited, where its army was known to be untouched, and the motives of its retreat understood, it was for battles that preparation was to be made.

"And with what means? Why was not liberty offered to them in 1807? Lithuania was then rich and populous. Since that time the continental system, by closing up the only outlet for its productions, had impoverished it, while Russian foresight had thinned its population of recruits, and more recently by a multitude of nobles, peasants, wagons, and cattle, which the Russian army had carried away with it."

To these causes they added "the famine resulting from the severity of the season in 1811, and the damage to which the over-rich wheats of those countries are subject. But why not make an appeal to the provinces of the south? In that quarter there were men, horses, and provisions of all kinds. They had nothing to do but to drive Tormasoff and his army out of them. Schwartzenberg was, perhaps, marching in that direction; but was it to the Austrians, the uneasy usurpers of Gallicia, that the liberation of Volhynia ought to be confided? Would they station liberty so near slavery? Why did not they send Frenchmen and Poles there? But then it would be necessary to halt, to carry on the war more methodically, and allow time for organisation; while Napoleon, doubtless urged by his distance from his own territory, by the daily expense of provisioning his immense army, depending on that alone, and hurrying after victory, sacrificed every thing to the hope of finishing the war at a single blow."

Here the speakers were interrupted: these reasons, though true, appeared insufficient excuses. "They concealed the most powerful cause of the immobility of their countrymen; it arose from the interested attachment of their grandees to the crafty policy of Russia, which flattered their vanity, respected their usages, and secured their rights over the peasants, whom the French came to set free. Doubtless, national independence appeared to them too dear a purchase at such a price."

This reproach was well founded, and although it was not personal, the Lithuanian generals became irritated at it. One of them exclaimed, "You talk of our independence; but it must be in great peril, since you, at the head of 400,000 men, are afraid to commit yourselves by its recognition; for you have recognised it neither by words nor actions. You have placed auditors, men quite new, at the head of an administration equally new, to govern our provinces. They imperiously levy heavy contributions, but they forget to inform us for whom it is that we are making such sacrifices as are only made for one's country. They exhibit to us the emperor everywhere, but the republic hitherto nowhere. You have held out no object for our movements, and yet complain of their being unsteady. Persons whom we do not respect as countrymen, you set over us as our chiefs. Notwithstanding our entreaties, Wilna remains separated from Warsaw; disunited as we thus are, you require of us that confidence in our strength which union alone can give. The soldiers you expect from us are offered you; 30,000 would be now ready; but you have refused them the arms, clothing, and money, which we want."

All these imputations might still have been combated; but he added: "True, we do not haggle for liberty, but we find that in fact it is not disinterestedly offered. Wherever you go, the report of your excesses precedes your march: nor are they partial, since your army marches upon a line of fifty leagues in front. Even at Wilna, notwithstanding the multiplied orders of your emperor, the suburbs have been pillaged, and it is natural that a liberty which brings such licentiousness with it should be mistrusted.

"What then do you expect from our zeal? A happy countenance, acclamations of joy, accents of gratitude?—when every day each of us is apprised that his villages and granaries are devastated; for the little which the Russians did not carry away with them, your famishing columns have devoured. In their rapid marches, a multitude of marauders of all nations, against whom it is necessary to keep on the watch, detach themselves from their flanks.

"What do you require more? that our countrymen should throng your passage; bring you their grain and cattle; that they should offer themselves completely armed and ready to follow you? Alas! what have they to give you? Your pillagers take all; there is not even time allowed to make you the offer. Turn your eyes towards the entrance of the imperial head-quarters. Do you see that man? He is all but naked; he groans and extends towards you a hand of supplication. That unhappy man who excites your pity, is one of those very nobles whose assistance you look for: yesterday, he was hurrying to meet you, full of ardour, with his daughter, his vassals, and his wealth; he was coming to offer himself to your emperor; but he met with some Wurtemberg pillagers on his way, and was robbed of every thing; he is no longer a father,—he is scarcely a man."

Every one groaned, and hastened to relieve him. Frenchmen, Germans, Lithuanians, all agreed in deploring those disorders, for which no one could find a remedy. How, in fact, was it possible to restore discipline among such immense masses, pushed on so precipitately, conducted by so many leaders of different manners, characters, and countries, and forced to resort to plunder for subsistence?

In Prussia, the emperor had caused the army to supply itself with provisions for only twenty days. This was as much as was necessary for the purpose of gaining Wilna by a battle. Victory was to have done the rest, but that victory was postponed by the flight of the enemy. The emperor might have waited for his convoys; but as by surprising the Russians he had separated them, he did not wish to forego his grasp and lose his advantage. He, therefore, pushed forward on their track 400,000 men, with twenty days' provisions, into a country which had been incapable of feeding the 20,000 Swedes of Charles XII.

It was not from want of foresight; for immense convoys of oxen followed the army, either in herds, or harnessed to provision cars. Their drivers had been organised into battalions; but being tired out with the slow pace of these heavy animals, they either slaughtered them, or suffered them to die of want. A great number, however, got as far as Wilna and Minsk; some even reached Smolensk, but too late; they could only be of service to the recruits and reinforcements which followed us.

Besides this, Dantzic contained so much corn, that she alone might have fed the whole army: she supplied Königsberg. Her provisions had ascended the Pregel in large barges up to Vehlau, and in lighter craft as far Insterburg. The other convoys went by land from Königsberg to Labiau, and from thence, by means of the Niemen and the Villa, to Kowno and Wilna. But the waters of the Vilia having shrunk so much through drought as to be incapable of floating these transports, it became necessary to find other means of conveyance.

Napoleon hated contractors. It was his wish that the administration of the army should organise the Lithuanian wagons; 500 were assembled, but the appearance of them disgusted him. He then permitted contracts to be made with the Jews, who are the only traders in the country; and the provisions stopped at Kowno at last arrived at Wilna; but the army had already left it.

1. Six out of the seven members were chosen from the higher class of the nobility: they were Count Saltan, Prince Alexander Sapieha, Count Potocki, Count Sierakowski, Count Prozor, and Count Tysenhaus. The seventh, M. Sniadecki, represented the university of Wilna, of which he was the President.—*Ed.*

2. This is incorrect. The three Polish gentlemen to whom M. Segur alludes, were three interpreters on the staff of Berthier. With respect to the guard of honour, Napoleon had restricted it to the number of fifty; but many more joined it.—*Ed*.

CHAPTER IV

DISTRESS OF THE FRENCH ARMY

IT was the largest column, that of the centre, which suffered most; it followed the road which the Russians had ruined, and of which the French advanced guard had just completed the spoliation. The columns which proceeded by lateral routes found necessaries there, but were not sufficiently careful in collecting and in economising them.

The responsibility of the calamities which this rapid march occasioned ought not, therefore, to be laid entirely on Napoleon; for order and discipline were maintained in the army of Davoust; it suffered less from dearth: it was nearly the same with that of Prince Eugene. When pillage was resorted to in these two corps, it was always with method, and nothing but necessary injury was inflicted; the soldiers were obliged to carry several days' provisions, and prevented from wasting them. The same precautions might have been taken elsewhere; but, whether it was owing to the habit of making war in fertile countries, or to habitual ardour of constitution, many of the other chiefs thought much less of administering than of fighting.

Napoleon was, therefore, most frequently compelled to shut his eyes to a system of plunder which he vainly prohibited: he was too well aware, also, of the attraction which that mode of subsistence had for the soldier; that it made him love war, because it enriched him; that it gratified him, by the authority which it frequently gave him over classes superior to his own; that in his eyes it had all the charms of a war of the poor against the rich; finally, that the pleasure of feeling and proving himself the strongest, was under such circumstances incessantly repeated and brought home to him.

Napoleon, however, grew indignant at the intelligence of these excesses. He issued a threatening proclamation, and he directed moveable columns of French and Lithuanians to see to its execution. We, too, who were irritated at the sight of the pillagers, were eager to pursue and punish them; but when we had stripped them of the bread, or the cattle which they had been stealing; when we saw them slowly retiring, sometimes eyeing us with a look of concentrated despair, sometimes bursting into tears; when we heard them murmuring, that, "not content with giving them nothing, we wrested every thing from them, and that we must, therefore, mean to let them perish of hunger;" we, then, in our turn, accused ourselves of barbarity to our own people, called them back, and restored them their prey. In truth, it was imperious necessity which impelled to plunder. The officer himself only lived on the share which his soldiers allowed him.

A position of so much excess engendered fresh excesses. These rugged men, with arms in their hands, when assailed by so many immoderate wants, could not remain moderate. When they arrived near any habitations, they were famished; at first they asked, but, either for want of being understood, or from the refusal or impossibility of the inhabitants to satisfy their demands, and of their inability to wait, altercations generally arose; then, as they became more and more exasperated with hunger, they became furious, and after turning either cottage or palace topsy-turvy, without finding the subsistence they were in quest of, they, in the violence of their despair, accused the inhabitants of being their enemies and revenged themselves on the proprietors by destroying their property.

There were some who actually destroyed themselves, rather than proceed to such extremities; others, after having done so: these were the youngest. They placed their foreheads on their muskets, and blew out their brains in the middle of the highroad. But many became hardened; one excess led them on to another, as people often get angry with the blows which they inflict. Among the latter, some vagabonds took vengeance of their distresses even upon the person; in the midst of so inauspicious an aspect of nature, they became denaturalised; abandoned to themselves at so great a distance from home, they imagined that every thing was allowed them, and, that their own sufferings authorised them to make others suffer.

In an army so numerous, and composed of so many nations, it was natural also to find more malefactors than in smaller ones: the causes of so many evils induced fresh ones; already weakened by hunger, it was necessary to make forced marches in order to escape from it, and to reach the enemy. At night, when they halted, the soldiers thronged into the houses; there, worn out equally by fatigue and want, they threw themselves upon the first dirty straw they met with.

The most robust had barely spirits left to knead the flour which they found, and to light the ovens with which all those wooden houses were provided; others had scarcely strength to go a few paces in order to make the fires necessary to cook some food: their officers, exhausted like themselves, feebly gave orders to take more care, and neglected to see that their orders were obeyed. A piece of burnt wood, at such times escaping from the ovens, or a spark from the fire of the bivouacs, was sufficient to set fire to a castle or a whole village, and to cause the deaths of many unfortunate soldiers who had taken refuge in them. These disasters, however, were very rare in Lithuania.

The emperor was not ignorant of these details, but he was already committed. Even at Wilna, all these disorders had occurred; the Duke of Treviso, among others, informed him of them. "From the Niemen to the Vilia, he had," he said, "seen nothing but ruined habitations, and baggage and provision-wagons abandoned; they were found dispersed on the highways and in the fields, overturned, broken open, and their contents scattered here and there, and pillaged, as if they had been taken by the enemy: he should have imagined himself following a defeated army. Ten thousand horses had been killed by the cold rains of the great storm, and by the unripe rye, which had become their new and only food. Their carcases were lying encumbering the road: they sent forth a mephitic smell, impossible to breathe,—a new scourge, which some compared to famine; but the last was much more terrible: several soldiers of the young guard had already perished of hunger."

Up to that point Napoleon listened with calmness, but here he abruptly interrupted the speaker. Wishing to escape from distress by incredulity, he exclaimed, "It is impossible! where are their twenty days' provisions? Soldiers well commanded never die of hunger."

A general, the author of this last report, was present. Napoleon turned towards him, appealed to him, and pressed him with questions; and that general, either from weakness or uncertainty, replied, "that the individuals referred to had not died of hunger, but from intoxication."

The emperor then remained convinced that the privations of the soldiers had been exaggerated to him. As to the rest, he exclaimed, "The loss of the horses must be borne with; of some equipages, and even some habitations; it was a torrent that rolled away: it was the worst side of the picture of war; an evil exchanged for a good; to misery her share must be given; his treasures, his benefits would repair the loss: one great result would make amends for all; he only required a single victory; if sufficient means remained for accomplishing that, he should be satisfied."

The duke remarked, that a victory might be overtaken by a more methodical march, followed by the magazines; but he was not listened to. Those to whom this marshal (who had just returned from Spain,) complained, replied to him, "That, in fact, the emperor grew angry at the account of evils, which he considered irremediable, his policy imposing on him the necessity of a prompt and decisive victory."

They added, "that they saw too clearly that the health of their leader was impaired; and that being compelled, meanwhile, to throw himself into positions more and more critical, he could not survey, without ill humour, the difficulties which he passed by, and suffered to accumulate behind him; difficulties which he then affected to treat with contempt, in order to disguise their importance, and preserve the energy of mind which he himself required to surmount them. This was the reason that, being already disturbed and fatigued by the new and critical situation into which he had thrown himself, and impatient to escape from it, he kept marching on, always pushing his army forward, in order to bring matters sooner to a termination."

Thus it was that Napoleon was constrained to shut his eyes to facts. It is well known that the greater part of his ministers were not flatterers. Both facts and men spoke sufficiently; but what could they teach him? Of what was he ignorant?

Had not all his preparations been dictated by the most clear-sighted prudence? What could be said to him, which he had not himself said and written a hundred times? It was after having anticipated the minutest details, prepared for every inconvenience, and provided every thing for a slow and methodical war, that he divested himself of all these precautions, that he abandoned all these preparations, and suffered himself to be hurried away by habit, by the necessity of short wars, of rapid victories, and sudden treaties of peace.

CHAPTER V

PROGRESS OF THAT ARMY

IT was in the midst of these grave circumstances that Balachoff, a Russian, a minister of the Russian emperor, presented himself with a flag of truce at the French advanced posts. He was received; and the army, now become less ardent, indulged the hope of peace.

He brought this message from Alexander to Napoleon, "That it was not yet too late to negociate; a war which the soil, the climate, and the character of Russia, rendered interminable, was begun; but all accommodation had not become impossible, and from one bank of the Niemen to the other they might yet come to an understanding."[1] He, moreover, added, "that his master declared in the face of Europe, that he was not the aggressor; that his ambassador at Paris, in demanding his passports, did not consider himself as having broken the peace; that thus the French had entered Russia without a declaration of war." There were, however, no fresh overtures, either verbal or written, proposed by Balachoff.

The choice of the bearer of this flag of truce had been remarked; he was the minister of the Russian police; that office required an observant spirit, and it was thought that he was sent to exercise it amongst us. What rendered us more suspicious of the character of the negociator was, that the negociation appeared to have no character, unless it were that of great moderation, which, under the actual circumstances, was taken for weakness.

Napoleon did not hesitate. He had not been able to stop at Paris; should he then draw back at Wilna? What would Europe think of him? What result could he offer to the French and allied armies as a justification for so many fatigues; for such vast movements; for such enormous individual and national expenditure: it would be at once confessing himself vanquished. Besides his language before so many princes, since his departure from Paris, had pledged him as much as his actions; so that, in fact, he found himself as much compromised before his allies as he did before his enemies. Even then, it is said, the warmth of conversation with Balachoff carried him to still greater lengths. "What had brought him to Wilna? What did the Emperor of Russia want with him? Did he pretend to resist him? He was only a parade general. As to himself, his head was his counsellor; from that every thing proceeded. But as to Alexander,—who was there to counsel him? Whom had he to oppose to him? He had only three generals,—Kutusoff, whom he did not like, because he was a Russian;—Beningsen, superannuated six years ago, and now in his second childhood;—and Barclay: the last could certainly manœuvre; he was brave; he understood war; but he was a general only good for a retreat." And he added, "You all fancy you understand the art of war because you have read Jomini; but if his book could have taught it you, do you think that I would have allowed him to publish it?" In this conversation, of which the above is the Russian version, it is certain that he added, "that, however, the Emperor Alexander had friends even in the imperial head-quarters." Then, pointing out Caulaincourt to the Russian minister, "there," said he, "is a knight of your emperor; he is a Russian in the French camp."

Probably Caulaincourt did not sufficiently comprehend, that by that expression Napoleon only wished to prepare for himself a negociator who was agreeable to Alexander; for as soon as Balachoff was gone, he advanced towards the emperor, and in an angry tone, asked him why he had insulted him? exclaiming, "that he was a Frenchman! a true Frenchman! that he had proved it already; and would prove it again by repeating, that this war was impolitic and dangerous; that it would destroy his army, France, and himself. That, moreover, as he had just insulted him, he should quit him; that all that he asked of him was a division in Spain, where nobody wished to serve, and the furthest possible from his presence." The emperor attempted to appease him; but not being able to obtain a hearing, he withdrew, Caulaincourt still pursuing him with his reproaches. Berthier, who was present at this scene, interposed without effect. Bessières, more in the back-ground, had vainly tried to keep back Caulaincourt by holding him by the coat.

The next day, Napoleon was unable to bring his grand equerry into his presence, without formal and repeated orders. At length he soothed him by caresses, and by the expression of an esteem and attachment which Caulaincourt well deserved. But he dismissed Balachoff with verbal and inadmissible proposals.

Alexander mad no reply to them; the full importance of the step he had just taken was not at the time properly comprehended. He could no longer either address himself to Napoleon, or even return him any answer. It was the last word previous to an irreparable breach; and that circumstance rendered it remarkable.

Meantime, Murat pursued the flying steps of that victory which was so much coveted; he commanded the cavalry of the advanced guard; he at last reached the enemy on the road to Swentziany, and drove him in the direction of Druïa. Every morning the Russian rear-guard appeared to have escaped him; every evening he overtook it again, and attacked it, but always in a strong position, after a long march, too late, and before his men had taken any refreshment; there was, consequently, every day fresh combats, producing no important results.

Other chiefs, by other routes, followed the same direction. Oudinot passed the Vilia beyond Kowno, and in Samogitia, to the north of Wilna, at Deweltowo, and at Vilkomir, had already fallen in with the enemy, whom he drove before him towards Dünabourg. In this manner he marched on, to the left of Ney and the King of Naples, whose right was flanked by Nansouty. From the 15th of July, the, river Dwina, from Disna to Dünabourg, had been approached by Murat, Montbrun, Sebastiani, and Nansouty, by Oudinot and Ney, and by three divisions of the 1st corps, placed under the orders of the Count de Lobau.

It was Oudinot who presented himself before Dünabourg: he made an attempt on that town, which the Russians had vainly attempted to fortify. This too eccentric march of Oudinot displeased Napoleon. The river separated the two armies. Oudinot re-ascended it in order to put himself in communication with Murat; and Wittgenstein, in order to form a junction with Barclay. Dünabourg remained without assailants, and without defenders.

On his march, Wittgenstein had a view, from the right bank, of a van-guard of French cavalry, which occupied Druiga with too negligent a security. Encouraged by the approach of night, he made one of his corps pass the river, and on the 15th, in the morning, the advanced posts of one of our brigades were surprised, sabred, and carried off. After this, Wittgenstein recalled his troops to the right bank, and pursued his way with his prisoners, among whom was a French general. This *coup-de-main* gave Napoleon reason to hope for a battle; believing that Barclay was resuming the offensive, he suspended, for a short time, his march upon Witepsk, in order to concentrate his forces and direct them according to circumstances. This hope, however, was of short duration.

During these events, Davoust, at Osmiana, to the south of Wilna, had got sight of some scouts of Bagration, who was already anxiously seeking an outlet towards the north. Up to that time, short of a victory, the plan of the campaign adopted at Paris had completely succeeded. Aware that the enemy was extended over too long a defensive line, Napoleon had broken it by briskly attacking it in one direction, and by so doing had thrown back and driven its largest mass upon the Dwina; while Bagration, whom he had not brought into contact till five days later, was still upon the Niemen. During an interval of several days, and along a front of eighty leagues, the manœuvre was the same as that which Frederic the Second had often employed upon a line of two leagues, and for the space of a few hours.

Already Doctoroff, and several scattered divisions of each of these two separate masses had only escaped by favour of the extent of the country, of chance, and of the usual causes of that ignorance, which always exists during war, as to what passes close at hand in the ranks of an enemy.

Some persons have asserted that there was too much circumspection or too much negligence in this first operation of the invasion; that after passing the Vistula, the assailing army had received orders to march with all the precautions of one that was attacked; that the aggression once commenced, and Alexander having fled, the advanced guard of Napoleon ought to have reascended the two banks of the Vilia with more celerity and more in advance, and that the army of Italy should have followed this movement more closely. Perhaps Doctoroff, who commanded the left wing of Barclay, being forced to cross our line of attack in order to fly from Lida toward Swentziany, might then have been made prisoner. Pajol repulsed him at Osmiana; but he escaped by Smorgoni. Nothing but his baggage was taken; and Napoleon laid the blame of his escape on Prince Eugene, although he had himself prescribed to him every one of his movements.

But the army of Italy, the Bavarian army, the 1st corps and the guard, very soon occupied and surrounded Wilna. There it was that, stretched out over his maps (which he was obliged to examine in that manner, owing to his short sight, a defect, which he shared with Alexander the Great and Frederic the Second,)[2] Napoleon followed the course of the Russian army; it was divided into two unequal masses: one with its emperor towards Drissa, the other with Bagration, who was still in the direction of Myr.

Eighty leagues in front of Wilna, the Dwina and the Borysthenes separate Lithuania from old Russia. At first, these two rivers run parallel to each other from east to west, leaving between them an interval of about twenty-five leagues of unequal, woody, and marshy soil. They arrive in that manner from the interior of Russia, on its frontiers; at this point, at the same time, and as if in concert, they turn off: the one abruptly at Orcha towards the south; the other, near Witepsk, towards the north-west. It is in that new direction that their course traces the frontiers of Lithuania and old Russia.

The narrow space which these two rivers leave between them before taking this opposite direction seems to constitute the entrance, and as it were the gates of Muscovy. It is the nucleus of the roads which lead to the two capitals of that empire.

Napoleon's whole attention was directed to that point. By the retreat of Alexander upon Drissa, he foresaw that which Bagration would attempt to make from Grodno towards Witepsk, through Osmiana, Minsk, and Docktzitzy, or by Borizoff; he determined to prevent it, and instantly pushed forward Davoust towards Minsk, between these two hostile bodies, with two divisions of infantry, the cuirassiers of Valence, and several brigades of light cavalry.

On his right, the king of Westphalia was to drive Bagration on Davoust, who would cut off his communication with Alexander, make him surrender, and get possession of the course of the Borysthenes; while, on his left, Murat, Oudinot, and Ney, who were already before Drissa, were to hold in check Barclay and his emperor in their front; he himself, with the *élite* of his army, the army of Italy, the Bavarian army, and three divisions detached from Davoust, designed to march upon Witepsk between Davoust and Murat, ready to join one or the other of them; in this manner penetrating and interposing between the two hostile armies, forcing himself between them and beyond them; finally, keeping them separate, not only by that central position, but by the uncertainty which it would create in Alexander as to which of his two capitals it would be requisite for him to defend. Circumstances would decide the rest.

Such was Napoleon's plan on the 10th of July at Wilna; it was written in this form on that very day under his dictation, and corrected by his own hand, for one of his chiefs, the individual who was to have the principal part in its execution. Immediately, the movement, which was already begun, became general.

1. Balachoff was authorised to propose an armistice, and a negociation for peace, on condition that Napoleon would repass the Niemen. Napoleon is said to have replied, that he was willing to negociate in the position which he occupied.—*Ed.*

2. Napoleon was not short-sighted.—*Ed.*

CHAPTER VI

A PERILOUS SITUATION

THE king of Westphalia then diverged from the Niemen at Grodno, with a view to repass it at Bielitza, to overpower the right of Bagration, put it to the rout, and pursue it.

This Saxon, Westphalian, and Polish army had to do with a general and a country both difficult to conquer. It fell to its lot to invade the elevated plain of Lithuania, where are the sources of the rivers which empty their waters into the Black and the Baltic seas. But the soil there is slow in determining their inclination and their current, so that the waters stagnate and overflow the country to a great extent. Some narrow causeways passed over those woody and marshy plains; they formed there long defiles, which Bagration had no difficulty in defending against the king of Westphalia. The latter attacked him carelessly; his advanced guard only three times encountered the enemy, at Nowogrodeck, at Myr, and at Romanoff. The first rencontre was entirely to the advantage of the Russians; in the two others, Latour-Maubourg remained master of a sanguinary and contested field of battle.

At the same time, Davoust, proceeding from Osmiana, extended his force towards Minsk and Ygumen, behind the Russian general, and made himself master of the outlet of the defiles, in which the King of Westphalia was compelling Bagration to engage himself.

Between this hostile general and his retreat was a river which takes its source in an infectious marsh; its uncertain, slow, and languid

current, across a rotten soil, does not belie its origin; its muddy waters
flow towards the south-east; its name[1] possesses a fatal celebrity, for
which it is indebted to our misfortunes.

The wooden bridges, and long causeways, which, in order to
approach it, had been thrown over the adjacent marshes, abut upon
a town named Borizoff, situated on its left bank, on the Russian side.
This bank is generally higher than the right; a remark applicable to
all the rivers which, in this country run in the direction of one pole
to the other, their eastern bank commanding their western bank, as
Asia does Europe.[2]

This passage was important; Davoust anticipated Bagration there,
by taking possession of Minsk on the 8th of July, as well as the entire
country from the Vilia to the Berezina; accordingly when the Russian
prince and his army, summoned by Alexander to the north, pushed
forward their piquets, in the first instance upon Lida, and afterwards
successively upon Olzania, Vieznowo, Troki, Bolzoï, and Sobsnicki,
they came in contact with Davoust, and were forced to fall back upon
their main body. They then lent their course a little more in the rear
and to the right, and made a new attempt on Minsk, but there again
they found Davoust. A scanty platoon of that marshal's van-guard was
entering by one gate, when the advanced guard of Bagration presented
itself at another; on which the Russian retreated once more into his
marshes, towards the south.

At this intelligence, observing Bagration and 40,000 Russians cut
off from the army of Alexander, and enveloped by two rivers and two
armies, Napoleon exclaimed, "I have them!" In fact, it only required
three marches more to have hemmed in Bagration completely. But
Napoleon, who since accused Davoust of suffering the escape of
the left wing of the Russians by remaining four days in Minsk, and
afterwards, with more justice, the King of Westphalia, had just then
placed that monarch under the orders of the marshal. It was this
change, which was made too late, and in the midst of an operation,
which destroyed the unity of it.

This order arrived at the very moment that Bagration, repulsed
from Minsk, had no other retreat open to him than a long and narrow
causeway. It passes over the marshes of Nieswig, Shlutz, Glusck, and

Bobruisk. Davoust wrote to the king to push the Russians briskly into this defile, the outlet of which at Glusck he was about to occupy. Bagration would never have been able to get out of it. But the king, already irritated by the reproaches which the uncertainty and dilatoriness of his first operations had brought upon him, could not suffer a subject to be his commander; he abandoned his army, without leaving any one in his place, or without even communicating, if we are to credit Davoust, to any of his generals, the orders which he had just received. He was permitted to retire into Westphalia without his guard; which he accordingly did.

Meanwhile Davoust vainly waited for Bagration at Glusck. That general, finding himself no longer pressed by the Westphalian army, was enabled to make a new *detour* towards the south, to get to Bobruisk, and there cross the Berezina, and reach the Borysthenes near Bickoff. There again, if the Westphalian army had had a commander, if that commander had pressed the Russian leader more closely, if he had replaced him at Bickoff, when he came in collision with Davoust at Mohileff, it is certain that in that case Bagration, enclosed between the Westphalians, Davoust, the Borysthenes, and the Berezina, would have been compelled to conquer or to surrender. We have seen that the Russian prince could not pass the Berezina but at Bobruisk, nor reach the Borysthenes, except in the direction of Novoï-Bickoff, forty leagues to the south of Orcha, and sixty leagues from Witepsk, which it was his object to reach.

Finding himself so far driven out of his track, he hastened to regain it by reascending the Borysthenes, to Mohileff. But, there again he found Davoust, who had anticipated him there as he had done at Lida, by passing the Berezina at the very point at which Charles XII. had formerly crossed it.

The marshal, however, had not expected to find the Russian prince on the road to Mohileff. He believed him to be already on the left bank of the Borysthenes. Their mutual surprise turned in the first instance to the advantage of Bagration, who cut off a whole regiment of his light cavalry. At that time Bagration had with him 35,000 men, Davoust only 12,000. On the 23rd of July, the latter chose an elevated ground, defended by a ravine, and flanked by two woods. The

Russians had no means of extending themselves on this field of battle; they, nevertheless, accepted the challenge. Their numbers were there useless; they attacked like men sure of victory; they did not even think of profiting by the woods, in order to turn Davoust's right.

These Muscovites said that, in the middle of the contest they were seized with a panic at the idea of finding themselves in the presence of Napoleon; for each of the enemy's generals imagined him to be opposed to them, Bagration at Mohileff; and Barclay at Drissa. He was believed to be in all places at once: so greatly does renown magnify the man of genius! so strangely does it fill the world with his fame! and convert him into an omnipresent and supernatural being!

The attack was violent and obstinate on the part of the Russians, but without scientific combination. Bagration was roughly handled, and again compelled to retrace his steps. He finally crossed the Borysthenes at Novoï-Bickoff, where he entered the Russian interior, and finally united with Barclay beyond Smolensk.

Napoleon disdained to attribute this disappointment to the ability of the enemy's general; he placed it entirely to the incapacity of his own. He already discovered that his presence was necessary every where, which rendered it every where impossible. The circle of his operations was so much enlarged, that, being compelled to remain in the centre, his presence was wanting on the whole of the circumference. His generals, exhausted like himself, too independent of each other, too much separated, and at the same time too dependent upon him, ventured to do less of themselves, and frequently waited for his orders. His influence was weakened over so great an extent. It required too great a soul for so great a body; his, vast as it was, was not sufficient for the purpose.

But at length, on the 16th of July, the whole army was in motion. While all were hurrying and exerting themselves in this manner, he himself was still at Wilna, which he caused to be fortified. He there ordered a levy of eleven Lithuanian regiments. He established the Duke of Bassano as governor of Lithuania, and as the centre of administrative, political, and even military communication between him, Europe, and the generals commanding the different corps which were not to follow him to Moscow.

This ostensible inactivity of Napoleon at Wilna lasted twenty days. Some thought that, being then in the centre of his operations with a strong reserve, he awaited the event, in readiness to direct his motions either towards Davoust, Murat, or Macdonald; others thought that the organisation of Lithuania, and the politics of Europe, to which he was more proximate at Wilna, detained him in that city; or that he did not anticipate any obstacles worthy of him till he reached the Dwina; a circumstance in which he was not deceived, but by which he was too much flattered. The precipitate evacuation of Lithuania by the Russians seemed to dazzle his judgment; of this Europe will be the best judge; his bulletins repeated his language.

"Here then is that Russian empire, so formidable at a distance! It is a desert, for which its scattered population is wholly insufficient. They will be vanquished by its very extent, which ought to defend them. They are barbarians. They are scarcely possessed of arms. They have no recruits in readiness. Alexander will require more time to collect them than he (Napoleon) will take to reach Moscow. It is true that, from the moment of the passage of the Niemen, the atmosphere has been incessantly deluging or burning up the unsheltered soil; but this calamity is less an obstacle to the rapidity of our advance, than an impediment to the flight of the Russians. They are conquered without a combat, by their weakness alone; by the memory of our victories; by the remorse which dictates the restitution of that Lithuania which they have acquired neither by peace nor war, but solely by treachery."

To these motives of the stay, perhaps too protracted, which Napoleon made at Wilna, those who were nearest to his person have added another. They remarked to each other, "that a genius so vast as his, and always increasing in activity and audacity, was not now seconded as it had been formerly by a vigorous constitution. They were surprised at finding their chief no longer insensible to the heat of a burning atmosphere; and they remarked to each other with melancholy forebodings, the tendency to corpulence which his frame had now acquired; the certain forerunner of premature decay."

Some of them attributed this to his frequent use of the bath. They were ignorant, that, far from being a habit of luxury, this had become to him an indispensable relief from a bodily ailment of a serious and alarming character,[3] which his policy carefully concealed, in order not to excite cruel expectations in his adversaries.

Such is the inevitable and unhappy influence of the most trivial causes over the destiny of nations. It will be shortly seen—when the profoundest combinations, which ought to have secured the success of the boldest, and perhaps the most useful enterprise in a European point of view, came to be developed—how, at the decisive moment, on the plains of the Moskwa, nature paralysed the genius, and the man was wanting to the hero. The numerous battalions of Russia could not have defended her; a stormy day, a sudden attack of fever, were her salvation.

It will be only just and proper to revert to this observation, when, in examining the picture which I shall be forced to trace of the battle of the Moskwa, I shall be found repeating all the complaints, and even the reproaches, which an unusual inactivity and languor extorted from the most devoted friends and constant admirers of this great man. Most of them, as well as those who have subsequently given an account of the battle, were unaware of the bodily sufferings of a chief, who, in the midst of his depression, exerted himself to conceal their cause. That which was eminently a misfortune, these narrators have designated as a fault.

Besides, at 800 leagues distance from one's home, after so many fatigues and sacrifices, at the instant when we saw victory escaping from our grasp, and an alarming futurity reveal itself, it was natural for us to be severe; and we had suffered too much to be quite impartial.

As for myself, I shall not conceal what I witnessed, in the persuasion that truth is of all tributes that which is alone worthy of a great man; of that illustrious captain, who so often contrived to extract prodigious advantages from every occurrence, not excepting his reverses; of that man who raised himself to so great an eminence, that posterity will scarcely be enabled to distinguish the clouds scattered over his glory.

1. The Berezina.

2. This is not quite correct. Of the rivers to the north of Moscow, the western banks are loftier than the eastern.—*Ed.*

3. The *dysuria*, or retention of urine.

CHAPTER VII

THE RUSSIANS RETREAT

MEANTIME, he was apprised that his orders were fulfilled, his army united, and that a battle claimed his presence. He at length departed from Wilna on the 16th of July, at half-past eleven at night; he stopped at Swentziani, while the heat of the 17th was most oppressive; on the 18th he was at Klubokoe: taking up his residence at a monastery, whence he observed that the village which it commanded bore more resemblance to an assemblage of savage huts than to European habitations.

An address of the Russians to the French had just been dispersed throughout his army. He found in it some idle abuse, coupled with a nugatory and unskilful invitation to desert. His anger was excited at its perusal; in his first agitation, he dictated a reply, which he tore; then a second, which experienced the same fate; at length a third, with which he was satisfied. It was that which was, at the time, read in the journals, under the signature of a French grenadier. In this manner he dictated even the most trivial letters, which issued from his cabinet or from his staff; he was perpetually reducing his ministers and Berthier to the condition of mere secretaries. His mind still retained its activity, although his body was weighed down; their united action, however, began to fail; and this was one cause of our misfortune.

In the midst of these occupations he learned that Barclay had, on the 18th, abandoned his camp at Drissa, and that he was marching towards Witepsk. This movement opened his eyes. Detained by the check which Sebastiani had received near Drula, and more especially by the rains and bad state of the roads, he found (though perhaps too late) that the occupation of Witepsk was urgent and decisive; that that city alone was eminently aggressive, in as much as it separated two rivers, and the two hostile armies. From that position he would be enabled to turn the broken army of his rival, cut him off from his southern provinces, and crush his weakness with superior force. He concluded that, if Barclay had anticipated him in reaching that capital, he would doubtless defend it: and there, perhaps, he was to expect that so-much-coveted victory, which had escaped him on the Vilia. He, therefore, instantly directed all his corps on Beszenkowiczi: thither he summoned Murat and Ney, who were then near Polotsk, where he left Oudinot. He himself proceeded from Klubokoe (where he was surrounded by his guard, the Italian army, and three divisions detached from Davoust), to Kamen, always in a carriage, except during the night, either from necessity, or perhaps with a view to keep his soldiers in ignorance of the inability of their chief to share their fatigues.[1]

Till that time, the greater part of the army had proceeded with astonishment at finding no enemy; they had now become habituated to the circumstance. By day the novelty of the places, and impatience to get to their journey's end, occupied their attention; at night the necessity of choosing or making for themselves a place of shelter; of finding food and dressing it. The soldiers were so much engaged by so many cares, that they considered themselves less employed in making war than a fatiguing journey; but if the war and the enemy were to fall back always thus, how much farther should they have to go in search of them? At length, on the 25th, the report of cannon was heard, and the army, as well as the emperor, indulged their hopes of a victory and peace.

This was in the direction of Beszenkowiczi. Prince Eugene had there encountered Doctoroff, who commanded Barclay's rear-guard. In following his leader from Polotsk to Witepsk, he cleared his way on the left bank of the Dwina to Beszenkowiczi, the bridge of which he burnt as he retired. The viceroy, on capturing this town, came in sight of the Dwina, and re-established the passage; the few Russian troops left in observation on the other side feebly opposed the operation. When Napoleon contemplated, for the first time, this river, his new conquest, he censured sharply, and not unjustly, the defective construction of the bridge which made him master of the two banks.

It was no puerile vanity which induced him then to cross that river, but anxiety to see with his own eyes how far the Russian army had proceeded on its march from Drissa to Witepsk, and whether he might not attack it on its passage, or anticipate its arrival at the latter city. But the direction taken by the enemy's rear-guard, and the information obtained from some prisoners, convinced him that Barclay had been before-hand with him; that he had left Wittgenstein in front of Oudinot, and that the Russian general-in-chief was in Witepsk. He was, indeed, already prepared to dispute with Napoleon the possession of the defiles which cover that capital.

Napoleon having observed on the right bank of the river nothing but the remains of the rear-guard, returned to Beszenkowiczi. His various divisions arrived there at the same time by the northern and western roads. His orders of march had been executed with so much precision, that all the corps which had left the Niemen, at different epochs, and by different routes, notwithstanding obstacles of every description, after a month of separation, and at a hundred leagues' distance from the point of their departure, found themselves all reunited at Beszenkowiczi, where they arrived on the same day, and nearly at the same hour.

Great disorder was naturally the result; numerous columns of cavalry, infantry, and artillery, presented themselves on all sides; contests took place for precedence; and each corps, exasperated with fatigue and hunger, was impatient to get to its destination. Meanwhile, the streets were blocked up with a crowd of orderlies, staff-officers, valets, saddle-horses, and baggage. They ran through the city in tumultuous groups; some looking for provisions; others for forage, and a few for lodgings; there was a constant crossing and jostling; and as the influx augmented every instant, chaos in a short time reigned throughout.

In one quarter, *aides-de-camp*, the bearers of urgent orders, vainly sought to force a passage; the soldiers were deaf to their remonstrances, and even to their orders: hence arose quarrels and outcries; the noise of which united with the beating of drums, the oaths of the wagoners, the rumbling of the baggage-carts and cannon, the commands of the officers, and, finally, with the tumult of the regular contests which took place in the houses, the entrances of which one party attempted to force, while others, already established there, prepared to defend.

At length, towards midnight, all these masses, which were nearly confounded together, got disentangled; the accumulation of troops gradually moved off in the direction of Ostrowno, or were distributed in Beszenkowiczi; and the most profound silence succeeded the most frightful tumult.

This great concentration, the multiplied orders which came from all parts, the rapidity with which the various corps were pushed forward, even during the night—all announced the expectation of a battle on the following day. In fact, Napoleon not having been able to anticipate the Russians in the possession of Witepsk, was determined to assail them in that position but the latter, after having entered by the right bank of the Dwina, had passed through that city, and were now come to meet him, in order to defend the long defiles which protect it.

On the 25th of July, Murat proceeded towards Ostrowno with his cavalry. At the distance of two leagues from that village, Domon, Du Coëtlosquet, Carignan, and the 8th hussars, were advancing in column upon a broad road, lined by a double row of large birch trees. These hussars had nearly reached the summit of a hill, from which they could only get a glimpse of the smallest portion of a corps, composed of three regiments of cavalry of the Russian guard, and six pieces of cannon. There was not a single sharp-shooter to cover their line.

The colonels of the 8th imagined themselves preceded by two regiments of their division, which had marched across the fields on the right and left of the road, and from the view of which they were precluded by the double row of trees. But these corps had halted; and the 8th, already considerably in advance of them, still kept marching on, persuaded that what it perceived through the trees, at 150 paces' distance, in its front, were these two regiments, of which, without being aware of it, it had got the start.

The immobility of the Russians completed the error into which the chiefs of the 8th had fallen. The order to charge seemed to them to be a mistake; they sent an officer to reconnoitre the troop which was before them, and still marched on without suspicion. Suddenly they beheld their officer sabred, knocked down, made prisoner, and the enemy's cannon bringing down their hussars. They now hesitated no longer, and without losing time to form their line under the enemy's fire, they dashed through the trees, and rushed forward to extinguish it. At the first onset they seized the cannon, dispersed the regiment that was in the centre of the enemy's line, and destroyed it. During the confusion caused by this first success, they observed the Russian regiment on the right, which they had passed, remaining motionless with astonishment: upon this they turned round, attacked it in the rear, and dispersed it. In the midst of this second victory, they perceived the third regiment on the enemy's left, which was giving way in confusion, and endeavouring to retreat; towards this third enemy they briskly returned, with all the men they could muster, and attacked and dispersed it in the midst of its retreat.

Animated by this success, Murat drove the enemy into the wood of Ostrowno, where he seemed to conceal himself. That monarch endeavoured to penetrate the wood, but a strong resistance obstructed the attempt.

The position of Ostrowno was well chosen and commanding; those who were posted there could see without being seen; it intersected a main road; it had the Dwina on the right, a ravine in front, and a thick wood close to it on the left. It was, moreover, in communication with magazines; it covered them, as well as Witepsk, the capital of these countries. Ostermann advanced in haste to defend it.

On his side, Murat, always as prodigal of his life, now that he was a victorious monarch, as he had formerly been when only an obscure private soldier, persisted in his attack upon the wood, not withstanding the heavy fire which proceeded from it. But he was soon made sensible that a furious onset was fruitless here. The ground carried by the hussars of the 8th was disputed with him; and his advance-column, composed of the divisions Bruyères and Saint Germain, and of the 8th corps of infantry, was compelled to maintain itself there against an army.

They defended themselves as victors always do, by attacking. Each hostile corps, as it presented itself to assail our flanks, was in turn assaulted. Their cavalry were driven back into the woods, and their infantry broken at the point of the sabre. Our troops, nevertheless, were getting fatigued with victory, when the division Delzons arrived; the king promptly pushed it forward on the right, toward the line of the enemy's retreat, who now became uneasy, and no longer disputed the victory.

These defiles are several leagues in length. The same evening the Viceroy rejoined Murat, and the next day they found the Russians in a new position. Pahlen and Konownitzin had united with Ostermann. After having repulsed the Russian left, the two French princes were pointing out to the troops of their right wing the position which was to serve them as a *point d'appui*, from which they were to make the attack, when suddenly a great clamour arose on their left: their eyes were instantly turned that way; the cavalry and infantry of that wing had twice attacked the enemy, and been twice repulsed; the Russians, emboldened by this success, were issuing in multitudes, and with frightful cries, from their wood. The daringness and fervour of attack had passed over to them, while the French exhibited the wavering and timidity of defence.

A battalion of Croats, and the 84th regiment, vainly attempted to make a stand; their line was gradually diminished; the ground in front of them was strewed with their dead; behind them, the plain was covered with their wounded, who had retired from the battle, with those who carried them, and with many others, who, under pretence of supporting the wounded, or of being wounded themselves successively abandoned their ranks. A rout accordingly began. Already the artillery corps, who are always picked men, perceiving themselves no longer supported, began retiring with their pieces; a few minutes longer, and the troops of all arms, in their flight towards the same defile, would have there met each other; thence would have resulted a confusion, in which the voices and efforts of their officers would have been lost, where all the elements of resistance would have been confounded together and rendered useless.

It is said that Murat, irritated at this sight, darted forward to the head of a regiment of Polish lancers; and that the latter, excited by the presence of the king, animated by his words, and, moreover, transported with rage at the sight of the Russians, followed him precipitately. Murat had only wished to stimulate them and impel them against the enemy: it did not become him to throw himself with them into the midst of a conflict, in which he could neither be able to see nor to command; but the Polish lances were already couched and condensed behind him; they covered the whole width of the ground; and they pushed him before them with all the rapidity of their steeds; he could neither move off to one side, nor halt; he had no alternative but to charge in front of the regiment, just where he had placed himself in order to harangue it; an alternative to which, like a true soldier, he submitted with the best possible grace.[2]

At the same time, general Anthouard ran to his artillerymen, and general Girardin to the 106th regiment, which he halted, rallied, and led back against the Russian right wing, whose position he carried, as well as two pieces of cannon and the victory; on his side general Piré attacked and turned the left of the enemy. Fortune having again changed sides, the Russians withdrew into their forest.

Meanwhile, their left continued obstinately to defend a thick wood, the advanced position of which broke our line. The 92nd regiment, intimidated by the heavy fire which issued from it, and bewildered by a shower of balls, remained immoveable, neither daring to advance nor retreat, restrained by two opposite fears—of danger and shame— and escaping neither; but general Belliard, who was speedily followed by general Roussel, hastened to encourage them by his words, and incite them by his example, and the wood was carried.

By this success, a strong column which had advanced on our right, in order to turn it, was itself turned; Murat perceived this, and instantly drawing his sword, exclaimed, "Let the bravest follow me!" But this territory is intersected with ravines which protected the retreat of the Russians, who all plunged into a forest of two leagues in depth, which was the last natural curtain which concealed Witepsk from our view.

After so warm a contest, the King of Naples and the Viceroy were hesitating about committing themselves to so covered a country, when the Emperor came up: both hastened to his presence, in order to show him what had been done, and what still remained to be done. Napoleon immediately ascended the highest rising ground, which was nearest to the enemy. From thence his genius, soaring over every obstacle, soon penetrated the mystery of the forests, and the depths of the mountains before him; he gave his orders without hesitation; and the same woods which had arrested the audacity of the two princes, were traversed from end to end. In short, that very evening, Witepsk could discern, from the summit of her double eminence, our light troops emerging into the plain by which she is surrounded.

Here, every thing contributed to stop the Emperor; the night, the multitude of hostile fires which covered the plain, an unknown country, which it was necessary to reconnoitre, in order to direct his divisions across it, and especially the time requisite to enable the crowd of soldiers to disengage themselves from the long and narrow defile through which they had to pass. A halt was therefore ordered, for the purpose of taking breath, reconnoitring, rallying, refreshing, and getting their arms ready for the next day. Napoleon slept in his tent on an eminence to the left of the main road, and behind the village of Kukowiaczi.

1. The real cause of Napoleon travelling in a carriage is thus stated by General Gourgaud:—"The active life which he led in camp was subordinate to military operations. When the army was following up, or was near the enemy, he was habitually with it on horseback. When it was engaged in great manœuvres, and operations were carried on at considerable distances, he waited till the corps which were in march had nearly attained their assigned positions. He remained till then at his headquarters. There he devoted his attention to the internal administration of France, and replied to the reports which were daily sent to him by his ministers at Paris. For he governed the empire at the same time that he directed the army. Economical of his time, he calculated the moment of his departure so as to be at the head of his troops

exactly when his presence became necessary. He therefore rapidly proceeded thither in a carriage. But even, during his journey, he was not idle. He was employed in reading despatches, and, still more frequently, he received reports from his generals, and answered them on the spot. Expresses from Paris were also sometimes delivered to him at the same time. A lamp in the back of the vehicle lighted it during his nocturnal journeys, and enabled him to write as if he had been in his cabinet. At the doors were always his aides-de-camp and orderly officers, and a brigade of saddle-horses followed with the escort."—*Ed.*

2. This statement is erroneous. Murat voluntarily headed the charge.—*Ed.*

CHAPTER VIII

WITEPSK

ON the 27th, the emperor appeared at the advanced posts before sunrise; its first rays exhibited to him at last the Russian army encamped on an elevated plain, which commanded all the avenues of Witepsk. The river Luczissa, which has worn itself a deep channel, flowed at the foot of this position. In advance of it, 10,000 horse and some infantry made a show of defending its approaches; the infantry was in the centre, on the main road; its left in woody uplands; all the cavalry on the right in double lines, supported by the Dwina.

The front of the Russians was no longer opposite to our column, but upon our left; it had changed its direction with that of the river, a bend of which had removed it farther from us. The French column, after having crossed, by means of a narrow bridge, the ravine which divided it from the new field of battle, was obliged to deploy by a change of front to the left, with the right wing forward, in order to preserve the support of the river on that side, and so confront the enemy: on the banks of this ravine, near the bridge, and to the left of the main road, there was an insulated hillock which had already attracted the notice of the Emperor. From that point he could see both armies, being stationed on the flank of the field of battle, like the second in a duel.

Two hundred Parisian *voltigeurs* of the 9th regiment of the line were the first to debouch; they were immediately pushed forward to the left, in front of the whole Russian cavalry, like them supporting themselves by the Dwina, and marking the left of the new line: the 16th horse chasseurs followed, and then some light pieces. The Russians coolly allowed us to defile before them, and mature our attack.

Their inactivity was favourable to us; but the King of Naples, whose brain was intoxicated by the general notice he attracted, yielding to his usual impetuosity, urged on the chasseurs of the 16th against the whole body of the Russian cavalry. All eyes then beheld with terror that feeble French line, broken on its march by the deep ravines which intersected the ground, advance to attack the enemy's masses. These unfortunate men, feeling themselves sacrificed, proceeded with hesitating steps to certain destruction. In consequence, at the first movement made by the lancers of the Russian guard, they turned their backs; but the ravines, which it was necessary to pass, obstructed their flight; they were overtaken, and precipitated into these hollows, where many of them perished.

At sight of this Murat, grieved beyond measure, rushed, sabre in hand, into the midst of this medley, with the sixty officers and horsemen who surrounded him. His boldness so astonished the Russian lancers, that they halted. While this prince was engaged, and the *piquer* who followed him saved his life by severing the arm of an enemy which was raised over his head, the remains of the 16th rallied, and went to seek shelter close to the 53rd regiment, which protected them.

This successful charge of the lancers of the Russian guard had carried them as far as the foot of the hillock from which Napoleon was directing the different corps. Some chasseurs of the French guard had just dismounted from their horses, according to custom, in order to form a circle around him; a few discharges from their carabines drove off the assailant lancers. The latter, being thus repulsed, encountered on their return the two hundred Parisian *voltigeurs,* whom the flight of the 16th horse chasseurs had left alone between the two armies. These they attacked, and all eyes were instantly fixed on the engagement.

Both armies concluded these foot soldiers to be lost; but though alone, they did not despair. In the first instance, their captains, by dint of hard fighting, obtained possession of a ground intersected by crevices and thickets which bordered on the Dwina; there the whole of them were soon collected, led by their warlike habits, by the desire of mutual support, and by the danger which stared them in the face. In this emergency, as always happens in imminent dangers, each looked to his neighbour; the young ones to their seniors, and all of them to their chiefs, in order to read in their countenances what they had to hope, to fear, or to perform; each aspect was replete with confidence, and all relying on their comrades, every one relied with greater confidence upon himself.

The ground was skilfully turned to account. The Russian lancers, entangled in the bushes, and obstructed by the crevices, couched their long lances in vain; they were struck by our people's balls while they were endeavouring to penetrate their ranks, and fell, wounded, to the earth; their bodies, and those of their horses, added to the difficulties of the ground. At length they became discouraged, and took to flight. The joyful shouts of our army, the crosses of honour, which the emperor instantly sent to the bravest of the group, his words, afterwards perused by all Europe,—all taught these valiant soldiers the extent of a glory which they had not yet estimated; the noblest actions generally appearing quite ordinary to those who perform them. They had imagined themselves on the point of being killed or taken; and found themselves almost at the same instant victorious and rewarded.

Meanwhile, the army of Italy and the cavalry of Murat, followed by three divisions of the first corps, which had been confided, since they left Wilna, to Count de Lobau, attacked the high-road and the woods which formed the support of the enemy's left. The engagement was, in the first instance, very animated; but it terminated abruptly. The Russian vanguard retreated precipitately behind the ravine of the Luczissa, to avoid being driven into it. The enemy's army was then entirely collected on the opposite bank, and presented a united force of 80,000 men.

Their determined countenance, in a strong position, and in front of a capital, deceived Napoleon; he conceived that they would regard it as a point of honour to maintain their ground. It was only eleven o'clock; he ordered the attack to cease, in order to have an opportunity of exploring tranquilly the whole front of the line, and to prepare for a decisive battle on the following day. In the first instance, he proceeded to post himself on a rising ground among the light troops, in the midst of whom he breakfasted. Thence he observed the enemy's army, a ball from which wounded an officer very near him. The subsequent hours he spent in reconnoitring the ground, and in waiting for the arrival of the other corps.

Napoleon announced a battle for the following day. His parting words to Murat were these:—"To-morrow at five o'clock, the sun of Austerlitz!" These words afford an explanation of the suspension of hostilities in the middle of the day, in the midst of a success which filled the troops with enthusiasm. They were astonished at this inactivity at the moment of overtaking an army, the pursuit of which had completely exhausted them.[1] Murat, who had been daily deluded by a similar expectation, remarked to the Emperor that Barclay only made a demonstration of boldness at that hour, in order to be enabled more tranquilly to effect his retreat during the night. Finding himself unable to convince his chief, he rashly proceeded to pitch his tent on the banks of the Luczissa, almost in the midst of the enemy. It was a position which gratified his desire of hearing the first symptoms of their retreat, his hope of disturbing it, and his adventurous character.

Murat was deceived, and yet he appeared to have been most clear-sighted; Napoleon was in the right, and yet, the event placed him in the wrong; such are the freaks of fortune! The Emperor of the French had correctly appreciated the designs of Barclay. The Russian general believing Bagration to be still near Orcha, had resolved upon fighting, in order to give him time to rejoin him. It was the intelligence which he received that very evening, of the retreat of Bagration by Novoï-Bickoff towards Smolensk, which suddenly changed his determination.

In fact, by daybreak on the 28th, Murat sent word to the Emperor that he was about to pursue the Russians, who had already disappeared. Napoleon still persisted in his opinion, obstinately affirming that the whole enemy's army was in front of him, and that it was necessary to advance with circumspection; this occasioned a considerable delay. At length he mounted his horse; every step he took destroyed his illusion;

and he soon found himself in the midst of the camp which Barclay had just abandoned.

Every thing about it exhibited the scientific knowledge of war; its advantageous site; the symmetry of all its parts; the exact and exclusive nicety in the use to which each of them had been destined the order and neatness which thence resulted;[2] in fine, nothing left behind, not one weapon, nor a single valuable; no trace, nothing in short, in this sudden nocturnal march, which could demonstrate, beyond the bounds of the camp, the route which the Russians had taken; there appeared more order in their defeat, than in our victory! Though conquered, their flight left us lessons by which conquerors never profit: whether it be that good fortune is contemptuous, or that it waits for misfortune to correct it.

A Russian soldier, who was surprised asleep under a bush, was the solitary result of that day, which was expected to be so decisive. We entered Witepsk, which was found equally deserted with the camp of the Russians. Some filthy Jews and Jesuits were all that remained; they were interrogated, but without effect. All the roads were abortively reconnoitred. Were the Russians gone to Smolensk? Had they re-ascended the Dwina? At length, a band of irregular cossacks attracted us in the latter direction, while Ney explored the former. We marched six leagues over a deep sand, through a thick dust, and a suffocating heat. Night arrested our march in the neighbourhood of Agha-ponovchtchina.

While parched, fevered, and exhausted by fatigue and hunger, the army met with nothing there but muddy water, Napoleon, the King of Naples, the Viceroy, and the Prince of Neufchatel, held a council in the imperial tents, which were pitched in the court-yard of a castle, situated upon an eminence to the left of the main road.

"That victory which was so fervently desired, so rapidly pursued, and rendered more necessary by the lapse of every succeeding day, had, it seemed, just escaped from our grasp, as it had at Wilna. True, we had come up with the Russian rear-guard; but was it that of their army? Was it not more likely that Barclay had fled towards Smolensk by way Rudnia? How far, then, must we pursue the Russians, in order to compel them to fight? Did not the necessity of organising re-conquered Lithuania, of establishing magazines and hospitals, of fixing a new centre of repose, of defence, and departure for a line of operations which prolonged itself in so alarming a manner:— did not every thing, in short, decidedly prove the necessity of halting on the borders of old Russia?"

An affray had just happened, not far from that, respecting which Murat was silent. Our vanguard had been repulsed; some of the cavalry had been obliged to dismount, in order to effect their retreat; others had been unable to bring off their attenuated horses, otherwise than by dragging them by the bridle. The Emperor having interrogated Belliard on the subject, that general frankly declared, that the regiments were already very much weakened, that they were harassed to death, and stood in absolute need of rest; and that if they continued to march for six days longer, there would be no cavalry remaining, and that it was high time to halt.

To these motives were added the effects of a consuming sun reflected from burning sands. Exhausted as he was, the Emperor now decided; the course of the Dwina and of the Borysthenes marked out the French line. The army was thus quartered on the banks of these two rivers, and in the interval between them; Poniatowski and his Poles at Mohileff; Davoust and the first corps at Orcha, Dubrowna, and Luibowiczi; Murat, Ney, the army of Italy and the guard, from Orcha and Dubrowna to Witepsk and Suraij. The advanced posts at Lyadi, Inkowo, and Velij, opposite to those of Barclay and Bagration; for these two hostile armies, the one flying from Napoleon, across the Dwina, by Drissa and Witepsk, the other, escaping Davoust across the Berezina and the Borysthenes, by way of Bobruisk, Bickoff, and Smolensk, had just succeeded in forming a junction in the interval bounded by these two rivers.

The great divisions of the army detached from the central body were then stationed as follows: To the right, Dombrowski, in front of Bobruisk, and opposed to the corps of 12,000 men commanded by the Russian general Hoertel.

To the left, the Duke of Reggio and St. Cyr, at Polotsk and at Bieloé, on the Petersburgh road, which was defended by Wittgenstein and 30,000 men.

At the extreme left were Macdonald and 38,000 Prussians and Poles, before Riga. They extended their line towards the right upon the Aa, and in the direction of Dünabourg.

At the same time, Schwartzenberg and Regnier, at the head of the Saxon and Austrian corps, occupied, towards Slonim, the interval between the Niemen and the Bug, covering Warsaw and the rear of the grand army, which was menaced by Tormasoff. The Duke of Belluno was on the Vistula with a reserve of 40,000 men; while Augereau assembled an eleventh army at Stettin.

As to Wilna, the Duke of Bassano remained there, surrounded by the envoys of several courts. That minister governed Lithuania, communicated with all the chiefs, sent them the instructions which he received from Napoleon, and forwarded the provisions, recruits, and stragglers as fast as they arrived.

As soon as the Emperor had come to a decision, he returned to Witepsk with his guard: there, on the 28th of July, on entering the imperial head-quarters, he took off his sword, and throwing it carelessly on the maps with which the tables were covered, exclaimed; "Here I stop! here I must look round me; rally; refresh my army, and organise Poland. The campaign of 1812 is finished; that of 1813 will do the rest."

1. The delay was absolutely necessary, in order to afford time for accurately reconnoitring the Russian position.—*Ed*.

2. General Gourgaud, by whom this camp was minutely examined, declares it to have been extremely irregular, and dirty, and in such disorder that no estimate could be formed of the number of men and animals which had bivouacked in it.—*Ed*.

BOOK V

CHAPTER I

MARCH TO SMOLENSK

WITH the conquest of Lithuania, the object of the war was attained, and, yet, the war appeared scarcely to have commenced; for places only had been vanquished, and not men. The Russian army was unbroken; its two wings, which had been separated, by the rapidity of our first onset, had once more united with it. We were in the finest season of the year. It was in this situation that Napoleon believed himself irrevocably decided to halt on the banks of the Borysthenes and the Dwina. At that time, he could much more easily deceive others as to his intentions, as he actually deceived himself.

His line of defence was already traced upon his maps; the battering cannon were proceeding towards Riga; the left of the army would rest on that strong place; thence, proceeding to Dünabourg and Polotsk, it would maintain a menacing defensive. Witepsk, so easy to fortify, and its woody heights, would serve as an entrenched camp for the centre. Thence, towards the south, the Berezina and its marshes, covered by the Borysthenes, supply no other passage but a few defiles; a very few troops would be sufficient to guard them. Further on, Bobruisk marked out the right of this great line, and orders were given to obtain possession of that fortress. In addition, an insurrection of the populous provinces of the south was calculated on; they would assist Schwartzenberg in expelling Tormasoff, and the army would be increased by their numerous Cossacks. One of the greatest proprietors of these provinces, a nobleman in whom every thing was distinguished, even to his external appearance, hastened to join the liberators of his country. He it was whom the emperor intended for the leader of this insurrection.

In this position nothing would be wanting. Courland would support Macdonald; Samogitia, Oudinot; the fertile plains of Glubokoë, the Emperor; the southern provinces would supply the rest. In addition, the grand magazine of the army was at Dantzic; its intermediate ones at Wilna and Minsk. In this manner the army would be connected with the country which it had just set free; and all things appertaining to that country—its rivers, marshes, productions, and inhabitants, would be united with us: all things would be agreed for the purposes of defence.

Such was Napoleon's plan. He was at that time seen exploring Witepsk and its environs, as if to reconnoitre places where he was likely to make a long residence. Establishments of all kinds were formed there. Thirty-six ovens, capable of baking at once 29,000 pounds of bread were constructed. Neither was utility alone attended to; embellishment was also considered. Some stone houses, spoiled the appearance of the square of the palace; the emperor ordered his guard to pull them down, and to clear away the rubbish. Indeed, he was already anticipating the pleasures of winter; Parisian actors must come to Witepsk; and as that city was abandoned, spectators of the fair sex must be attracted from Warsaw and Wilna.

His star at that time enlightened his path: happy had it been for him, if he had not afterwards mistaken the promptings of his impatience for the inspirations of genius. But whatever may be said, it was by himself alone that he suffered himself to be hurried on; for in him every thing proceeded from himself; and it was a vain attempt to seduce his prudence. In vain did one of his marshals then promise him an insurrection of the Russians, in consequence of the proclamations which the officers of his advanced guard had been instructed to disseminate. Some Poles had intoxicated that general with inconsiderate promises, dictated by the delusive hope common to all exiles, with which they flatter the ambition of the leaders who rely upon them.

But Murat was the individual whose incitements were most frequent and animated. Tired of repose, and insatiable of glory, that monarch, who considered the enemy to be within his grasp, was unable to repress his emotions. He quitted the advanced guard, went to Witepsk, and in a private interview with the Emperor gave way to his impetuosity. He accused the Russian army of cowardice; according to him, it had failed in the *rendezvous* before Witepsk, as if it had been an affair of a duel. It was a panic-struck army, which his light cavalry alone was sufficient to put to flight. This ebullition extorted a smile from Napoleon; but in order to moderate his fervour he said to him, "Murat! the first campaign in Russia is finished: let us here plant our eagles. Two great rivers mark out our position; let us raise block-houses on that line; let our fires cross each other on all sides; let us form in square battalion; cannon at the angles and the exterior; let the interior contain our quarters and our magazines: 1813 will see us at Moscow—at Petersburgh. The Russian war is a three years' war."

It was thus that his genius conceived every thing in masses, and his eye expatiated over an army of 400,000 men as if it were a regiment.

That very day he loudly addressed an administrator in the following words: "As for you, sir, you must take care to provide subsistence for us in these quarters; for," added he, in a loud voice, and addressing himself to some of his officers, "we shall not repeat the folly of Charles the Twelfth." But his actions in a short time belied his words; and there was a general astonishment at his indifference in giving the necessary orders for so great an establishment. To the left no instructions were sent to Macdonald, nor was he supplied with the means of obtaining possession of Riga. To the right, it was Bobruisk which it was necessary to capture; this fortress stands in the midst of an extensive and deep marsh; and it was to a body of cavalry that the task of besieging it was committed.

Napoleon, in former times, scarcely ever gave orders without the possibility of being obeyed; but the prodigies of the war of Prussia had since occurred, and from that time the idea of impossibility was never admitted. Every thing was ordered to be attempted, because up to that time every thing had succeeded. This at first gave birth to great exertions, all of which, however, were not fortunate. His followers got discouraged; but their chief persevered; he had become accustomed to command every thing; those whom he commanded got accustomed not to execute every thing.

Dombrowski, however, was left before that fortress with his Polish division, which Napoleon stated at 8000 men, although he knew very well that it did not at that time amount to more than 1200;[1] but such was his custom; either because he calculated on his words being repeated, and that they would deceive the enemy; or that he wished, by this exaggerated estimate, to make his generals feel all that he expected from them.

Witepsk remained for survey. From the windows of its houses the eye looked down perpendicularly into the Dwina, or to the very bottom of the precipices by which its walls are surrounded. In these countries the snow remains long upon the ground; it filters through its least solid parts, which it penetrates to a great depth, and which it dilutes and breaks down. Hence those deep and unexpected ravines, which no declination of the soil gives reason to foresee, which are imperceptible at some paces from their edge, and which on those vast plains surprised and suddenly arrested the charges of cavalry.

The French would not have required more than a month to render that city strong enough even to stand a regular siege: the natural strength of the place was such as to require little assistance from art, but that little was denied it. At the same time, a few millions, which were indispensable to effect the levy of the Lithuanian troops, were refused to them. Prince Sangutsko was to have gone and commanded the insurrection in the south, but he was detained in the imperial head-quarters.

But the moderation of the first discourses of Napoleon had not deceived the members of his household. They recollected that, at the first view of the deserted camp of Barclay, and of Witepsk abandoned, when he heard them congratulating each other on this conquest, he turned sharply round to them and exclaimed, "Do you think then that I have come so far to conquer these huts?" They also knew perfectly, that when he had a great object in view, he never devised any other than a vague plan, preferring to take counsel of opportunity; a system more conformable to the promptitude of his genius.

In other respects, the whole army was loaded with the favours of its commander. If he happened to meet with convoys of wounded, he stopped them, informed himself of their condition, of their sufferings, of the actions in which they had been wounded, and never quitted them without consoling them by his words; or making them, partakers of his bounty.

He bestowed particular attention on his guard; he daily reviewed some part of them, lavished commendation, and sometimes blame; but the latter seldom fell on any but the administrators; which pleased the soldiers, and diverted their complaints.

Every day he went and visited the ovens, tasted the bread, and satisfied himself of the regularity of all the distributions. He frequently sent wine from his table to the sentinel who was nearest to him. One day he assembled the *élite* of his guards for the purpose of giving them a new leader; he made them a speech, and with his own hand and sword introduced him to them; afterwards he embraced him in their presence. So many attentions were ascribed, by some, to his gratitude for the past; by others, to his exigency for the future.

The latter saw clearly that Napoleon had at first flattered himself with the hope of receiving fresh overtures of peace from Alexander, and that the misery and debility of his army had occupied his attention. It was necessary to allow the long train of stragglers and sick sufficient time, the one for joining their corps, and the latter for reaching the hospitals. Finally, to establish these hospitals, to collect provisions, recruit the horses, and wait for the hospital-wagons, the artillery, and the pontoons, which were still laboriously dragging after us across the Lithuanian sands. His correspondence with Europe must also have occupied his attention. To conclude, a destructive atmosphere stopped his progress! Such, in fact, is that climate; the weather is always in the extreme—always in excess; it either parches or inundates, burns up or freezes, the soil and its inhabitants, for whose protection it appears expressly framed; a perfidious climate, the heat of which debilitated our bodies, in order to render them more accessible to the frosts by which they were shortly to be pierced.

The Emperor was not less sensible of its effects than others; but when he found himself somewhat refreshed by repose, when no envoy from Alexander made his appearance, and his first dispositions were completed, he became impatient. He was observed to grow restless; whether it was that inactivity annoyed him, as it does all men of active habits; and that he preferred danger to the weariness of expectation, or that he was agitated by that desire of acquisition, which, with the greater part of mankind, has greater influence than the pleasure of preserving, or the fear of losing.

It was then especially that the image of captive Moscow besieged him; it was the boundary of his fears, the object of his hopes; possessed of that, he would possess everything. From that time it was foreseen that an ardent and restless genius like his, and accustomed to short cuts, would not wait eight months, when he felt his object within his reach, and when twenty days were sufficient to attain it.

We must not, however, be too hasty in condemning this extraordinary man for weaknesses common to all men. We shall presently hear from himself; we shall see how much his political position tended to render complex his military position. At a later period, we shall be less tempted to blame the resolution he was now about to take, when it is seen that the fate of Russia depended upon only one more day's health, which failed Napoleon, even on the very field of the Moskwa.

In the first instance he appeared hardly bold enough to confess to himself a project of such great temerity. But by degrees, he assumed courage to look it in the face. He then began to deliberate, and the state of great irresolution which tormented his mind affected his whole frame. He was observed to wander about his apartments, as if pursued by some dangerous temptation. Nothing could rivet his attention; he every moment began, quitted, and resumed his occupation; he walked about without any object; inquired the hour, and remarked the weather; completely absorbed, he stopped, then hummed a tune with an absent air, and again began walking about.

In the midst of his perplexity, he occasionally addressed the persons whom he met with such half sentences as "Well, what shall we do? Shall we stay where we are, or advance? How is it possible to stop short in the midst of so glorious a career?" He did not wait for their reply, but still kept wandering about, as if he was looking for something for somebody to terminate his indecision.

At length, quite sinking under the weight of such important considerations, and in a manner overwhelmed with this great uncertainty, he would throw himself on one of the beds which he had caused to be laid on the floor of his apartments. His body, exhausted by the heat, and the struggles of his mind, could only bear a light garment; in this manner did he pass a portion of his day at Witepsk.

But when his body was at rest, his spirit was only the more active. "What numerous motives urged him towards Moscow? How support at Witepsk the *ennui* of seven winter months?—he who till then had always been the assailant, was about to be reduced to a defensive position; a part unworthy of him, of which he had no experience, unsuitable to his genius.

Moreover, at Witepsk, nothing had been decided, and yet, at what a distance was he already from France! Europe, then, would at length behold him stopped, him whom nothing had been able to stop. Would not the duration of the enterprise augment its danger? Ought he to allow Russia time to arm herself completely? How long could he protract this uncertain condition without impairing the charm of his infallibility, (which the resistance of Spain had already enfeebled,) and without engendering dangerous hopes in Europe? What would be thought, if it were known that a third of his army, dispersed or sick, were no longer in the ranks? It was indispensable, therefore, to dazzle the world speedily by the éclat of a great victory, and hide so many sacrifices under a heap of laurels."

Then, if he remained at Witepsk, he considered that he should have the *ennui,* the whole expense, all the inconveniences and anxieties of a defensive position to bear; while at Moscow there would be peace, abundance, a reimbursement of the expenses of the war, and immortal glory. He persuaded himself that boldness was now his only prudential course; that it is the same with all hazardous undertakings, as with faults, in which there is always risk at the beginning, but frequently gain at the conclusion; the more inexcusable they are, the more they require to be successful. That it was indispensable, therefore, to consummate this undertaking, to push it to the utmost, astonish the universe, beat down Alexander by his daring, and carry off a prize which might compensate so many losses.

Thus it was, that the same danger which perhaps ought to have recalled him to the Niemen, or kept him stationary on the Dwina, urged him towards Moscow! Such is the nature of false positions; every thing in them is perilous; temerity is prudence; there is only a choice of errors; there is no hope but in those of the enemy, and in chance.

Having at last determined, he hastily arose, as if not to allow time to his own reflections to renew so painful a state of uncertainty; and already quite full of the plan which was to secure his conquest, he hastened to his maps; they presented to his view the cities of Smolensk and Moscow; "the great Moscow, the holy city;" names which he repeated with complacency, and which served to add new fuel to his ambitious flame. Fired with this prospect, his spirit, replete with the energy of his mighty conception, appears possessed by the genius of war. His voice deepens; his eye flashes fire; and his countenance darkens; his attendants retreat from his presence, struck with mingled awe and respect; but at length his plan is fixed; his determination taken; his order of march traced out. Instantly the internal struggle by which he had been agitated subsided; and no sooner was he delivered of his terrible conception, than his countenance resumed its usual mild and tranquil character.

1. On the contrary, this division consisted of twelve brigades of infantry, and a brigade of cavalry consisting of 9000 men, with twenty-four pieces of artillery. It was not ordered to besiege, but to blockade Bobruisk.—*Ed.*

CHAPTER II

DISCUSSIONS
WITH THE OFFICERS

HIS resolution once taken, he was anxious that it should satisfy his counsellors; he conceived that by persuading them, they would be actuated by greater zeal, than by commanding their obedience. It was, moreover, by their sentiments, that he was enabled to judge of those of the rest of his army; in short, like all other men, the silent discontent of his household disturbed him. Surrounded by disapproving countenances, and opinions contrary to his own, he felt himself uncomfortable. And, besides, to obtain their assent to his plan, was in some degree to make them share the responsibility of it, which possibly weighed upon his mind.

But all the officers about his person opposed his plan; each in the way that marked his peculiar character: Berthier, with a sorrowful countenance, with lamentations, and even with tears; Lobau and Caulaincourt with a frankness, which, in the first, was stamped by a cold and haughty bluntness, excusable in so brave a warrior; and which, in the second, was persevering even to obstinacy, and impetuous even to violence. The emperor repelled their observations with some ill-humour; he exclaimed, addressing himself more especially to his aide-de-camp, as well as to Berthier, "that he had enriched his generals too much; that all they now aspired to was to follow the pleasures of the chase, and to display their brilliant equipages in the capital: and that, doubtless, they had become disgusted with war." When their honour was thus attacked, there was no longer any reply to be made; they merely bowed and remained silent. During one of his impatient fits, he told one of the generals of his guards, "you were born in a *bivouac*, and in a *bivouac* you will die."

As to Duroc, he at first signified his disapprobation by a chilling silence, and afterwards by short answers, reference to accurate reports, and brief remarks. To him the Emperor admitted, "that he saw clearly enough that the Russians wanted to draw him on; but that, nevertheless, he must proceed as far as Smolensk; that there he would establish his head-quarters; and that in the spring of 1818, if Russia did not previously make peace, she would be ruined; that Smolensk was the key of the two roads to Petersburgh and Moscow that he must get possession of it; and that he would then be able to march on both those capitals at once, in order to destroy every thing in the one, and preserve every thing in the other."

Here the grand marshal observed to him, that he was not more likely to make peace at Smolensk, or even at Moscow, than he was at Witepsk: and that, in removing to such a distance from France, the Prussians constituted an intermediate body, on whom little reliance could be placed. But the emperor replied, that on that supposition, as the Russian war no longer offered him any advantageous result, he ought to renounce it; and if so, he must turn his arms against Prussia, and compel her to pay the expenses of the war.

It was now Daru's turn. This minister is straightforward even to stiffness, and possesses immoveable firmness. The grand question of the march upon Moscow produced a discussion which lasted for eight successive hours, and at which only Berthier was present. The emperor having desired his minister's opinion of the war; "It is not a national war," replied Daru; "the introduction of some English merchandise into Russia, and even the restoration of the kingdom of Poland, are not sufficient reasons for engaging in so distant a war; neither your troops nor ourselves understand its necessity or its objects, and to say the least, all things recommend the policy of stopping where we now are."

The Emperor rejoined, "Did they take him for a madman? Did they imagine he made war from inclination? Had they not heard him say that the wars of Spain and Russia were two ulcers which ate into the vitals of France, and that she could not bear them both at once?

"He was anxious for peace; but in order to treat for it, two persons were necessary and he was only one. Had a single letter from Alexander yet reached him?

"What, then, should he wait for at Witepsk? Rivers, it was true, traced out there the line of a position; but, during the winter, there were no longer any rivers in this country. It was, therefore, a visionary line which they traced out; it was rather a line of demarcation than of separation. It was requisite, therefore, to constitute an artificial line; to construct towns and fortresses capable of defying the elements, and every species of scourge; to create every thing, land and atmosphere; for every thing was deficient, even provisions unless, indeed, he chose to drain Lithuania and render her hostile, or ruin ourselves; for if they were at Moscow, they might take what they pleased; here it was necessary to pay for every thing. Consequently," continued he, "you cannot enable me to live at Witepsk, nor shall I be able to protect you in it; both of us, therefore, are here out of our proper element.

"That if he returned to Wilna, he might there, indeed, more easily find supplies, but that he should not be in a better condition to defend himself; that in that case it would be necessary for him to fall back to the Vistula, and to lose Lithuania. Whereas at Smolensk, he would be sure to gain either a decisive battle, or at least, a fortress and a position on the Dnieper.

"That he perceived clearly that their thoughts were dwelling on Charles the Twelfth; but that if the expedition to Moscow wanted a fortunate precedent, it was because it had wanted a man capable of undertaking it; that in war, fortune went for one-half in every thing; that if people always waited for a complete assemblage of favourable circumstances, nothing would ever be undertaken; that we must begin, in order to finish; that there was no enterprise in which every thing concurred, and that, in all human projects, chance had its share; that, in short, it was not the rule which created the success, but the success the rule; and that, if he succeeded by new means, that success would create new principles.

"Blood has not yet been spilled," he added, "and Russia is too powerful to yield without fighting. Alexander can only negociate after a great battle. If it is necessary, I will even proceed to the holy city in search of that battle and I will gain it. Peace waits for me at the gates of Moscow. But, with his honour thus saved, if Alexander still persists, I will negociate with the boyards, or even with the population of that capital; it is numerous, united, and consequently enlightened. It will understand its own interests, and comprehend the value of liberty." He concluded by saying, that "Moscow hated Petersburgh; that he would take advantage of their rivalry; that the results of such a jealousy were incalculable."

It was in this manner that the Emperor, in the warmth of conversation, revealed the nature of his hopes. Daru replied, "That war was a game which he played well, in which he was always the winner, and that it was natural to infer, that he took a pleasure in playing it. But that, in this case, it was not so much men as nature which it was necessary to conquer; that already the army was diminished one-third by desertion, sickness, or famine.

"If provisions failed at Witepsk, what would be the case farther on? The officers whom he had sent to procure them, either never re-appeared, or returned empty handed. That the small quantity of flour, or the few cattle which they had succeeded in collecting, were immediately consumed by the imperial guard; that the other divisions of the army were heard to murmur, that it exacted and absorbed every thing, that it constituted as it were, a privileged class. The hospital and provision-wagons, as well as the droves of cattle, were not able to come up. The hospitals were insufficient for the sick; provisions, room, and medicines, were all wanting in them.

"All things, consequently, admonished them to halt, and with so much the more effect, as they could not calculate on the favourable disposition of the inhabitants beyond Witepsk. In conformity with his secret orders, they had been sounded, but without effect. How could men be roused to insurrection, for the sake of a liberty whose very name they did not understand? What influence could be obtained over a people almost savages, without property, and without wants? What could be taken from them? With what could they be tempted?

Their only property was their life, which they carried with them into regions of almost infinite space."

Berthier added, "that if we were to proceed forward, the Russians would have in their favour our too much elongated flanks, famine, and especially their formidable winter; while in staying where he was, the emperor would enlist the latter on his side, and render himself master of the war; that he would fix it within his reach, instead of following its deceitful, wandering, and undecided flight."

Such were the replies of Berthier and Daru. The emperor mildly listened to their observations, but oftener interrupted them by subtle arguments; putting the question according to his wishes, or shifting it when it became too pressing. But however disagreeable might be the truths which he was obliged to hear, he listened to them patiently, and replied with equal patience. Throughout this discussion, his conversation and whole deportment were remarkable for ease, simplicity, and good-humour, which, indeed, he almost always preserved to those about him; a circumstance which sufficiently accounts for the affection, which, notwithstanding so many misfortunes, was entertained for him, by those who lived on terms of intimacy with him.

Still dissatisfied, the emperor summoned successively several of the generals of his army; but his questions were such as indicated their answers: and many of these chiefs, born in the capacity of soldiers, and accustomed to obey his voice, were as submissive to him in these conversations as they were upon the field of battle.

Others waited the issue, in order to give their opinion; concealing their dread of a reverse, in the presence of a man who had always been fortunate, as well as their opinion, lest success might on some future day reproach them for it.

The greater part signified their approbation, being perfectly convinced that were they even to incur his displeasure by recommending him to stop, he would not be the less certain to advance. As it was necessary to incur fresh dangers, they preferred meeting them with an appearance of good-will. They found it more convenient to be wrong with him, than right against him.

But there was one individual, who, not content with approving his design, encouraged it. Prompted by a culpable ambition, he increased

Napoleon's confidence, by exaggerating the force of his own division, for after incurring so many fatigues, unaccompanied by danger, it was a great merit in those chiefs who preserved the greatest number of men around their eagles. The emperor was thus gratified on his weak side, and the time for rewards was approaching. In order to make himself more agreeable, the individual in question boldly took upon himself to vouch for the ardour of his soldiers, whose lank visages but ill accorded with the boasting of their leader. The emperor gave credit to this ardour, because it pleased him, and because he only saw the soldiers at reviews; occasions when his presence, the military pomp, the mutual excitation produced by great assemblages, imparted fervour to the mind; when, in short, all things, even to the secret orders of the chiefs, dictated an appearance of enthusiasm.

But in fact it was only his guard that thus occupied his attention. In the army, the soldiers complained of his non-appearance. "They no longer saw him," they said, "except in days of battle, when they had to die for him, but never to supply them with the means of existence. They were all there to serve him, but he seemed no longer there to serve them."

In this manner did they suffer and complain: without sufficiently considering that what they complained of was one of the inseparable evils of the campaign. The dispersion of the different corps, being indispensable for the sake of procuring subsistence in these deserts, necessarily kept Napoleon at a distance from his soldiers. His guard could hardly find subsistence and shelter in his immediate neighbourhood; the rest were out of his sight. It is true that many imprudent acts had recently been committed; several convoys of provisions belonging to other corps were on their passage daringly retained at the imperial head-quarters, for the use of the guard, by whose order is not known. This violence, added to the jealousy which such bodies of men always inspire, created discontent in the army.

The emperor was ignorant of these complaints; but another cause of anxiety tormented him. At Witepsk alone, there were 3000 of his soldiers attacked by the dysentery, which was extending its ravages over his whole army. The rye which they were eating in soup was its principal cause. Their stomachs, accustomed to bread, rejected this cold and indigestible food, and the emperor urged his physicians to find a remedy for its effects. One day he appeared less uneasy. "Davoust," said he, "has found out what the medical men could not discover; he has just sent to inform me of it; all that is required is to roast the rye before preparing it;" and his eyes sparkled with hope as he questioned his physician, who declined giving any opinion until the experiment was tried. The emperor instantly called two grenadiers of his guard; he seated them at table, close to him, and made them begin the trial of this nourishment so prepared. It did not succeed with them, although he added to it some of his own wine, which he himself poured out for them.

Respect, however, for the conqueror of Europe, and the necessity of circumstances, supported them in the midst of their numerous privations. They saw that they were too deeply embarked; that a victory was necessary for their speedy deliverance; and that he alone could give it them. Misfortune, moreover, had purified the army; all that remained of it could not fail to be its *élite,* both in mind and body. In order to have got so far as they had done, what trials had they not withstood! Ennui, and the uncomfortableness of their miserable cantonments, were sufficient to agitate such men. To remain, appeared to them insupportable; to retreat, impossible; it was, therefore, imperative to advance.

The great names of Smolensk and Moscow inspired no alarm. In ordinary times, and with ordinary men, that unknown region, these new nations, and the distance which magnifies all things, would have been sufficient to discourage. But these were exactly the circumstances which most attracted them. The soldiers' chief pleasure was in hazardous situations, which were rendered more interesting by the greater proportion of danger they involved, and on which new dangers conferred a more striking air of singularity; emotions full of charm for active spirits, which had tasted of every thing, and which, therefore, required new scenes to excite them.

Ambition was, at that time, completely unshackled; every thing inspired the passion for glory; they had been launched into a boundless career. How was it possible to measure the ascendency which a powerful emperor must have acquired, or the strong impulse which he had given them?—an emperor, capable of telling his soldiers after the victory of Austerlitz, "I will allow you to name your children after me; and if among them there should prove one worthy of us, I will leave him every thing I possess, and name him my successor."

CHAPTER III

PARTIAL SUCCESSES
ON BOTH SIDES

THE junction of the two wings of the Russian army, in the direction of Smolensk, had compelled Napoleon also to approximate his various divisions. No signal of attack had yet been given, but the war involved him on all sides; it seemed to tempt his genius by success, and to stimulate it by reverses. On his left, Wittgenstein, equally in dread of Oudinot and Macdonald, remained between the two roads from Polotsk and Dünaburgh, which meet at Sebez. The duke of Reggio's orders had been to keep on the defensive. But neither at Polotsk nor at Witepsk was there any thing found in the country which disclosed the position of the Russians. Tired of feeling nothing of them on any side, the marshal determined to go in quest of them himself. On the 1st of August, therefore, he left general Merle and his division on the Drissa, to protect his baggage, his great park of artillery, and his retreat; he pushed Verdier towards Sebez, and made him take a position on the high road, in order to mask the movement which he was meditating. He himself, turning to the left with Legrand's infantry, Castex's cavalry and Aubry's light artillery, advanced as far as Yakoubowo, on the road to Osweïa.

As chance would have it, Wittgenstein, at the same moment, was marching from Osweïa to Yakoubowo; the hostile armies unexpectedly met each other in front of that village. It was late in the day; the shock was violent, but of short duration; night put an end to the combat, and postponed its decision.

The marshal found himself engaged, with a single division, in a deep and narrow pass, surrounded with woods and hills, all the declivities of which were opposed to us. He was hesitating, however, whether he should quit that confined position, on which all the enemy's fire was about to be concentrated, when a young Russian staff-officer, scarcely emerged from boyhood, came dashing heedlessly into our posts, and was taken, with the despatches of which he was the bearer. We learned from them, that Wittgenstein was marching with all his forces to attack and destroy our bridges over the Dwina. Oudinot felt it necessary to retreat, in order to rally and concentrate his forces in a less unfavourable position; in consequence, as frequently happens in retrograde marches, some stragglers and baggage fell into the hands of the Russians.

Wittgenstein, elated by this easy success, pushed it beyond all bounds. In the first transport of what he regarded as a victory, he ordered Koulnieff, and 12,000 men, to pass the Drissa, in order to pursue Albert and Legrand. The latter had made a halt; Albert hastened to inform the marshal. They covered their detachment by a rising ground, watched all the movements of the Russian general, and observing him rashly venturing himself into a defile between them and the river, they rushed suddenly upon him, overthrew and killed him; taking from him also eight pieces of cannon and 2000 men.[1]

Koulnieff is said to have died like a hero; a cannon-ball broke both his legs, and threw him prostrate on his own cannon; where, observing the French approaching, he tore off his decorations, and, in a transport of anger at his own temerity, condemned himself to die on the very spot where his error was committed, commanding his soldiers to leave him to his fate. The whole Russian army regretted him; it imputed this misfortune to one of those individuals whom the caprice of Paul had made into generals, at the period when that emperor was quite new to power, and conceived the idea of entering his peaceable inheritance in the character of a triumphant conqueror.

Rashness passed over with the victory from the Russian to the French camp; this unexpected success elated Casa-Bianca and his Corsican battalions; they forgot the error to which they were indebted for it, they neglected the recommendation of their general, and without reflecting that they were imitating the imprudence by which they had just profited, they precipitated themselves upon the flying footsteps of the Russians. They proceeded, headlong, in this manner for two leagues, and were only reminded of their temerity by finding themselves alone in presence of the Russian army. Verdier, forced to engage in order to support them, was already compromising the rest of his division, when the duke of Reggio hurried up, relieved his troops from this peril, led them back behind the Drissa, and on the following day resumed his first position under the walls of Polotsk. There he found Saint Cyr and the Bavarians, who increased the force of his corps to 35,000 men. As to Wittgenstein, he tranquilly took up his first position at Osweïa. The result of these four days was very unsatisfactory to the emperor.

Nearly about the same time intelligence was brought to Witepsk that the advanced guard of the viceroy had gained some advantages near Suraij; but that in the centre, near the Dnieper, at Inkowo, Sebastiani had been surprised by superior numbers, and defeated.

Napoleon was then writing to the duke of Bassano to announce daily fresh victories to the Turks! True or false was of no consequence, provided the communications produced the effect of suspending their treaty with Russia. He was still engaged in this task, when deputies from Red Russia arrived at Witepsk, and informed Duroc, that they had heard the report of the Russian cannon announcing the peace of Bucharest. That treaty, signed by Kutusoff, had just been ratified.

At this intelligence, which Duroc transmitted to Napoleon, the latter was deeply mortified. He was now no longer astonished at Alexander's silence. At first, it was the tardiness of Maret's negociations to which he imputed this result; then, to the blind stupidity of the Turks, to whom their treaties of peace were always more fatal than their wars; lastly, to the perfidious policy of his allies, all of whom, taking advantage of the distance, and in the obscurity of the seraglio, had, doubtless, dared to unite against their common dictator.

This event rendered a prompt victory still more necessary to him. All hope of peace was now at an end. He had just read the proclamations of Alexander. Being addressed to a rude people, they were necessarily unrefined: the following are some passages of them: "The enemy, with unexampled perfidy, has announced the destruction of our country. Our brave soldiers burn to throw themselves on his battalions, and to destroy them; but it is not our intention to allow them to be sacrificed on the altars of this Moloch. A general insurrection is necessary against the universal tyrant. He comes, with treachery in his heart, and loyalty on his lips, to chain us by means of his legions of slaves. Let us drive away this race of locusts. Let us carry the cross in our hearts, and the sword in our hands. Let us pluck his fangs from this lion's mouth, and overthrow the tyrant, whose object is to overthrow the earth."

The emperor was incensed. These reproaches, these successes, and these reverses, all contributed to stimulate his mind. The forward movement of Barclay, in three columns, towards Rudnia, which the check at Inkowo had disclosed, and the vigorous defensive operations of Wittgenstein, promised the approach of a battle. He had to choose between that, and a long, painful, and sanguinary defensive war, to which he was unaccustomed, which was difficult to maintain at such a distance from his reinforcements, and encouraging to his enemies.

Napoleon accordingly decided; but his decision, without being rash, was grand and bold, like the enterprise itself. Having determined to detach himself from Oudinot, he first caused him to be reinforced by Saint-Cyr's corps, and ordered him to connect himself with the duke of Tarentum; having resolved also to march against the enemy, he did it by changing in front of him, and within his reach, but without his knowledge, the line of his operations at Witepsk for that of Minsk.[2] His manœuvre was so well combined, he had accustomed his lieutenants to so much punctuality, secrecy, and precision, that in four days, while the surprised hostile army could find no traces of the French army before it, the latter would by this plan find itself in a mass of 185,000 men on the left flank and rear of that enemy, which but just before had presumed to think of taking him by surprise.

Meantime, the extent and the multiplicity of the operations which on all sides claimed Napoleon's presence, still detained him at Witepsk. It was only by his letters, that he could make his presence universally felt. His head alone laboured for the whole, and he indulged himself in the thought that his urgent and repeated orders would suffice to make nature herself obedient to him.

The army only subsisted by its exertions, and from day to day; it had not provisions for twenty-four hours: Napoleon ordered that it should provide itself for fifteen days. He was incessantly dictating letters. On the 10th of August he addressed eight to the Prince of Eckmühl, and almost as many to each of his other lieutenants. In the first, he concentrates every thing round himself, in conformity with his leading principle, "that war is nothing else than the art of assembling on a given point, a larger number of men than your enemy." It was in this spirit that he wrote to Davoust: "Bring up Latour-Maubourg. If the enemy remain at Smolensk, as I have reason to suppose, it will be a decisive affair, and we can not have too much numerical strength. Orcha will become the pivot of the army. Every thing leads me to believe that there will be a great battle at Smolensk; hospitals will, therefore, be requisite; they will be necessary at Orcha, Dombrowna, Mohileff, Kochanowo, Bobr, Borizoff, and Minsk."

It was then particularly that he manifested extreme anxiety about the provisioning of Orcha. It was on the 10th of August, at the very moment when he was dictating this letter, that he gave his order of march. In four days, all his army would be assembled on the left bank of the Borysthenes, and in the direction of Liady. He departed from Witepsk on the 13th, after having remained there a fortnight.

1. The Russian loss is said to have been 3000 men and 14 pieces of cannon.— *Ed.*

2. The design of Napoleon was to pass his army rapidly to the left bank of the Dnieper, and reach Smolensk before the Russians, which would place him on their flank or rear.—*Ed.*

BOOK VI

CHAPTER I

CROSSING THE BORYSTHENES

IT was the check at Inkowo which decided Napoleon; ten thousand Russian horse, in an affair with the advanced guard, had overthrown Sebastiani and his cavalry. The intrepidity and reputation of the defeated general, his report, the boldness of the attack, the hope, nay, the urgent necessity, of a decisive engagement, all led the emperor to believe, that their numbers alone had carried the day, that the Russian army was between the Dwina and the Dnieper, and that it was marching against the centre of his cantonments: this was actually the fact.

The grand army being dispersed, it was necessary to collect it together. Napoleon had resolved to defile with his guard, the army of Italy, and three of Davoust's divisions, before the front of attack of the Russians; to abandon his Witepsk line of operation, and take that of Orcha; and, lastly, to throw himself with 183,000 men on the left of the Dnieper and of the enemy's army. Covered by the river, his plan was to get beyond it, for the purpose of reaching Smolensk before the enemy; if successful, he should have separated the Russian army not only from Moscow, but from the whole centre and south of the empire; it would be confined to the north; and he would have accomplished at Smolensk, against Bagration and Barclay united, what he had in vain attempted at Witepsk against the army of Barclay alone.

Thus the line of operation of so large an army was about to be suddenly changed; 200,000 men, spread over a tract of more than fifty leagues, were to be all at once brought together, without the knowledge of the enemy, within reach of him, and on his left flank. This was, undoubtedly, one of those grand determinations which, executed with the unity and rapidity of their conception, change instantaneously the face of war, decide the fate of empires, and display the genius of conquerors.

As we marched from Orcha to Liady, the French army formed a long column on the left bank of the Dnieper. In this mass, the first corps, that of Davoust, was distinguished by the order and harmony which prevailed in its divisions. The fine appearance of the troops, the care with which they were supplied, and the attention that was paid to make them careful of their provisions, which the improvident soldier is apt to waste; lastly, the strength of these divisions, the happy result of this severe discipline, all caused them to be acknowledged as the model of the whole army.

Gudin's division was the only one wanting; owing to an ill-written order, it had been wandering for twenty-four hours in marshy woods; it arrived, however, but diminished by three hundred combatants; for such errors are not to be repaired but by forced marches, under which the weakest are sure to sink.

The emperor traversed in a day the hilly and woody tract which separates the Dwina from the Borysthenes; it was in front of Rassasna that he crossed the latter river. Its distance from our home, the very antiquity of its name, every thing connected with it, excited our curiosity. For the first time, the waters of this Muscovite river were about to bear a French army, and to reflect our victorious arms. The Romans had known it only by their defeats: it was down this same stream that the savages of the north, the children of Odin and of Rurik, had descended to plunder Constantinople. Long before we could perceive it, our eyes sought it with ambitious impatience; we came to a narrow river, straitened between woody and uncultivated banks; it was the Borysthenes which presented itself to our view in this humble form. At this sight all our proud thoughts were humbled, and they were soon totally banished by the necessity of providing for our most urgent wants.

The emperor slept in his tent in advance of Rassasna; next day the army marched together, ready to draw up in order of battle, with the emperor on horseback in the midst of it. The advanced guard drove before it two pulks of Cossacks, who resisted only till they had gained time to destroy some bridges and some trusses of forage. The villages, deserted by the enemy, were plundered as soon as we entered them: we passed through them in the greatest haste and disorder.

The streams were crossed by fords which were soon spoiled; the regiments which came afterwards passed over in other places, wherever they could. No one gave himself much concern about such details, which were neglected by the general staff: no person was left to point out the danger, where there was any, or the road, if there were several. Each corps seemed to look to itself alone, each division, each individual to be unconnected with the rest; as if the fate of one had not depended on that of the other.

The army everywhere left stragglers behind it, and men who had lost their way, whom the officers passed without noticing; there would have been too many to find fault with; and besides, each was too much occupied with himself to attend to others. Many of these men were marauders, who feigned illness or a wound, as a pretence for separating from the rest, which there was not time to prevent, and which will always be the case in large armies, that are urged forward with such precipitation, as individual order cannot exist in the midst of general disorder.

As far as Liady the villages appeared to us to be more Jewish than Polish; the Lithuanians sometimes fled at our approach; the Jews always remained; nothing could have induced them to forsake their wretched habitations; they might be known by their thick pronunciation, their voluble and hasty way of speaking, the vivacity of their motions, and their complexion animated by the base passion of lucre. We noticed in particular their eager and piercing looks, their faces and features lengthened out into acute points, which a malicious and perfidious smile cannot widen; their tall, slim, and supple form; the earnestness of their demeanour, and lastly, their beards, usually red, and their long robes, tightened round their loins by a leather girdle; for every thing but their filthiness distinguishes them from the Lithuanian peasants; every thing about them bespeaks a degraded people.

They seem to have conquered Poland, where they swarm; and the whole substance of which they extract. Formerly their religion, and at present the sense of a reprobation too long universal, have made them the enemies of mankind; of old they attacked with arms, at present by cunning. This race is abhorred by the Russians, perhaps on account of its enmity to image-worship, while the Muscovites carry their adoration of images to idolatry. Finally, whether from superstition or rivalry of interests, they have forbidden them their country: the Jews were obliged to put up with their contempt, which their impotence repaid with hatred; but they detested our pillage still more. Enemies of all, spies to both armies, they sold one to the other from resentment or fear, according to occasion, and because there is nothing that they would not sell.

At Liady the Jews ended, and Russia Proper commenced; our eyes were therefore relieved from their disgusting presence, but other wants made us regret them; we missed their active and officious services, which money could command, and their German jargon, the only language which we understood in these deserts, and which they all speak, because they require it in their traffic.

CHAPTER II

SURPRISE OF
NEWEROWSKOI'S CORPS

ON the 15th of August, at three o'clock, we came in sight of Krasnoë, a town constructed of wood, which a Russian regiment made a show of defending; but it detained marshal Ney no longer than the time necessary to come up with and overthrow it. The town being taken, there were seen beyond it 6000 Russian infantry in two columns, while several squadrons covered the retreat. This was the corps of Newerowskoi.

The ground was unequal, but bare, and suitable for cavalry. Murat took possession of it; but the bridges of Krasnoë were broken down, and the French cavalry was obliged to move off to the left, and to defile to a great distance in bad fords, in order to come up with the enemy. When our troops were in presence of the latter, the difficulty of the passage which they had just left behind them, and the bold countenance of the Russians, made them hesitate: they lost time in waiting for one another and deploying, but finally the first effort dispersed the enemy's cavalry.

Newerowskoi, finding himself uncovered, drew together his columns, and formed them into a compact square, so thick, that Murat's cavalry penetrated several times into it, without being able to break through or to disperse it.

It is even true that our first charges failed at the distance of twenty paces from the front of the Russians: whenever the latter found themselves too hard pressed, they faced about, steadily waited for us, and drove us back with their small arms; after which, profiting by our disorder, they immediately continued their retreat.

The Cossacks were seen striking with the shafts of their lances, such of their foot-soldiers as lengthened the line of march, or stepped out of their ranks; for our squadrons harassed them incessantly, watched all their movements, threw themselves into the smallest intervals, and instantly carried off all that separated from the main body; they even penetrated into it twice, but a little way, the horses remaining, as it were, stuck fast in that thick and unyielding mass.

Newerowskoi had one very critical moment: his column was marching on the left of the high road through a field of rye not yet cut, when all at once it was stopped by a long fence, formed of a stout palisade; his soldiers, pressed by our movements, had not time to make a gap in it, and Murat sent the Wurtembergers against them to make them lay down their arms; but while the head of the Russian column was surmounting the obstacle, their rearmost ranks faced about and stood firm. They fired badly, it is true, most of them into the air, like persons who are frightened; but so near, that the smoke, the flash, and the reports of so many shot, frightened the Wurtemberg horses, and threw them into confusion.

The Russians embraced that moment to place between them and us that barrier which was expected to prove fatal to them. Their column profited by it to rally and gain ground. At length some French cannon came up, and they alone were capable of making a breach in this living fortress.

Newerowskoi hastened to reach a defile, where Grouchy had been ordered to anticipate him; but Murat, deceived by a false report, had diverted the greatest part of that general's cavalry in the direction of Elnia, and Grouchy had only 600 horse remaining with him. He made the 8th chasseurs dash forward to the defile, but it found itself too weak to stand against so strong a column. The vigorous and repeated charges made by that regiment, by the 6th hussars and the 6th lancers, on the left bank of that dense mass, which was protected by the double row of birch trees that lined each side of the road, were insufficient, and Grouchy's applications for assistance were not attended to, either because the general who followed him was kept back by the difficulties of the ground, or that he was not sufficiently sensible of the importance of the combat. It was nevertheless great, since there was between Smolensk and Murat but this one Russian corps, and had that been defeated, Smolensk might have been surprised without defenders, taken without a battle, and the enemy's army cut off from his capital. But this Russian division at length succeeded in gaining a woody ground where its flanks were covered.

Newerowskoi retreated like a lion; still he left on the field of battle 1200 killed, 1000 prisoners, and eight pieces of cannon. The French cavalry had the honour of that day. The attack was as furious as the defence was obstinate; it had the more merit, having only the sword to employ against both fire and sword; the enlightened courage of the French soldier being besides of a more exalted nature than that of the Russians, who are mere docile slaves, whose existence is less happy, and in whose bodies the severity of the climate has blunted sensibility.

As chance would have it, the day of this success vas the emperor's birth-day. The army had no idea of celebrating it. In the disposition of the men and of the place, there was nothing that harmonised with such a celebration; empty acclamations would have been lost amid those vast deserts. In our situation, there was no other festival than the day of a complete victory.

Murat and Ney, however, in reporting their success to the emperor, paid homage to that anniversary, and caused a salute of 100 guns to be fired. The emperor remarked, with displeasure, that in Russia it was necessary to be more sparing of French powder; the answer was, that it was Russian powder which had been taken the preceding day. The idea of having his birth-day celebrated at the expense of the enemy drew a smile from Napoleon. It was admitted that this very rare species of flattery became such men.

Prince Eugene also considered it his duty to carry him his good wishes. The emperor said to him, "Every thing is preparing for a battle; I shall gain it, and we shall see Moscow." The prince kept silence, but as he retired, his remark in answer to the questions of marshal Mortier was, "Moscow will be our ruin!" Thus did disappprobation begin to be expressed. Duroc, the most reserved of all, the friend and confidant of the emperor, loudly declared that he could not foresee the period of our return. Still it was only among themselves that the great officers indulged in such remarks, for they were aware that, as the decision was now taken, all of them would have to concur in its execution; they felt that the more dangerous their situation became, the more need there was of courage; and that the least expression likely to cool the general ardour, would be almost an act of treason; hence it was that those who by silence, nay, even by words, opposed the emperor in his tent, appeared out of it full of confidence and hope. This attitude was dictated by honour; the multitude has imputed it to flattery.

Newerowskoi, almost crushed, hastened to shut himself up in Smolensk. He left behind him some Cossacks to burn the forage; the houses were spared.

CHAPTER III

MOVEMENTS OF THE RUSSIAN ARMY

WHILE the grand army was thus ascending the Dnieper, along its left bank, Barclay and Bagration, placed between that river and the lake of Kasplia, towards Inkowo, believed themselves to be still in presence of the French army. They hesitated; twice instigated by the counsel of quarter-master-general Toll, they resolved to force the line of our cantonments, and twice, dismayed at so bold a determination, they stopped short in the midst of the movement they had commenced for that purpose. At length, too timid to take any other counsel than their own, they appeared to have left their decision to circumstances, and to wait our attack, in order to regulate their defence by it.

It might also be perceived, from the unsteadiness of their movements, that there was not a good understanding between these two chiefs. In fact, their situation, their disposition, their very origin, every thing about them was at variance. On the one hand, the cool valour, the scientific, methodical, and tenacious genius of Barclay, whose mind, German like his birth, was for calculating everything, even the chances of the hazard, bent on owing all to his tactics, and nothing to fortune; on the other, the martial, bold, and vehement instinct of Bagration, an old Russian of the school of Suwarrow, dissatisfied at being placed under a general who was his junior in the service—terrible in battle, but acquainted with no other book than nature, no other instructor than memory, no other counsels than his own inspirations.

This old Russian, on the frontiers of Russia Proper, trembled with shame at the idea of retreating farther without fighting. In the army all shared his ardour; it was supported on the one hand by the patriotic pride of the nobles, by the success at Inkowo, by the inactivity of Napoleon at Witepsk, and by the severe remarks of those who were not responsible; on the other hand, by a nation of peasants, tradesmen, and soldiers, who saw us on the point of treading their sacred soil, with all the horror that such profanation could excite. All, in short, demanded a battle.

Barclay alone was against fighting. His plan, which has been erroneously attributed to England, had been formed in his mind so far back as the year 1807; but he had to combat his own army as well as ours; and though he was both commander-in-chief and minister, he was neither Russian enough, nor victorious enough, to win the confidence of the Russians. He possessed that of Alexander alone.

Bagration and his officers hesitated to obey him. The point was to defend their native land, to devote themselves for the salvation of all; it was the affair of each, and all imagined that they had a right to examine. Thus their ill fortune distrusted the prudence of their general; whilst, with the exception of a few chiefs, our good fortune trusted implicitly to the boldness, hitherto always prosperous, of ours; for in success to command is easy; no one inquires whether it is prudence or fortune that guides. Such is the situation of military chiefs; when successful, they are blindly obeyed by all; when unfortunate, they are criticised by all.

Hurried away, notwithstanding, by the general impulse, Barclay had just yielded to it for a moment, collected his forces near Rudnia, and attempted to surprise the French army, dispersed as it was. But the feeble blow which his advanced guard had just struck at Inkowo had alarmed him. He trembled, paused, and imagining every moment that he saw Napoleon approaching in front of him, on his right, and everywhere excepting on his left, which was covered as he thought by the Dnieper; he lost several days in marches and counter-marches. He was in this state of uncertainty, when all at once Newerowskoi's cries of distress resounded in his camp. To attack was now entirely out of the question; his troops ran to arms, and hurried towards Smolensk for the purpose of defending it.

Murat and Ney were already attacking that city; the former with his cavalry, at the place where the Borysthenes enters its walls; the latter, with his infantry, where it issues from them, and on woody ground intersected by deep ravines. The marshal's left was supported by the river, and his right by Murat, whom Poniatowskoi, coming direct from Mohileff, arrived to reinforce.

In this place two steep hills contract the channel of the Borysthenes; on these hills Smolensk is built. That city has the appearance of two towns, separated by the river and connected by two bridges. That on the right bank is the most modern, and is wholly occupied by traders; it is open, but overlooks the other, of which it is nevertheless but a dependency.

The old town, occupying the elevated plain and slopes of the left bank, is surrounded by a wall twenty-five feet high, eighteen thick, three thousand fathoms in length, and defended by twenty-nine massive towers, an indifferent earthen citadel of five bastions, which commands the Orcha road, and a wide ditch, which serves as a covered way. Some outworks and the suburbs intercept the view of the approaches to the Mohileff and Dnieper gates; they are defended by a ravine, which, after encompassing a great part of the town, becomes deeper and steeper as it approaches the Dnieper, on the side next to the citadel.

The deluded inhabitants were quitting the temples, where they had been praising God for the victories of their troops, when they saw them hastening up, bloody, vanquished, and flying before the victorious French army. Their disaster was unexpected, and their consternation so much the greater.

Meanwhile, the sight of Smolensk inflamed the impatient ardour of marshal Ney; we know not whether he unseasonably called to mind the wonders of the Prussian war, when citadels fell before the sabres of our cavalry, or whether, at the outset, he designed only to reconnoitre this first Russian fortress; at any rate he approached too near; a ball struck him on the neck; incensed, he despatched a battalion against the citadel, through a shower of balls and bullets, which swept away two-thirds of his men; the remainder proceeded, and were only stopped by the Russian walls; a few only returned. Little notice was taken of the heroic attempt which they had made, because it was a fault of their general's, and useless into the bargain.[1]

Cooled by this check, Marshal Ney retired to a sandy and woody height bordering the river. He was surveying the city and its environs, when he imagined that he could discern troops in motion on the other side of the river: he ran to fetch the emperor, and conducted him through coppices and dingles to avoid the fire of the place.

Napoleon, on reaching the height, beheld a cloud of dust enveloping long black columns glistening with a multitude of arms: these masses advanced so rapidly that they seemed to run. It was Barclay,—Bagration,—nearly 120,000 men: in short, the whole Russian army.

Transported with joy at this sight, Napoleon clapped his hands, exclaiming, "At last I have them!" There could be no longer any doubt of it; this surprised army was hastening up to throw itself into Smolensk, to pass through it, to deploy under its walls, and at length to offer us that battle which was so ardently desired. The moment that was to decide the fate of Russia had at last arrived!

The emperor immediately went through the whole line, and allotted to each his place. Davoust, and next to him Count Lobau, were to deploy on the right of Ney: the guard in the centre, as a reserve, and farther off the army of Italy. The place of Junot and the Westphalians was indicated; but a false movement had carried them out of the way. Murat and Poniatowski formed the right of the army; those two chiefs already threatened the city: he made them draw back to the margin of a coppice, and leave vacant before them a spacious plain, extending from this wood as far as the Dnieper. It was a field of battle which he offered to the enemy. The French army, thus posted, had defiles and precipices at its back; but Napoleon concerned himself little about retreat;[2] he thought only of victory.

Bagration and Barclay were meanwhile returning at full speed towards Smolensk; the first to save it by a battle, the other to cover the flight of its inhabitants and the evacuation of its magazines: he was determined to leave us nothing but its ashes. The two Russian generals arrived panting on the heights on the right bank; nor did they again take breath till they saw that they were still masters of the bridges which connect the two towns.

Napoleon then caused the enemy to be harassed by a host of riflemen, for the purpose of drawing him to the left bank of the river, and ensure a battle for the following day. It is asserted that Bagration would have fallen in with his views, but that Barclay did not expose him to the temptation. He despatched him to Elnia, and took upon himself the defence of Smolensk.

Barclay had imagined that the greatest part of our army was marching upon Elnia, to get between Moscow and the Russian army. He deceived himself by the disposition, so common in war, of imputing to one's enemy designs contrary to those which he demonstrates. For the defensive, being uneasy in its nature, frequently magnifies the offensive, and fear, heating the imagination, causes it to attribute to the enemy a thousand projects of which he never dreamt. It is possible, too, that Barclay, having to cope with a colossal foe, felt authorised to expect from him gigantic movements.

The Russians themselves have since reproached Napoleon with not having adopted that manœuvre; but have they considered, that to proceed thus to place himself beyond a river, a fortified town, and a hostile army, to cut off the Russians from the road to their capital, would have been cutting off himself from all communication with his reinforcements, his other armies, and Europe? Those are not capable of appreciating the difficulties of such a movement, who are astonished that it was not made, without preparation in two days, across a river and a country both unknown, with such masses, and in the middle of another combination, the execution of which was not yet completed.

Be that as it may, in the evening of the 16th Bagration commenced his march for Elnia. Napoleon had just had his tent pitched in the middle of his first line, almost within reach of the guns of Smolensk, and on the brink of the ravine which encircles the city. He summoned Murat and Davoust: the former had just observed among the Russians, movements indicative of a retreat. Every day since the passage of the Niemen, he had been accustomed to see them thus escape him; he did not therefore believe that there would be any battle the following day. Davoust was of a contrary opinion. As for the emperor, he had no hesitation in believing what he wished.

1. The attack was made for the purpose of driving the enemy into the citadel, that Ney might reconnoitre it.—*Ed.*

2. There were two great roads open for the retreat of the French.—*Ed.*

CHAPTER IV

CAPTURE OF SMOLENSK

ON the 17th, by day-break, the hope of seeing the Russian army drawn up before him awoke Napoleon; but the field which he had prepared for it remained empty: he persisted, nevertheless, in his illusion, in which Davoust participated; it was to his side that he proceeded. Dalton, one of the generals of that marshal, had seen some hostile battalions quit the city and range themselves in order of battle. The emperor seized this hope, which Ney, jointly with Murat, combated in vain.

But while he was still full of hopes and expectations, Belliard, tired of this uncertainty, ordered a few horse to follow him; he drove a band of Cossacks into the Dnieper, above the town, and saw on the opposite bank the road from Smolensk to Moscow covered with artillery and troops on the march. There was no longer any doubt that the Russians were in full retreat. The emperor was apprised that he must renounce all hopes of a battle, but that his cannon might, from the opposite bank, annoy the retrograde march of the enemy.

Belliard even proposed to send part of the army across the river, to cut off the retreat of the Russian rear-guard, which was entrusted with the defence of Smolensk; but the party of cavalry sent to discover a ford went two leagues without finding one, and drowned several horses in the search. There was nevertheless a wide and commodious crossing about a league above the city. Napoleon himself, in his agitation, turned his horse that way. He proceeded several wersts in that direction, tired himself, and returned.

From that moment he seemed to consider Smolensk as a mere place of passage, of which it was absolutely necessary to gain possession by main force, and without loss of time. But Murat, prudent when not heated by the presence of the enemy, and who, with his cavalry, had nothing to do in an assault, disapproved of his resolution.

To him so violent an effort appeared useless; when the Russians were retiring of their own accord; and in regard to the plan of overtaking them, he observed, that "since they would not fight, we had followed them far enough, and it was high time to stop."

The emperor replied: but the rest of their conversation was not overheard. As, however, the king afterwards declared that "he had thrown himself at the knees of his brother, and conjured him to stop, but that Napoleon saw nothing but Moscow; that honour, glory, rest, every thing for him was there: that this Moscow would be our ruin!"— it was obvious what had been the cause of their disagreement.[1]

So much is certain, that when Murat quitted his brother-in-law, his face wore the expression of deep chagrin; his motions were abrupt; a gloomy and concentrated vehemence agitated him; and the name of Moscow several times escaped his lips.

Not far off, on the left bank of the Dnieper, a formidable battery had been placed, at the spot where Belliard had perceived the retreat of the enemy. The Russians had opposed to us two still more formidable. Every moment our guns were shattered, and our ammunition-wagons blown up. It was into the midst of this volcano that the king urged his horse: there he stopped, alighted, and remained motionless. Belliard warned him that he was sacrificing his life to no purpose, and without glory. The king answered only by pushing on still farther. Those around him no longer doubted, that despairing of the issue of the war, and foreseeing future disasters, he was seeking death in order to escape them. Belliard, however, insisted, and observed to him, that his temerity would be the destruction of those about him. "Well then," replied Murat, "do you retire, and leave me here by myself." All refused to leave him; when the king angrily turning about, tore himself from this scene of carnage, like a man who is suffering violence.

Meanwhile a general assault had been ordered. Ney had to attack the citadel, and Davoust and Lobau the suburbs, which cover the walls of the city. Poniatowski, already on the banks of the Dnieper, with sixty pieces of cannon, was again to descend that river to the suburb which borders it, to destroy the enemy's bridges, and to intercept the retreat of the garrison. Napoleon gave orders, that, at the same time, the artillery of the guard should batter the great wall with its twelve pounders, which were ineffective against so thick a mass. It disobeyed, and directed its fire into the covered way, which it cleared.

Every manœuvre succeeded at once, excepting Ney's attack, the only one which ought to have been decisive; but which was neglected. The enemy was driven back precipitately within his walls; all who had not time to regain them perished; but, in mounting to the assault, our attacking columns left a long and wide track of blood, of wounded and dead.

It was remarked, that one battalion, which presented itself in flank to the Russian batteries, lost a whole rank of one of its platoons by a single bullet, twenty-two men were felled by the same blow.

Meanwhile the army, from an amphitheatre of heights, contemplated with silent anxiety the conduct of its brave comrades; but when it saw them darting through a shower of balls and grape shot, and persisting with an ardour, a firmness, and a regularity, quite admirable; then it was that the soldiers, warmed with enthusiasm, began clapping their hands. The noise of this glorious applause was such as even to reach the attacking columns. It rewarded the devotion of those warriors; and although in Dalton's single brigade, and in the artillery of Reindre, five chiefs of battalion, 1500 men, and the general himself fell, the survivors still say, that the enthusiastic homage which they excited was a sufficient compensation to them for all their sufferings.

On reaching the walls of the place, they screened themselves from its fire, by means of the outworks and buildings, of which they had gained possession. The fire of musketry continued; and from the report, redoubled by the echo of the walls, it seemed to become more and more brisk. The emperor grew tired of this; he would have withdrawn his troops. Thus the same blunder which Ney had made a battalion commit the preceding day, was again repeated by the whole army; the one had cost 300 or 400 men, the other 5,000 or 6,000; but Davoust persuaded the emperor to persevere in his attack.

Night came on. Napoleon retired to his tent, which had been placed in a more secure situation than the day before; and the count Lobau, who had made himself master of the ditch, but could no longer maintain his ground there, ordered shells to be thrown into the city to dislodge the enemy. Thick black columns of smoke were presently seen rising from several points; these were soon lighted at intervals by flickering flashes, then by sparks, and at last long spires of flame burst from all parts. It was like a great number of distinct fires. It was not long before they united and formed but one vast blaze, which, whirling about as it rose, covered Smolensk, and entirely consumed it, with a dismal roaring.

Count Lobau was dismayed by so great a disaster, which he believed to be his own work. The emperor, seated in front of his tent, contemplated in silence this awful spectacle. It was as yet impossible to ascertain either the cause or the result, and the night was passed under arms.

About three in the morning, one of Davoust's subalterns ventured to the foot of the wall, which he scaled without noise. Emboldened by the silence which reigned around him, he penetrated into the city; all at once several voices and the Sclavonian accent were heard, and the Frenchman, surprised and surrounded, thought that he had nothing to do but to sell his life as dearly as he could, or to surrender. The first rays of the dawn, however, showed him, in those whom he mistook for enemies, some of Poniatowski's Poles. They had been the first to enter the city, which Barclay had just evacuated.

After Smolensk had been reconnoitred and its approaches cleared, the army entered within the walls; it traversed the reeking and blood-stained ruins with its accustomed order, pomp, and martial music, triumphing over the deserted wreck, and having no other witness of its glory but itself. A show without spectators, an almost fruitless victory, a sanguinary glory, of which the smoke that surrounded us, and seemed to be our only conquest, was but too faithful an emblem.

1. General Gourgaud, from personal knowledge, denies this conversation to have taken place.—*Ed.*

CHAPTER V

THE RESULTS OF VICTORY

WHEN the Emperor knew that Smolensk was entirely occupied, and the conflagration almost extinguished, and when day and the different reports had sufficiently instructed him; when in short, he saw that there, as at Niemen, at Wilna, at Witepsk, the phantom of victory, which allured him forward, and which he always imagined himself to be on the point of seizing, had once more eluded his grasp, he proceeded slowly towards his barren conquest.

But in the first place, according to his custom, he inspected the field of battle in order to appreciate the value of the attack, the merit of the resistance, and the loss on both sides. He found it strewed with a great number of Russian dead, and very few of ours. Most of them, especially the French, had been stripped; they might be known by the whiteness of their skin, and by their forms less bony and muscular than those of the Russians. Melancholy review of the dead and dying! a dismal account to make up and deliver! The pain felt by the emperor might be inferred from the contraction of his features and his irritation; but in him policy was a second nature, which soon imposed silence on the first.

Moreover, this numbering of the dead on the day after an engagement was as delusive as it was disagreeable; for most of ours had been previously removed, but those of the enemy left in sight; an expedient adopted with a view to prevent unpleasant impressions being made on our own troops, as well as from the natural impulse which causes us to collect and assist our own dying, and to pay the last duties to our own dead, before we think of those belonging to the enemy.

The emperor, nevertheless, asserted in his bulletin, that his loss on the preceding day was much smaller than that of the Muscovites; that the conquest of Smolensk made him master of the Russian salt works, and that his minister of finance might reckon upon twenty-four additional millions. It is neither true nor probable, that he suffered himself to be the dupe of such illusions: yet it was believed that he was then turning against himself that faculty of imposing upon others, of which he knew how to make such important use.

Continuing his reconnoissance, he came to one of the gates of the citadel, near the Borysthenes, facing the suburb on the right bank, which was still occupied by the Russians. There, surrounded by marshals Ney, Davoust, Mortier, the grand-marshal Duroc, Count Lobau, and another general, he sat down on some mats before a hut, not so much to observe the enemy, as to relieve his heart from the load which oppressed it, and to seek, in the flattery or in the ardour of his generals, encouragement against facts and against his own reflections.

He talked long, vehemently, and without interruption. "What a disgrace for Barclay, to have given up, without fighting, the key of old Russia! and yet what a field of honour he had offered to him! How advantageous it was for him! A fortified town to support and take part in his efforts! The same town and a river to receive and cover the wreck of his army, if defeated!

"And what would he have had to fight? An army, numerous indeed, but straitened for want of room, and having nothing but precipices for its retreat. It had given itself up, in a manner to his blows. Barclay had wanted nothing but resolution.

"It was, therefore, all over with Russia. She had no army but to witness the fall of her cities, and not to defend them. For, in fact, on what more favourable ground could Barclay make a stand? What position would he determine to dispute? He, who had forsaken that Smolensk, called by him Smolensk the holy, Smolensk the strong, the key of Moscow, the bulwark of Russia, which, as it had been given out, was to prove the grave of the French! We should presently see the effect of this loss on the Russians; we should see their Lithuanian soldiers, nay even those of Smolensk, deserting their ranks, indignant at the abandonment of their capital without a struggle."

Napoleon added, that "authentic intelligence had made him acquainted with the weakness of the Russian divisions; that most of them were already much reduced; that they suffered themselves to be destroyed in detail, and that Alexander would soon cease to have an army. The mob of peasants armed with pikes, whom we had just seen in the train of their battalions, sufficiently demonstrated to what shifts their generals were reduced."

While the emperor was thus talking, the balls of the Russian riflemen were whizzing about his ears; but he was worked up by his subject. He launched out against the enemy's general and army, as if he would have destroyed them by his reasoning, because he could not by victory. No one answered him; it was evident that he was not asking advice; that he had been talking all this time to himself; that he was contending against his own reflections, and that, by this torrent of conjectures, he was seeking to impose upon himself, and endeavouring to make others participators in the same illusions.

Indeed, he did not give any one time to interrupt him. As to the weakness and disorganisation of the Russian army, nobody believed it; but what could be urged in reply? He appealed to positive documents, those which had been sent to him by Lauriston; but the truth is, that these had been altered, under the idea of correcting them: for the estimate of the Russian forces by Lauriston, the French minister in Russia, was correct; but according to accounts less deserving of credit, though more flattering, this estimate had been diminished one-third.

After an hour's conversation, the emperor, looking at the heights on the right bank, which were nearly abandoned by the enemy, concluded with exclaiming, that "the Russians were women, and that they acknowledged themselves vanquished!" He strove to persuade himself that these people had, from their contact with Europe, lost their rude and savage valour. But their preceding wars had instructed them, and they had arrived at that point, at which nations still possess all the primitive virtues, in addition to those they have acquired.

At length, he again mounted his horse. It was then the grand-marshal observed to one of us, that "if Barclay had committed so very great a blunder in refusing battle, the emperor would not have been so extremely anxious to convince us of it." A few paces farther, an officer, sent not long before to prince Schwartzenberg, presented himself: he reported that Tormasoff and his army had appeared in the north, between Minsk and Warsaw, and that they had marched upon our line of operations. The capture of a Saxon brigade at Kobrynn, the grand-duchy over-run, and Warsaw alarmed, had been the first results of this aggression; but Regnier had summoned Schwartzenberg to his aid. Tormasoff had then retreated to Gorodeczna, where he halted on the 12th of August, between two defiles, in a plain surrounded by woods and marshes, but accessible in the rear of his left flank.

Regnier, skilful before an action, and an excellent judge of ground, knew how to prepare battles; but when the field became animated, when it was covered with men and horses, he lost his self-possession, and rapid movements seemed to dazzle him. At first, therefore, that general perceived at a glance the weak side of the Russians; he bore down upon it, but instead of breaking into it by masses and with impetuosity, he merely made successive attacks.

Tormasoff, forewarned by these, had time to oppose, at first, regiments to regiments, then brigades to brigades, and lastly divisions to divisions. By favour of this prolonged contest, he gained the night, and withdrew his army from the field of battle, where a rapid and simultaneous effort might have destroyed it. Still, he lost some pieces of cannon, a great quantity of baggage, and four thousand men, and retired behind the Styr, where he was joined by Tchitchakoff, who was hastening with the army of the Danube to his succour.

This battle, though far from decisive, preserved the grand-duchy: it confined the Russians, in this quarter, to the defensive, and gave the emperor time to win a battle.

During this recital, the tenacious genius of Napoleon was less struck with these advantages in themselves, than with the support they gave to the illusion which he had just been holding forth to us: accordingly, still adhering to his original idea, and without questioning the aide-de-camp, he turned round to his auditory, and, as if continuing his former conversation, he exclaimed: "There you see, the poltroons! they allow themselves to be beaten even by Austrians!" Then casting around him a look of apprehension, "I hope," added he, "that none but Frenchmen hear me." He then asked if he might rely on the good faith of Prince Schwartzenberg, for which the aide-de-camp pledged himself; nor was he mistaken, though the event seemed to belie his confidence.

Every word which the emperor had uttered merely proved his disappointment, and that a great hesitation had again taken possession of his mind; for in him success was less communicative, and decision less verbose. At length he entered Smolensk. In the passage through its massive walls, count Lobau exclaimed, "What a fine head for cantonments!" This was the same thing as advising him to stop there; but the emperor returned no other answer to this counsel than a stern look.

This look, however, soon changed its expression, when it had nothing to rest upon but ruins, among which our wounded were crawling, and heaps of smoking ashes, where lay human skeletons, dried and blackened by the fire. This great destruction confounded him. What a harvest of victory! That city, where his troops were at length to find shelter, provisions, a rich booty, the promised reward for so many hardships, was but a ruin on which he should be obliged to bivouac! No doubt his influence over his men was great, but could it extend beyond nature? What were they to think?

Here, it is right to observe that the sufferings of the army did not want for an interpreter. He knew that his soldiers asked one another "for what purpose they had been marched eight hundred leagues, to find nothing but muddy water, famine, and bivouacs on heaps of ashes: for such were all their conquests; they possessed nothing but what they had brought with them. If it was necessary to drag every thing along with them, to transport France into Russia, wherefore had they been required to quit France?"

Several of the generals themselves began to tire: some were arrested by illness, others murmured. "What the better were they for his having enriched them, if they could not enjoy their wealth? for his having given them wives, if he made them widowers by a continual absence?

for his having bestowed on them palaces, if he forced them to live abroad incessantly on the bare ground, amidst frost and snow?—for every year the hardships of war increased; fresh conquests compelling them to go farther in quest of fresh enemies. Europe would soon be insufficient: he would want Asia too."

Many, especially among our allies, ventured to think, that we should lose less by a defeat than by victory: a reverse would perhaps disgust the emperor with the war; at least it would bring it more within our reach.

The generals who were nearest to Napoleon were astonished at his confidence. "Had he not already in some measure quitted Europe? and if Europe were to rise against him, he would have no subjects but his soldiers, no empire but his camp: even then, one-third of them, being foreigners, would become his enemies." Such was the language of Murat and Berthier. Napoleon, irritated at finding in his two chief-lieutenants, and at the very moment of action, the same uneasiness with which he was himself struggling, vented his ill-humour against them: he overwhelmed them with it, as frequently happens in the household of princes, who are least sparing of those of whose attachment they are most sure; an inconvenience attending favour, which counterbalances its advantages.

After his spleen had vented itself in a torrent of words, he summoned them back; but this time, dissatisfied with such treatment, they kept aloof. The emperor then made amends for his hastiness by caresses, calling Berthier "his wife," and his fits of passion "family quarrels."

Murat and Ney left him with minds full of sinister presentiments relative to this war, which at the first sight of the Russians they were themselves for carrying on with fury. For in them, whose character was entirely made up of action, inspiration, and first movements, there was no consistency: every thing was unexpected; the occasion hurried them away; impetuous, they varied in language, plans, and dispositions, at every step, just as the ground changed its appearance.

CHAPTER VI

STATE OF THE FRENCH ARMY

ABOUT the same time, Rapp and Lauriston presented themselves: the latter came from Petersburgh. Napoleon did not ask a single question of this officer on his arrival from the capital of his enemy. Aware, no doubt, of the frankness of his former aide-de-camp, and of his opinion respecting this war, he was apprehensive of receiving from him unsatisfactory intelligence.

But Rapp, who had followed our track, could not keep silence. "The army had advanced but a hundred leagues from the Niemen, and already it was completely altered. The officers who travelled post from the interior of France to join it, arrived dismayed. They could not conceive how it happened that a victorious army, without fighting, should leave behind it more wrecks than a defeated one.

"They had seen all who were marching to join the masses, and all who had separated from them in short, all who were not excited either by the presence of the chiefs, or by example, or by the war. The countenance of each troop, according to its distance from home, excited hope, anxiety, or pity.

"In Germany, as far as the Oder, where a thousand objects were incessantly reminding them of France, these recruits imagined themselves not wholly cut off from it; they were ardent and jovial: but beyond the Oder, in Poland, where the soil, productions, inhabitants, costumes, manners, in short every thing, to the very habitations, wore a foreign aspect; where nothing, in short, resembled their regretted native home; they began to be dismayed at the distance they had traversed, and their saddened faces already bore the stamp of fatigue and lassitude.

"By what an extraordinary distance must they then be separated from France, since they had already reached unknown regions, where every thing presented to them an aspect of such gloomy novelty! how many leagues had they travelled, and how many more they had yet to travel! The very idea of return was disheartening; and yet they were obliged to march on, to keep constantly marching! and they complained that, ever since they left France, their fatigues had been gradually increasing, and the means of supporting them continually diminishing."

The truth is, that wine first failed them, then beer, then spirits; and, lastly, they were reduced to water, which in its turn was frequently wanting. The same was the case with dry provisions, and also with every necessary of life; and in this gradual destitution, depression of mind kept pace with the successive debilitation of the body. Agitated by a vague inquietude, they marched on amid the dull uniformity of the vast and silent forests of dark pines. They crept among these large trees, bare and stript to their very tops, affrighted at their own weakness amid this immensity. They then conceived gloomy and absurd notions respecting the geography of these unknown regions; and, overcome by a secret horror, they hesitated to penetrate farther into such vast deserts.

From these sufferings, physical and moral, from these privations, from these continual bivouacs, which are as dangerous near the pole as under the equator, and from the infection of the air by the putrid carcasses of men and horses that strewed the roads, sprang two dreadful epidemics—the dysentery and the typhus fever. The Germans first felt their ravages; they are less nervous and less sober than the French; and they were less interested in a cause which they regarded as foreign to them. Out of 22,000 Bavarians who had crossed the Oder, 11,000 only reached the Dwina; and yet they had never been in action. This military march cost the French one-fourth, and the allies one half of their army.

Every morning the regiments started in order from their bivouacs; but scarcely had they proceeded a few steps, before their disconnected ranks became lengthened out into small and broken files; the weakest, being unable to follow, dropped behind: these unfortunate wretches beheld their comrades and their eagles getting farther and farther from them: they still strove to overtake, but at length lost sight of them, and then sank disheartened. The roads and the margins of the woods were studded with them: some were seen plucking the ears of rye to devour the grain: and they would then attempt, frequently in vain, to reach the hospital, or the nearest village. Great numbers thus perished.

But it was not the sick only that separated from the army: many soldiers, disgusted and dispirited on the one hand, and impelled by a love of independence and plunder on the other, voluntarily deserted their colours; and these were not the least resolute: their numbers soon increased, as evil begets evil by example. They formed bands, and fixed their quarters in the mansions and villages adjacent to the military road. There they lived in abundance. Among them there were fewer French than Germans; but it was remarked, that the leader of each of these little independent bodies, composed of men of several nations, was invariably a Frenchman.

Rapp had been a witness of all these disorders: on his arrival, his blunt honesty kept back none of these details from his chief; but the emperor merely replied, "I am going to strike a great blow, and all the stragglers will then rally."

With Sebastiani he was more explicit. The latter reminded him of his own words, when he had declared to him at Wilna, that he would not cross the Dwina, for to proceed farther this year would be hurrying to infallible destruction.

Sebastiani, like the others, laid great stress on the state of the army. "It is dreadful, I know," replied the emperor: "from Wilna, half of it consisted of stragglers; now they form two-thirds; there is, therefore, no time to be lost: we must extort peace; it is at Moscow. Besides, this army cannot now stop: with its composition, and in its disorganised state, motion alone keeps it together. One may advance at the head of it, but not stop or go back. It is an army of attack, not of defence; an army of operation, not of position."

It was thus that he spoke to those immediately about him; but to the generals commanding his divisions, he held a different language. Before the former, he manifested the motives which urged him forward; from the latter he carefully concealed them, and seemed to agree with them as to the necessity of stopping. This may serve to explain the contradictions which were remarked in his own language.

Thus, the very same day, in the streets of Smolensk, surrounded by Davoust and his generals, whose corps had suffered most in the assault of the preceding day, he said, that in the capture of Smolensk he was indebted to them for an important success, and that he considered that city as an excellent head of cantonments.

"Now," continued he, "my line is well covered; we will stop here; behind this rampart, I can rally my troops, let them rest, receive reinforcements, and our supplies from Dantzic. Thus the whole of Poland is conquered and defended: this is a sufficient result; it is gathering, in two months, the fruit that might be expected only from two years of war: it is therefore sufficient. Betwixt this and the spring, we must organise Lithuania, and recompose an invincible army; then, if peace should not come to seek us in our winter quarters, we will go and conquer it at Moscow."

He then told the marshal in confidence, that his motive for ordering him to proceed beyond Smolensk, was only to drive off the Russians to the distance of a few marches; but he strictly forbade him to involve himself in any serious affair. At the same time, it is true, he committed the vanguard to Murat and to Ney, the two rashest of his officers; and, unknown to Davoust, he placed that prudent and methodical marshal under the command of the impetuous King of Naples. Thus his mind seemed to be wavering between two great resolutions, and the contradictions in his words were communicated to his actions. In this internal conflict, however, it was remarked, what an ascendence his enterprising genius had over his prudence, and how the former so disposed matters as to give birth to circumstances which must necessarily hurry him away.

CHAPTER VIII

THE RUSSIANS
WITHDRAW FURTHER

MEANWHILE the Russians still defended the suburb on the right bank of the Dnieper. On our side, the 18th, and the night of the 19th, were employed in rebuilding the bridges. On the 19th of August, before daybreak, Ney crossed the river by the light of the suburb, which was on fire. At first, he saw there no enemies but the flames, and he began to climb the long and rugged declivity on which it stands. His troops proceeded slowly and with caution, making a thousand circuits to avoid the fire. The Russians had managed it with skill: it met our men at every point, and obstructed the principal avenues.

Ney, and the foremost of his soldiers, advanced in silence into this labyrinth of flames, with anxious eye and attentive ear, not knowing but that the Russians might be waiting on the summit of the steep, to pour suddenly upon them, to overthrow and drive them back into the flames and the river. But they breathed more freely, relieved from the weight of a great apprehension, when they perceived on the crest of the ravine, at the branching-off of the roads to Petersburgh and Moscow, nothing but a band of Cossacks, who immediately fled by those two roads. Having neither prisoners nor inhabitants, nor spies, the ground was, as at Witepsk, the only thing they could interrogate. But the enemy had left as many traces in one direction as in the other, so that the marshal paused in uncertainty between the two until mid-day.

During this interval, a passage had been effected across the Borysthenes, at several points; the roads to the two hostile capitals were reconnoitred to the distance of a league, and the Russian infantry was discovered on that leading to Moscow. Ney would soon have overtaken it; but as that road skirted the Dnieper, he had to cross the streams which fall into it. Each of them, having excavated its own bed, marked the bottom of a valley, the opposite side of which was a position where the enemy posted himself, and which it was necessary to carry: the first, that of the Stubna, did not detain him long; but the hill of Valoutina, at the foot of which runs the Kolowdnia, became the scene of an obstinate conflict.

The cause of this resistance has been attributed to an ancient tradition of national glory, which represented this field of battle as ground consecrated by victory. But this superstition, worthy even still of the Russian soldier, is far beneath the more enlightened patriotism of their generals. It was necessity that here compelled them to fight: we have seen that the Moscow road, on leaving Smolensk, skirted the Dnieper, and that the fire of the French artillery, on the other bank, traversed it. Barclay durst not take this road at night, for fear of risking his artillery, baggage, and the wagons with the wounded, the rolling of which would have betrayed his retreat.

The Petersburgh road quitted the river more abruptly: two marshy cross-roads branched off from it to the right, one at the distance of two leagues from Smolensk, the other at four; they ran through woods, and rejoined the high road to Moscow, after a long circuit, the one at Bredichino, two leagues beyond Valoutina, the other farther off at Slobpnewa.

Into these defiles Barclay was bold enough to commit himself with his numerous horses and vehicles; so that this long and heavy column had thus to traverse two large arcs of a circle, of which the high road from Smolensk to Moscow, which Ney soon attacked, was the chord. Every moment, as always happens in such cases, the overturning of a carriage, the sticking fast of a wheel, or of a single horse, in the mud, or the breaking of a trace, stopped the whole. The sound of the French cannon, meanwhile, drew nearer, and seemed to have already got before the Russian column, and to be on the point of reaching and shutting up the outlet which it was striving to gain.

At length, after an undisturbed march, the head of the enemy's convoy came in sight of the high road, at the moment when the French had only to force the height of Valoutina and the passage of the Kolowdnia, in order to reach that outlet. Ney had furiously carried that of the Stubna; but Korff, being driven back upon Valoutina, had summoned to his aid the column which preceded him. It is asserted that the latter, being in disorder, and badly officered, hesitated to comply; but that Woronzoff, aware of the importance of that position, prevailed upon its commander to turn back.

The Russians defended themselves to defend every thing, cannon, wounded, baggage: the French attacked in order to take every thing. Napoleon had halted a league and a half in the rear of Ney. Conceiving that it was but an affair between his advanced guard and the rear of the enemy, he sent Gudin to the assistance of the marshal, rallied the other divisions, and returned to Smolensk. But this fight became a regular battle; 30,000 men were successively engaged in it on both sides: soldiers, officers, generals, encountered each other; the action was long, the struggle terrible; even night did not suspend it. At length, in possession of the summit, exhausted by the loss of strength and of blood, Ney, finding himself surrounded only by dead, dying, and obscurity, became fatigued; he ordered his troops to cease firing, to keep silence, and present bayonets. The Russians, hearing nothing more, were silent also, and availed themselves of the darkness to effect their retreat.

There was almost as much glory in their defeat as in our victory: the two chiefs carried their point, the one in conquering, the other in not being conquered till he had saved the Russian artillery, baggage, and wounded. One of the enemy's generals, (Toutchekoff,) the only one left unhurt on this field of carnage, endeavoured to escape from among our soldiers, by repeating the French word of command; he was recognised by the flashes of their fire-arms, and secured. Other Russian generals had perished; but the grand army sustained a still greater loss.

At the passage of the bridge over the Kolowdnia, which had been badly repaired, General Gudin, whose well-regulated valour loved to confront none but useful dangers, and who besides was rather a timid rider, had alighted from his horse to cross the stream, when, at that moment, a cannon-ball, skimming the surface of the ground, broke both his legs. When the tidings of this misfortune reached the emperor, they put a stop to every thing—to discussion and action. Every one was thunderstruck; the victory of Valoutina seemed no longer to be a success.

Gudin was conveyed to Smolensk, and there received the unavailing attentions of the emperor; but he soon expired. His remains were interred in the citadel of the city, to which they do honour: a worthy tomb for a soldier, who was a good citizen, a good husband, a good father, an intrepid general, just and gentle, a man both of principle and talent; a rare assemblage of qualities in an age when virtuous men are too frequently devoid of abilities, and men of abilities without virtue. It was a fortunate chance that he was worthily replaced; Gérard, the oldest general of brigade of the division, took the command of it, and the enemy, who knew nothing of our loss, gained nothing by the dreadful blow he had just dealt us.

The Russians, astonished at having been attacked only in front, conceived that all the military combinations of Murat were confined to following them on the high road. They therefore styled him in derision *"the general of the high roads,"* characterising him thus from the event, which tends more commonly to deceive than to enlighten.

In fact, while Ney was attacking, Murat scoured his flanks with his cavalry, without being able to bring it into action; woods on the left, and morasses on the right, obstructed his movements. But while they were fighting in front, they were both anticipating the effect of a flanking march of the Westphalians, commanded by Junot.

From the Stubna, the high-road, in order to avoid the marshes formed by the various tributary streams of the Dnieper, turned off to the left, ascended the heights, and diverged from the basin of the river, to which it afterwards returned in a more favourable situation. It had been remarked, that a by-road, bolder and shorter, as they all are, ran straight across these low marshy grounds, between the Dnieper and the high-road, which it rejoined behind the flat summit of Valoutina.

It was this cross-road which Junot pursued after crossing the river at Prudiszy. It soon led him into the rear of the left of the Russians, upon the flank of the columns which were returning to the assistance of their rearguard. His attack was all that was wanted to render the victory decisive.

Those who were engaged in front with marshal Ney would have been daunted at hearing an attack in their rear; while the uncertainty and disorder into which, in the midst of an action, it would have thrown the multitude of men, horses, and carriages, crowded together in one road, would have been irreparable; but Junot, though personally brave, was irresolute as a general. His responsibility alarmed him.

Meanwhile Murat, judging that he must have come up, was astonished at not hearing his attack. The firmness of the Russians opposed to Ney led him to suspect the truth. He left his cavalry, and crossing the woods and marshes almost alone, he hastened to Junot, and upbraided him with his inaction. Junot alleged in excuse, "that he had no orders to attack; his Wurtemberg cavalry was shy, its efforts feigned, and it would never be brought to charge the enemy's battalions."

These words Murat answered with actions. He rushed on at the head of that cavalry, which, with a different leader, were quite different troops; he urged them on, launched them against the Russians, overthrew their sharp shooters, returned to Junot and said to him, "Now finish the business: your glory and your marshal's staff are still before you!" He then left him to rejoin his own troops, and Junot, confounded, remained motionless. Too long about Napoleon, whose active genius directed every thing, both the plan and the details, he had learned only to obey: he wanted experience in command; besides, toil and wounds had made him an old man before his time.

That such a general should have been selected for so important a movement was not at all surprising; it is well known that the emperor was attached to him both from habit (for he was his oldest aide-de-camp) and from a secret foible, for as the presence of that officer was mixed up with all the recollections of his victories and his glory, he disliked to part from him. It is also reasonable to suppose that it flattered his vanity, to see men who had been his pupils commanding his armies; and it was moreover natural that he should have a firmer reliance on their attachment, than on that of others.

When, however, on the following day he inspected the places themselves, at sight of the bridge where Gudin fell, he made the remark, that it was not there he ought to have debouched; when afterwards gazing with an angry look, on the position which Junot had occupied, he exclaimed: "It was there, no doubt, that the Westphalians should have attacked! all the battle was there! what was Junot about?" His anger became so violent, that nothing could at first allay it. He called Rapp, and told him to take the command from the duke of Abrantes:—he would dismiss him from the army! he had irretrievably lost his marshal's staff! this blunder would probably block the road to Moscow against them: that to him, Rapp, he gave the command of the Westphalians; that he could speak to them in their own language, and would know how to make them fight." But Rapp refused the place of his old companion in arms; he appeased the emperor, whose anger always subsided quickly, as soon as it had vented itself in words.

But it was not merely on his left that the enemy had a narrow escape from being conquered; on his right he had run a still greater risk. Morand, one of Davoust's generals, had been despatched from that side through the forests; he marched along woody heights, and was, from the commencement of the action, on the flank of the Russians. A few paces more, and he would have debouched in the rear of their right. His sudden appearance would have infallibly decided the victory, and rendered it complete; but Napoleon, ignorant of the localities, had ordered him to be recalled to the spot where Davoust and himself had stopped.

In the army, we could not help asking ourselves, why the emperor, in making three officers, all independent of each other, combine for the same object, had not made a point of being on the spot, to give their movements the unity indispensable, and without his presence impossible. He, on the contrary, had returned to Smolensk, either from fatigue, or chiefly from not expecting so serious an affair; or finally, because, from the necessity of attending to every thing at once, he could not be in time, or completely, any where. In fact, the business of his empire and of Europe, having been suspended by the preceding days of activity, had accumulated. It was necessary to clear out his portfolios, and to give circulation to both civil and political affairs, which began to clog; it was, besides, urgent and glorious to date from Smolensk.

When, therefore, Borelli, second in command of Murat's staff, came to inform him of the battle of Valoutina, he hesitated about receiving him, and so deeply was he engaged in the business before him, that a minister had to interfere to procure that officer immediate admittance. The report of this officer agitated Napoleon. "What say you?" he exclaimed: "what! you are not enough! the enemy shows 60,000 men! Then it is a battle!" and he began storming at the disobedience and inactivity of Junot. When Borelli informed him of Gudin's mortal wound, Napoleon's grief was violent; he gave vent to it in repeated questions and expressions of regret; then with that strength of mind which was peculiar to him, he subdued his uneasiness, postponed his anger, suspended his chagrin, and giving himself up wholly to his occupation, he deferred until the morrow the charge of battles, for night had come on; but afterwards the hope of a battle roused him, and he appeared next morning with the day on the fields of Valoutina.

CHAPTER VIII

CONSEQUENCES OF VALOUTINA

NEY'S troops, and those of Gudin's division, deprived of their general, had drawn up there on the corses of their companions and of the Russians, amidst the stumps of broken trees, on ground trampled by the feet of the combatants, furrowed with balls, strewed with the fragments of weapons, tattered garments, military utensils, carriages overthrown, and scattered limbs; for such are the trophies of war, such the beauties of a field of victory.

Gudin's battalions appeared to be melted down to platoons; the more they were reduced, the prouder they seemed to be: close to them, one still breathed the smell of burnt cartridges and gun-powder, with which the ground and their apparel were impregnated, and their faces yet quite begrimed. The emperor could not pass along their front without having to avoid, to pass over, or to tread upon carcasses, and bayonets twisted by the violence of the shock. But over all these horrors he threw a veil of glory. His gratitude transformed this field of death into a field of triumph, where, for some hours, satisfied honour and ambition held exclusive sway.

He was sensible that it was high time to encourage his soldiers by commendations and rewards. Never, therefore, were his looks more kind; and as to his language, "this battle was the most glorious achievement in our military history; the soldiers who heard him were men with whom one might conquer the world; the slain warriors who died an immortal death." He spoke thus, well aware that it is more, especially amid such destruction that men think of immortality.

He was profuse in his rewards: on the 12th, 21st, 127th of the line, and the 7th light,[1] he conferred eighty-seven decorations and promotions; these were Gudin's regiments. The 127th had, before that time, marched without an eagle; for at that period it was necessary for a regiment to earn its colours in a field of battle, to prove, that in the sequel it would know how to preserve them there.

The emperor delivered the eagle to it with his own hands; he also satisfied Ney's corps. His favours were as great in themselves as they were in their form. The value of the gift was enhanced by the manner in which he bestowed it. He was successively surrounded by each regiment as by a family. There he addressed himself in a loud voice to the officers, subalterns, and privates, inquiring who were the bravest of all those brave men, or the most successful, and recompensing them on the spot. The officers named them, the soldiers confirmed, the emperor approved: thus, as he himself observed, the elections were made instantaneously, in a circle, in his presence, and confirmed with acclamations by the troops.

These paternal manners, which made the private soldier the military comrade of the ruler of Europe, these forms, which revived the still-regretted usages of the republic, delighted the troops. He was a monarch, but the monarch of the Revolution; and they could not but love a fortunate sovereign who led them on to fortune; in him there was every thing to excite, and nothing to reproach them.

Never did field of victory exhibit a spectacle more capable of exalting; the presentation of that richly merited eagle, the pomp of the promotions, the shouts of joy, the glory of those warriors, recompensed on the very spot where it had just been acquired; their valour proclaimed by a voice every accent of which rung throughout attentive Europe; by that great captain whose bulletins would carry their names over the whole world, and more especially among their countrymen, and into the bosoms of their families, which they would at once cheer and make proud: how many favours at once! they were absolutely intoxicated with them; he himself seemed at first to share their transports.

But when he was out of sight of his troops, the attitude of Ney and Murat, and the words of Poniatowski, who was as frank and judicious in council, as he was intrepid in the field, cooled him; and when the close heat of the day began to overpower him, and he learned from the reports that his men had proceeded eight leagues without overtaking the enemy, the spell was entirely dissolved. On his return to Smolensk, the jolting of his carriage over the relics of the fight, the stoppages caused on the road by the long file of the wounded who were crawling or being carried back, and in Smolensk itself by the tumbrils of amputated limbs about to be thrown away at a distance; in a word, all that is horrible and odious out of fields of battle, completely disarmed him. Smolensk was but one vast hospital, and the loud groans which issued from it drowned the shout of glory which had just been raised on the fields of Valoutina.

The reports of the surgeons were frightful; in that country a spirit distilled from grain is used instead of wine and brandy made from grapes. Narcotic plants are mixed with it. Our young soldiers, exhausted with hunger and fatigue, conceived that this liquor would cheer them; but its perfidious heat caused them to exhaust at once all the fire that was yet left in them, after which they sank into a state of debility, and became the victims of disease.

Others, less sober, or more weakened, were seized with dizziness, stupefaction, and torpor; they squatted into the ditches and on the roads. Their half-open, watery, and lack-lustre eyes seemed to watch, with insensibility, death gradually seizing their whole frame; they expired sullenly and without a groan.

At Wilna, it had not been possible to establish hospitals for more than six thousand sick; convents, churches, synagogues, and barns, served to receive the suffering multitude. In these dismal places, which were sometimes unhealthy, but still too few, and too crowded, the sick were frequently without food, without beds, without covering, and without even straw and medicines. The surgeons were, from their small number, inadequate to the duty; so that everything, even to the very hospitals, contributed to create disease, and nothing to cure. At Witepsk, 400 wounded Russians were left on the field of battle; 300 more were abandoned in the town by their army; and as the inhabitants had been taken away, these unfortunate wretches remained three days before they were discovered without assistance, huddled together pell mell, dead and dying, amidst the most horrible filth and infection; they were at length collected together and mixed with our own wounded, who, like those of the Russians, amounted to 700. Our surgeons tore up even their own shirts, and those of these poor creatures, to dress them; for there already began to be a scarcity of linen.

When at length the wounds of these unfortunate men began to heal, and they required nothing but wholesome food to complete their cure, they perished from want of sustenance; few either of the French or Russians escaped. Those who were prevented from going in quest of food by the loss of a limb, or by debility, were the first to sink. These disasters occurred wherever the emperor was not in person; his presence bringing, and his departure carrying, everything along with it; and his orders, in fact, not being scrupulously obeyed but within the circle of his own observation.

At Smolensk, there was no want of hospitals; fifteen spacious brick buildings were rescued from the flames; there were even found some wine, brandy, and a few medical stores; and our reserve wagons for the wounded at length rejoined us; but everything ran short. The surgeons were at work night and day; but the very second night, all the materials for dressing the wounded were exhausted; there was no more linen, and they were forced to use paper, found in the archives, in its stead. Parchment served for splinters, and coarse cloth for compresses; and they had no other substitute for lint except tow and birch cotton.

Our surgeons were overwhelmed with dismay: for three days an hospital of a hundred wounded had been forgotten; an accident led to its discovery: Rapp penetrated into that abode of despair. I will spare my reader the horror of a description of it. Wherefore communicate those terrible impressions which harrow up the soul? Rapp did not spare them to Napoleon, who instantly caused his own wine and a sum of money to be distributed among such of those unfortunate men as a tenacious life still animated, or whom a disgusting food had supported.

But to the vehement emotion which these reports excited in the bosom of the emperor, was superadded an alarming consideration. The conflagration of Smolensk was no longer, he saw, the effect of a fatal and unforeseen accident of war, nor even the result of an act of despair: it was the result of cool determination. The Russians had studied the time and means, and taken as great pains to destroy as are usually taken to preserve.

The same day the courageous answers of one of their popes (the only one found in Smolensk,) enlightened him still more in regard to the blind fury which had been excited in the whole Russian nation. His interpreter, alarmed by this animosity, conducted the pope to the emperor. The venerable priest first reproached him with firmness for his alleged sacrilegious acts: he knew not that it was the Russian general himself who had caused the storehouses and churches to be set on fire, and who had accused us of these outrages, in order that the mercantile class and the peasantry might not separate their cause from that of the nobility.

The emperor listened attentively. "But," said he to him at last, "has your church been burned?"—"No, sire," replied the pope, "God will be more powerful than you; he will protect it, for I have opened it to all the unfortunate people whom the destruction of the city has deprived of a home!"—"You are right," rejoined Napoleon, with emotion, "yes, God will watch over the innocent victims of war; he will reward you for your courage. Go, worthy priest, return to your post. Had all your popes followed your example, they had not basely betrayed the mission of peace which they received from heaven; if they had not deserted the temples which their presence alone renders sacred, my soldiers would have spared your holy edifices; for we are all Christians, and your God is our God."

With these words, Napoleon sent back the priest to his church, with an escort and some succours. A heart-rending shriek arose at the sight of the soldiers penetrating into this asylum. A crowd of terrified women and children thronged about the altar; but the pope, raising his voice, cried, "Be of good cheer: I have seen Napoleon; I have spoken to him. Oh! how have we been deceived, my children! the emperor of France is not the man that he has been represented to you. Learn that he and his soldiers worship the same God as we do. The war which he wages is not religious, it is a political quarrel with our emperor. His soldiers fight only against our soldiers. They do not slaughter, as we have been told, old men, women, and children. Cheer up, then, and let us thank God for being relieved from the painful duty of hating them as heathen, impious wretches, and incendiaries!" The pope then commenced a hymn of thanksgiving, in which they all joined with tearful eyes.

But these very words demonstrate how much the nation had been deceived. The rest of the inhabitants had fled. Henceforward, then it was not their army alone, it was the population, it was all Russia that fled before us. The emperor felt that, with this population, one of his most powerful engines of conquest was escaping from his hands.

1. On reaching the front of the 7th light, Napoleon ordered all the captains to form a circle round him and said, "Now shew me the best officer in the regiment." "Sire, they are all good." "Well, but point out to me the best." "Sire, they are all equally good." "Come, come, that is not an answer. Say, like Themistocles, I am the first, my neighbour is the second." Captain Moncey, who was wounded and absent, was then mentioned to him. "What!" said Napoleon, "Moncey, who was my page, the son of the marshal? Mention another." "Sire, he is the best." "Well, then, he shall have the decoration."—*Ed.*

CHAPTER IX

THE RUSSIAN PEASANTRY

EVER since our arrival at Witepsk, Napoleon had, in fact, employed two of his officers to sound the sentiments of these people. The object was to instil into them notions of liberty, and to compromise them in our cause by an insurrection more or less general. But there had been nothing to work upon, excepting a few straggling savage boors, whom the Russians had perhaps left as spies amongst us. This attempt had only served to betray his plan, and to put the Russians on their guard against it.

This expedient, moreover, was repugnant to Napoleon's nature, which was much more inclined to the cause of kings than to that of nations. He employed it but carelessly. Subsequently, at Moscow, he received several addresses from different heads of families. They complained that they were treated by the nobility like herds of cattle, which they might sell or barter at pleasure. They solicited Napoleon to proclaim the abolition of slavery, and in the event of his doing so, they offered to head several partial insurrections, which they promised speedily to render general.

These offers were rejected. We should have seen among a barbarous people a barbarous liberty, an ungovernable, a horrible licentiousness: a few partial revolts had formerly afforded a specimen of them. The Russian nobles, like the planters of St. Domingo, would have been ruined. The fear of this prevailed in the mind of Napoleon, and was confessed by him; it induced him to give up, finally, all attempts to excite a movement which he could not have regulated.

Besides, these masters had conceived a distrust of their slaves. Amidst so many dangers, they recognised this as the most urgent. They first worked upon the minds of their unfortunate serfs, debased by all sorts of servitude. Their priests, whom they are accustomed to believe, imposed upon them by delusive language; they persuaded these peasants that we were legions of devils, commanded by Antichrist, infernal spirits, whose very look would excite horror, and whose touch would contaminate. Such of our prisoners as fell into their hands, remarked that these poor creatures would not again make use of the vessels which they had used, and that they reserved them for the most filthy animals.

As we advanced, however, our presence would have refuted all these clumsy fables. But behold! these nobles fell back with their serfs into the interior of the country, as at the approach of a dire contagion. Property, habitations, all that could detain them, and be serviceable to us, were sacrificed. They interposed famine, fire, and the desert, between them and us; for it was as much against their serfs as against Napoleon, that this mighty resolution was executed. It was no longer, therefore, a war of kings that was to be prosecuted, but a war of class, a war of party, a war of religion, a national war, a combination of all sorts of war.

The emperor then first perceived the enormous magnitude of his enterprise; the farther he advanced, the more it became magnified. So long as he only encountered kings, to him, who was greater than all of them, their defeats were but sport; but the kings being conquered, he had now to do with people; and it was another Spain, but remote, barren, infinite, that he had found at the opposite extremity of Europe. He was daunted, hesitated, and paused.

At Witepsk, whatever resolution he might have taken, he wanted Smolensk, and till he should be at Smolensk, he seemed to have deferred coming to any determination. For this reason he was again seized with the same perplexity; it was now more embarrassing, as the flames, the prevalent epidemic, and the victims which surrounded him, had aggravated every thing; a fever of hesitation attacked him; his eyes turned towards Kieff, Petersburgh, and Moscow.

At Kieff, he should envelop Tchitchakoff, and his army; he should rid of annoyance the right flank and the rear of the grand army; he should cover the Polish provinces most productive of men, provisions, and horses; while fortified cantonments at Mohileff, Smolensk, Witepsk, Polotsk, Dünabourg, and Riga, would defend the rest. Behind this line, and during the winter, he might raise and organise the whole of ancient Poland, and hurl it in the spring upon Russia, oppose nation to nation, and render the contest equal.

At Smolensk, however, he was at the point where the Petersburgh and Moscow roads meet, twenty-nine marches from the first of these capitals, and fifteen from the other. Petersburgh was the centre of the government, the knot to which all the threads of the administration were united, the brain of Russia, the seat of her military and naval arsenals: by possessing himself of that, he would secure the only point of communication between Russia and England. The victory of Polotsk, of which he had just received intelligence, seemed to urge him in that direction. By marching in concert with Saint-Cyr upon Petersburgh, he should envelop Wittgenstein, and cause Riga to fall before Macdonald.

On the other hand, at Moscow, the nobility, as well as the nation, would be attacked in their property, and in their ancient honour; the road to that capital was shorter; it presented fewer obstacles and greater resources; the Russian main army, which he could not neglect, and which he must destroy, was there, together with the chances of a battle, and the hope of giving a shock to the nation, by striking it at the heart in this national war.

Of these three plans the latter appeared to him the only one practicable in spite of the advancing season. The history of Charles XII. was, nevertheless, before his eyes; not that of Voltaire, which he threw aside with impatience, regarding it as romantic and inaccurate; but the journal of Adlerfield, which he read, but which did not stop him. On comparing that expedition with his own, he found a thousand differences between them, on which he laid great stress; for who can be a judge in one's own cause? And of what use is the example of the past, in a world where there were never two men, two things, or two situations exactly alike?

At any rate, about this period the name of Charles XII. was frequently heard to drop from his lips.

CHAPTER X

DISSENSION AND DISCORD

BUT the news which arrived from all quarters excited his ardour quite as much as it had been raised at Witepsk. His lieutenants seemed to have done more than himself: the actions of Mohileff, Molodeczna, and Valoutina, were regular battles, in which Davoust, Schwartzenberg, and Ney, were conquerors; on his right, his line of operation seemed to be covered; the enemy's army was flying before him on his left, the duke of Reggio, after drawing Wittgenstein upon Polotsk, was attacked at Slowna, on the 17th of August. The attack of Wittgenstein was furious and obstinate; it failed; but he retained his offensive position, and marshal Oudinot was wounded. Saint-Cyr succeeded him in the command of that army, composed of about 30,000 French, Swiss, and Bavarians. The very next day this general, who disliked any command unless when he exercised it alone and in chief, availed himself of it, to give his measure to his own troops and to the enemy; but with the coolness and combination peculiar to his character.

From daybreak till five in the evening, he contrived to amuse the enemy by the proposal of an agreement to withdraw the wounded, and more especially by demonstrations of retreat. At the same time he silently rallied all his combatants, drew them up into three columns of attack, and concealed them behind the village of Spas, and in the hollow grounds.

At five o'clock, all being ready, and Wittgenstein's vigilance asleep, Saint-Cyr gave the signal; artillery immediately began firing, and his columns rushed forward. The Russians, being taken by surprise, made a vain resistance; their left was first broken, and their centre soon fled in disorder; they abandoned 1000 prisoners, 20 pieces of cannon, a field of battle covered with slain, and the offensive, which Saint-Cyr, being too weak, could only affect to resume, for the purpose of better defending himself.

In this short but severe and sanguinary conflict, the right wing of the Russians, which was supported by the Dwina, made an obstinate resistance. It was necessary to charge it with the bayonet, amidst a thick fire of grape-shot; but when it was supposed that there was no more to do but to pursue, all was nearly lost. Some Russian dragoons, according to some, and horse-guards, according to others, risked a charge on a battery of Saint Cyr's; a French brigade placed to support it advanced, but suddenly turned its back and fled through the midst of our cannon, which it prevented from being fired. The Russians reached them pell-mell with our men; they sabred the gunners, upset the pieces, and pursued our horse so closely, that the latter, more and more terrified, ran in disorder up their commander-in-chief and his staff, whom they overthrew. General Saint-Cyr was obliged to fly on foot. He threw himself into the bottom of a ravine, which sheltered him from the squall. The Russian dragoons were already close to Polotsk, when a prompt and skilful manœuvre of Berkheim and the 4th French cuirassiers put an end to this warm affair. The Russians betook themselves to the woods.

The following day Saint-Cyr sent a body of men in pursuit of them, but merely to ascertain their retreat, to fix his claim to the victory, and to reap some more of its fruits. During the two succeeding months, up to the 18th of October, Wittgenstein kept at a respectful distance.— The French general on his part, employed himself in observing the enemy, in keeping up his communications with Macdonald, with Witepsk, and Smolensk, in fortifying himself in his position at Polotsk, and, above all, in finding means of subsistence for his army.

In this action of the 18th, four generals, four colonels, and many officers, were wounded. Among them the army remarked the

Bavarian generals Deroy and Liben. They expired on the 22nd of August. These generals were of the same age, they had belonged to the same regiment, made the same campaigns, and proceeded at nearly an equal pace in their perilous career, which was gloriously terminated by the same death, and in the same battle. It was thought right, not to separate in the tomb these warriors, whom neither life nor death had been able to part; one grave received the remains of both.

On the news of this victory, the emperor sent to general Saint-Cyr the staff of marshal of the empire. He placed a great number of crosses at his disposal, and subsequently approved most of the promotions which were applied for.

Notwithstanding this success, the determination to proceed beyond Smolensk was too perilous for Napoleon to decide on it alone: it was requisite that he should contrive to be drawn into it. Beyond Valoutina, Ney's corps, which was fatigued, had been replaced by that of Davoust. Murat, as king, as brother-in-law to the emperor, and agreeably to his order, was to command it. Ney had submitted to this arrangement less from condescension than from conformity of disposition. They agreed in their ardour.

But Davoust, whose methodical and tenacious genius was a complete contrast to the fiery impetuosity of Murat, and who was rendered proud by the remembrance of and the titles derived from his two great victories, was piqued at being placed in this dependence. These haughty chiefs, who were about the same age, had been companions in war, and had mutually witnessed each other's elevation; they were both spoiled by the habit of having obeyed only a great man, and were by no means fit to command each other; Murat, especially, who was too often unable to command himself.

Davoust nevertheless obeyed, but with an ill grace, and imperfectly, as wounded pride generally does. He affected immediately to break off all direct correspondence with the emperor. The latter, surprised at this, ordered him to renew it, alleging his distrust of the reports of Murat. Davoust made a handle of this avowal, and again asserted his independence. Henceforward the vanguard had two leaders. Thus the emperor, fatigued, distressed, over-loaded with business of every kind, and forced to show indulgence to his lieutenants, divided his power as well as his armies, in spite of his precepts and his former example. Circumstances, which he had so often controlled, became stronger than him, and controlled him in their turn.

Meanwhile Barclay, having fallen back without resistance nearly as far as Dorogobouje, Murat had no need of Davoust, and no occasion presented itself for misunderstanding; but about eleven in the forenoon of the 23rd of August, a thick wood, a few wersts from that town, which the king of Naples wished to reconnoitre, was warmly disputed with him: he was obliged to carry it twice.

Murat, surprised at such a resistance at that early hour, pushed on, and piercing through this curtain, beheld the whole Russian army drawn up in order of battle. The narrow ravine of the Luja separated him from it: it was noon; the extent of the Russian lines, especially towards our right, the preparations, the hour, the place, which was that where Barclay had just rejoined Bagration, the choice of the ground, well suited for a general engagement, all gave him reason to anticipate a battle; and he sent a despatch to the emperor to apprise him of it.

At the same time he ordered Montbrun to pass the ravine on his right with his cavalry, in order to reconnoitre and get upon the left of the enemy. Davoust, and his five divisions of infantry, extended themselves on that side, and protected Montbrun: the king recalled them to his left, on the high-road, designing, it is said, to support Montbrun's flank movement by some demonstrations in front.

Davoust replied, that "this would be sacrificing our right wing, through which the enemy would get behind us on the high-road, our only means of retreat that thus he would force us to a battle, which he, Davoust, had orders to avoid, and which he would avoid, his force being insufficient, the position bad, and being moreover under the command of a leader in whom he had but little confidence." He then wrote immediately to Napoleon, urging him to come up without loss of time, if he would not have Murat engage without him.

On this intelligence, which he received in the night of the 24th of August, Napoleon joyfully threw aside his indecision; which to his enterprising and decisive genius was absolute torture: he hurried forward with his guard, and proceeded twelve leagues without halting;

but on the evening of the preceding day the enemy's army had again disappeared.

On our side, their retreat was attributed to the movement of Montbrun; on the part of the Russians to Barclay, and to a bad position chosen by the chief of his staff, who had taken up ground in his own disfavour, instead of making it serve to his advantage. Bagration was the first who perceived this error; his rage knew no bounds, and he proclaimed it treason.

Discord reigned in the Russian camp as well as in our advanced guard. Confidence in their commander, that strength of armies, was wanting; his every step seemed a blunder; each resolution that was taken the very worst. The loss of Smolensk had soured every body; the junction of the two *corps d'armée* increased the evil; the stronger the Russian force felt itself, the weaker did its general seem to it. The outcry against him became general; another leader was loudly called for. A few prudent men, however, interposed: Kutusoff was announced, and the humbled pride of the Russians awaited him in order to fight.

The emperor, on his part, who was already at Dorogobouje, no longer hesitated; he knew that he carried every where with him the fate of Europe; that wherever he might be, that would always be the place, where the destiny of nations would be decided; that he might therefore advance, fearless of the threatening consequences of the defection of the Swedes and Turks. Accordingly he neglected the hostile armies of Essen at Riga, of Wittgenstein before Polotsk, of Hoertell before Bobruisk, and of Tchitchakoff in Volhynia. They consisted of 120,000 men, whose number could not but keep gradually augmenting; he passed them, and suffered himself to be surrounded by them with indifference, well assured that all these vain obstacles of war and policy would be swept a by the very first thunderbolt which he should launch.

And yet, his column of attack, which was 185,000 strong at his departure from Witepsk, was already reduced to 157,000; it was diminished by 28,000 men, half of whom occupied Witepsk, Orcha, Mohileff, and Smolensk. The rest had been killed or wounded, or were straggling, and plundering in his rear our allies and the French themselves.

But 157,000 men were sufficient to destroy the Russian army by a complete victory, and to take Moscow. As to his base of operation, notwithstanding the 120,000 Russians by whom it was threatened, it appeared to be secure. Lithuania, the Dwina, the Dnieper, and lastly Smolensk, were or would soon be covered towards Riga and Dilnabourg by Macdonald and 32,000 men; towards Polotsk by Saint-Cyr, with 30,000; at Witepsk, Smolensk, and Mohileff, by Victor and 40,000; before Bobruisk, by Dombrowski and 12,000; and on the Bug by Schwartzenberg and Regnier, at the head of 45,000 men. Napoleon reckoned besides on the divisions of Loison and Durutte, 22,000 strong, which were already approaching Königsberg and Warsaw; and on reinforcements to the amount of 80,000, all of which would enter Russia before the middle of November.

He should thus have 280,000 men, including the Lithuanian and Polish levies, to support him, while, with 155,000 more, he made an incursion of ninety-three leagues; for such was the distance between Smolensk and Moscow.

But these 280,000 men were commanded by six different leaders, all independent of each other, and the most elevated of them, he who occupied the centre, and who seemed to be appointed to act as an intermediate link, to give some unity to the operations of the other five, was a minister of peace, and not of war.

Besides the same causes which had already diminished, by one-third, the French forces which first entered Russia, could not fail to disperse or to destroy a still greater proportion of all these reinforcements. Most of them were coming by detachments, formed provisionally into marching battalions, under officers new to them, whom they were to leave the first day, without the incentives of discipline, *esprit de corps*, or glory, and traversing an exhausted country, which the season and the climate would be rendering daily more bare and more rude.

Meanwhile Napoleon beheld Dorogobouje in ashes, like Smolensk, especially the quarter of the merchants, those who had most to lose, whom their riches might have detained or brought back amongst us, and who, from their situation, formed a kind of intermediate class, a commencement of the commons which liberty was likely to seduce.

He was perfectly aware that he was quitting Smolensk, as he had come thither, with the hope of a battle, which the indecision and discord of the Russian generals had as yet deferred; but his resolution was now taken; he would hear of nothing but what was calculated to support him in it. He persisted in pursuing the track of the enemy; his hardihood increased with their prudence; their circumspection he called pusillanimity, their retreat a flight; he despised, that he might hope.

BOOK VII

CHAPTER I

SUPPLY AND ORGANISATION

THE emperor proceeded with such expedition to Dorogobouje, that he was obliged to halt there, in order to wait for his army, and to allow Murat to pursue the enemy. He set out again on the 26th of August; the army marched in three columns abreast; the emperor, Murat, Davoust, and Ney in the centre, on the high road to Moscow; Poniatowski on the right; and the army of Italy on the left.

The principal column, that of the centre, found nothing on a road where its advanced guard itself had to subsist entirely on the leavings of the Russians: it could not digress from its direction, for want of time, in so rapid a march. Besides the columns on the right and left consumed every thing on either side of it. In order to live better, it ought to have set out later every day, halted earlier, and then extended itself more on the flanks during the night; which could not be done without imprudence when the enemy was so near at hand.

At Smolensk orders had been issued, as at Witepsk, to take, at starting, provisions for several days. The Emperor was aware of the difficulty of collecting them, but he reckoned upon the diligence of the officers and the troops; they had warning,—that was sufficient; they would contrive to provide themselves with necessaries. They had acquired the habit of doing so; and it was really a curious sight to observe the voluntary and continued efforts of so many men to follow a single individual to such great distances. The existence of the army was a prodigy that was daily renewed, by the active, industrious, and intelligent spirit of the French and Polish troops, by their habit of surmounting all difficulties, and by their fondness for the hazards and irregularities of this dreadful game of an adventurous life.

In the train of each regiment there were a multitude of those diminutive horses with which Poland swarms, a great number of carts of the country requiring to be incessantly replaced with fresh ones, and a drove of cattle. The baggage-wagons were driven by soldiers, for they turned their hands to every trade. They were missed in the ranks, it is true; but here the want of provisions, the necessity for transporting every thing with them, excused this prodigious train: it required a second army, as it were, to carry or draw what was indispensable for the first.

In this prompt organisation, adopted while on the march, the army had accommodated itself to all the local customs and difficulties; the genius of the soldiers had admirably made the most of the scanty resources of the country. As to the officers, as the general orders always took for granted regular distributions which were never made, each of them, according to the degree of his zeal, intelligence and firmness, appropriated to himself more or less of the spoil, and converted individual pillage into regular contributions.

For it was only by excursions on the flanks, and into an unknown country, that any provisions could be procured. Every evening, when the army halted, and the bivouacs were established, detachments, rarely commanded by divisions, sometimes by brigades, and most commonly by regiments, went in quest of necessaries, and penetrated into the country; a few wersts from the road they found all the villages inhabited, and were not very hostilely received; but as they could not make themselves understood, and besides wanted every thing, and that instantaneously, the peasants were soon seized with a panic and fled into the woods, whence they issued again as no very formidable partisans.

The detachments meanwhile plentifully regaled themselves, and rejoined their corps next day, or some days afterwards, laden with all they had collected; and it frequently happened that they were plundered in their turn by their comrades belonging to the other corps whom they chanced to fall in with. Hence arose animosities, which would have infallibly led to most sanguinary intestine conflicts, had not all been subsequently overtaken by the same misfortune, and involved in the horrors of a common disaster.

Until the return of their detachments, the soldiers who remained with their eagles lived on what they could find on the military road; in general it consisted of new rye, which they bruised and boiled. Owing to the number of cattle which followed them, there was less want of meat than of bread; but the length, and especially the rapidity, of the marches occasioned the loss of many of these animals: they were so suffocated by the heat and dust, that when they came to water, they ran into it with such eagerness that many of them were drowned, while others drank so immoderately, as to swell themselves out till they were unable to walk.

It was remarked now, as well as before we reached Smolensk, that the divisions of the first corps continued to be the most numerous; their detachments were better disciplined, brought back more, and did less injury to the inhabitants. Those who remained with their colours lived on the contents of their knapsacks, the regular appearance of which relieved the eye, fatigued with a disorder that was nearly universal.

Each of these knapsacks, reduced to what was strictly necessary in point of apparel, contained two shirts, two pair of shoes with nails, and a pair of extra soles, a pair of pantaloons and half-gaiters of cloth; a few articles requisite to personal cleanliness, a bandage, and a quantity of lint, and sixty cartridges.

In the two sides were placed four biscuits of sixteen ounces each; under these, and at the bottom, was a long, narrow linen bag, filled with ten pounds of flour. The whole knapsack and its contents, together with the straps and the hood, rolled up and fastened at top, weighed thirty-three pounds twelve ounces.

Each soldier carried also a linen bag, slung in the form of a shoulder-belt, containing two loaves of three pounds each. Thus with his sabre, his loaded knapsack, three flints, his turn-screw, his belt and musket, he had to carry fifty-eight pounds weight, and was provided with bread for four days, biscuit for four, flour for seven, and sixty rounds of ammunition.

Behind were carriages laden with provisions for six more days; but it was impossible to reckon with confidence on these vehicles, picked up on the spot, which would have been so convenient in any other country, with a smaller army, and in a more regular war.

When the flour bag was emptied, it was filled with any corn that could be found, and which was ground at the first mill, if any chanced to be met with; if not, by the hand-mills which followed the regiments, or which were found in the villages, for the Russians are scarcely acquainted with any others. It took sixteen men twelve hours to grind in one of them the corn necessary for one hundred and thirty men for one day.

As every house in this country has an oven, little want was felt on that score; bakers abounded; for the regiments of the first corps contained men of all trades, so that articles of food and clothing were all made or repaired by them during the march. They were colonies uniting the character of civilised and nomadic. The emperor had first conceived the idea, which the genius of the prince of Eckmühl made his own; he had every thing he wanted, time, place, and men to carry it into execution; but these three elements of success were less at the disposal of the other chiefs. Besides, their characters, being more impetuous and less methodical, would scarcely have derived the same advantages from it; with a less organising genius, they would therefore have had more obstacles to surmount; the emperor had not paid sufficient attention to these differences which were productive of baneful effects.

CHAPTER II

MURAT AND DAVOUST

IT was from Slawkowo, a few leagues beyond Dorogobouje, that Napoleon sent orders, on the 27th of August, to marshal Victor, who was then on the Niemen, to advance to Smolensk. This marshal's left was to occupy Witepsk, his right Mohileff, and his centre Smolensk. There he would succour Saint-Cyr, in case of need, serve for a point of support to the army of Moscow, and keep up his communications with Lithuania.

It was also from the same imperial head-quarters that he published the details of his review at Valoutina, with the intention of proclaiming to the present and future ages the names even of the private soldiers who had there distinguished themselves. But he added, that at Smolensk "the conduct of the Poles had astonished the Russians, who had been accustomed to despise them." These words drew from the Poles an outcry of indignation, and the emperor smiled at an anger which he had anticipated, and the effects of which were designed to fall exclusively on the Russians.

On this march he took delight in dating from the heart of Old Russia a number of decrees, which would be circulated in the meanest hamlets of France; from the desire of appearing to be present every where at once, and filling the earth more and more with his power: the offspring of that inconceivable and expanding greatness of soul, whose ambition was at first a mere plaything, but finally coveted the empire of the world.

It is true that at the same time there was so little order about him at Slawkowo, that his guard burned, during the night, to warm themselves, the bridge which they were ordered to guard, and the only one by which he could the next day leave his imperial quarters. This disorder, however, like many others, proceeded not from insubordination, but from thoughtlessness; it was corrected as soon as it was perceived.

The very same day Murat drove the enemy beyond the Osnia, a narrow river, but enclosed with high banks, and of great depth, like most of the rivers of this country; the effect of the snow, and which, at the period of its general melting, prevents inundations. The Russian rear-guard, covered by this obstacle, faced about and established itself on the heights of the opposite bank. Murat ordered the ravine to be examined, and a ford was discovered. It was through this narrow and insecure defile that he dared to march against the Russians, to venture between the river and their position; thus cutting off from himself all retreat, and turning a skirmish into a desperate action. In fact, the enemy descended in force from their height, and drove him back to the very brink of the ravine, into which they had well-nigh precipitated him. But Murat persisted in his error; he braved it out, and converted it into a success. The fourth lancers carried the position, and the Russians went to pass the night not far off; content with having made us purchase at a dear rate a quarter of a league of ground, which they would have given up to us for nothing during the night.

At the moment of the most imminent danger, a battery of the prince of Eckmühl twice refused to fire. Its commanding officer pleaded his instructions, which forbade him, upon pain of being broke, to fight without orders from Davoust. These orders arrived, in time, according to some, but too late according to others. I relate this incident, because, on the following day, it was the occasion of a violent quarrel between Murat and Davoust, in the presence of the emperor, at Semlewo.

The king reproached the prince with his tardy circumspection, and more especially with an enmity which dated from the expedition to Egypt. In the vehemence of his passion he told him, that if there was any quarrel between them they ought to settle it by themselves, but that the army ought not to be made the sufferers for it.

Davoust, irritated in his turn, accused the king of temerity; according to him "his thoughtless ardour was incessantly compromising his troops, and wasting to no purpose their lives, their strength, and their stores. It was necessary that the emperor should at last know what was daily occurring in his advanced guard. Every morning the enemy had disappeared before it; but this experience led to no alteration whatever in the march: the troops, therefore set out late, all keeping the high road, and forming a single column, and in this manner they advanced in the void till about noon.

"The enemy's rear-guard, ready to fight, was then discovered behind some marshy ravine, the bridges over which had been broken down, and which was commanded from the opposite bank. The light troops were instantly brought into action, then the first regiments of cavalry that were at hand, and then the artillery; but in general out of reach, or against straggling Cossacks, who were not worth the trouble. At length, after vain and sanguinary attempts made in front, the king took it into his head to reconnoitre the force and position of the enemy more accurately, and to manœuvre, and he sent for the infantry.

"Then, after having long waited in this endless column, the ravine was crossed on the left or on the right of the Russians, who retired under a fire of their small arms to a new position: where the same resistance, and the same mode of march and attack, exposed us to the same losses and the same delays.

"In this manner the king went on from position to position, till he came to one which was stronger or better defended. It was usually about five in the evening, sometimes later, rarely earlier; but in this case the tenacity of the Russians, and the hour, plainly indicated that their whole army was there, and was determined to pass the night on the spot.

"For it could not be denied that this retreat of the Russians was conducted with admirable order. The ground alone dictated it to them, and not Murat. Their positions were so well chosen, taken so seasonably, and each defended so exactly in proportion to its strength and the time which their general wished to gain, that in truth their movements seemed to form part of a plan which had been long determined on, carefully traced and executed with scrupulous exactness.

"They never abandoned a post till the moment before they were likely to be driven from it.

"In the evening they established themselves early in a good position, leaving under arms no more troops than were absolutely necessary to defend it, while the remainder rested and refreshed themselves."

Davoust added, that "so far from profiting by this example, the king paid no regard either to the hour, the strength of the situation, or the resistance; that he dashed on among his sharp-shooters, dancing about in front of the enemy's line, feeling it in every part; putting himself in a passion, giving his orders in a loud voice, and making himself hoarse with repeating them; exhausting every thing, cartouch-boxes, ammunition-wagons, men and horses, combatants and non-combatants, and keeping all the troops under arms till night had set in.

"Then, indeed, it was found necessary to desist, and take up their quarters where they were; but they no longer knew where to find necessaries. It was really pitiful to hear the soldiers wandering in the dark, groping about, as it were, for forage, water, wood, straw, and provisions, and then, unable to find their bivouacs again, calling out to one another during the whole night, lest they should lose themselves. Scarcely had they time to prepare their food, much less to sleep. Overwhelmed with fatigue, they cursed the authors of their hardships, till daylight and the enemy came to rouse them again.

"Nor was it the advanced guard alone that suffered in this manner, but the whole of the cavalry. Every evening Murat had left at a great distance behind him 20,000 men, on horseback and under arms, on the high-road. This long column had remained all day without eating or drinking amidst a cloud of dust, under a burning sky; ignorant of what was passing before it, advancing a few paces from one quarter of an hour to another, then halting to deploy among fields of rye, but without daring to take off the bridles and to allow their famished horses to feed, because the king kept them so incessantly on the alert. It was to advance five or six leagues that they thus passed sixteen tedious hours—particularly arduous for the cuirassier horses, which had more to carry than the others, though weaker, as the largest horses in general are, and requiring more food; hence their great carcasses were worn down to skeletons, their flanks collapsed, they crawled rather than walked, and every moment one was seen staggering, and another falling under his rider, who left him to his fate."

Davoust concluded with saying, that "in this manner the whole of the cavalry would perish: Murat, however, might dispose of that as he pleased, but as for the infantry of the first corps, so long as he had the command of it, he would not suffer it to be thrown away in that manner."

The king was not backward in replying. While the emperor was listening to them, he was at the same time playing with a Russian ball, which he kicked about with his foot. It seemed as if there was something in the misunderstanding between these chiefs which did not displease him. He attributed their animosity entirely to their ardour, well aware that of all passions glory is the most jealous.

The impatient ardour of Murat gratified his own. As the troops had nothing to live upon but what they found, every thing was consumed at the moment; for this reason it was necessary to make short work with the enemy, and to proceed rapidly. Besides, the general crisis in Europe was too strong, his situation too critical to remain there, and himself too impatient; he wished to bring matters to a close at any rate, in order to extricate himself.

The impetuosity of the king of Naples, therefore, seemed to suit his anxiety better than the methodical prudence of the prince of Eckmühl. Accordingly, when he dismissed them, he said mildly to Davoust, that "one person could not possess every species of merit; that he knew better how to fight a battle than to push a rear-guard: and that if Murat had pursued Bagration in Lithuania, he would probably not have allowed him to escape." It is even asserted that he reproached the marshal with his restless disposition which made him desirous of appropriating to himself the entire command; less, indeed, from ambition than zeal, and that all might go on better; but yet this zeal had its inconveniences. He then sent them away with an injunction to agree better in future.

The two chiefs returned to their commands, and to their animosity. As the war was confined to the head of the column, that also was the scene of their disputes.

CHAPTER III

FRENCH ADVANCES

ON the 28th of August, the army crossed the vast plains of the government of Viazma: it marched in all haste, the whole together, through fields, and several regiments abreast, each forming a short close column. The high-road was left for the artillery, its wagons, and those carrying the sick and wounded. The emperor, on horseback, was seen every where: Murat's letters and the approach to Viazma, deceived him once more with the hope of a battle: he was heard calculating on the march the thousands of cannon-balls which he would require to crush the hostile army.

Napoleon had assigned its place to the baggage: he published an order for burning all vehicles which should be seen among the troops, not excepting carts loaded with provisions, for they might embarrass the movements of the columns, and compromise their safety in case of an attack. Having met in his way with the carriage of general Narbonne, his aide-de-camp, he himself caused it to be set on fire, before the face of that general, and that instantaneously, without suffering it to be emptied; an order which was only severe, although it appeared harsh, because he himself began by enforcing its execution, which, however, was not followed up.

The baggage of all the different corps was therefore collected in the rear of the army: there was, from Dorogobouje, a long train of bat-horses and kibitkas, harnessed with ropes; these vehicles were laden with booty, provisions, military effects, men appointed to take care of them: lastly, sick soldiers, and the arms of both, which were rusting in them. In this column were seen many of the tall dismounted cuirassiers, bestriding horses no bigger than our asses, because they could not follow on foot for want of practice and of boots. On this confused and disorderly multitude, as well as on most of the marauders on our flanks, the Cossacks might have made some successful *coups-de-main*. They would thereby have harassed the army, and retarded its march, but Barclay seemed fearful of discouraging us: he put out his strength only against our advanced guard, and that but just sufficiently to slacken without stopping our progress.

This determination of Barclay's, the declining strength of the army, the quarrels between its chiefs, the approach of the decisive moment, gave great uneasiness to Napoleon. At Dresden, at Witepsk, and even at Smolensk, he had hoped in vain for a communication from Alexander. At Ribky, on the 28th of August, he appeared to solicit one: a letter from Berthier to Barclay, in no other respect worthy of notice, concluded with these words: "The emperor directs me to request you to present his compliments to the emperor Alexander; tell him that neither the vicissitudes of war nor any other circumstance, can diminish the friendship which he feels for him."

The same day, the 28th of August, the advanced guard drove back the Russians as far as Viazma; the army, thirsty from the march, the heat, and the dust, was in want of water; the troops disputed the possession of a few muddy pools, and fought near the springs, which were soon rendered turbid and exhausted; the emperor himself was forced to put up with this muddy beverage.

During the night, the enemy destroyed the bridges over the Viazma, plundered that town, and set it on fire. Murat and Davoust precipitately advanced to extinguish the flames. The enemy defended his conflagration, but the Viazma was fordable near the ruins of the bridges: one part of the advanced guard then attacked the incendiaries, and the other the fire, which they speedily subdued.

On this occasion some picked men were sent to the advanced guard, with orders to watch the enemy closely at Viazma, and ascertain whether they or our soldiers were the real incendiaries. Their report entirely dissipated the doubts which the emperor might still have entertained as to the fatal resolution of the Russians. They found in this town some resources, which pillage would soon have wasted. In passing through it, the emperor observed this disorder: he became exceedingly incensed, pressed his horse into the midst of the groups of soldiers, struck some, knocked down others, and caused a suttler to be seized, whom he ordered to be instantly tried and shot. But the meaning of the phrase from his lips was well known; it was known also that the more vehement his paroxysms of anger, the sooner they were followed by indulgence. A moment afterwards, they therefore merely placed in his way the unfortunate man on his knees, with a woman and several children by his side, whom they passed off for his family. The emperor, who had already cooled, inquired what they wanted, and ordered the man to be set at liberty.

He was still on horseback when he saw Belliard, for fifteen years the companion in war of Murat, and then the chief of his staff, coming towards him. Surprised at seeing him, the emperor fancied some misfortune had happened. Belliard first relieved his apprehensions, and then added, that "beyond the Viazma, behind a ravine, on an advantageous position, the enemy had shown himself in force and ready for battle; that the cavalry on both sides immediately engaged, and as the infantry became necessary, the king in person put himself at the head of one of Davoust's divisions, and drew it out to lead it against the enemy; but that the marshal hastened up calling to his men to halt, loudly censuring that manœuvre, harshly reproaching the king for it, and forbidding his generals to obey him: that Murat had then appealed to his superior military rank, and to the exigency of the occasion, but in vain: that, finally, he had sent him to the emperor to express his disgust for a command so contested, and to tell him that he must choose between him and Davoust."

This intelligence threw Napoleon into a passion: he exclaimed, that "Davoust was unmindful of all subordination; that he forgot the respect due to his brother-in-law, to him whom he had appointed his lieutenant;" and he sent Berthier with orders that Compans's division, the same which had been the subject of the altercation, should be thence-forward under the command of the king. Davoust did not vindicate the manner, but merely the motive of his conduct, either from prejudice against the habitual temerity of the king, from spleen, or that he was a better judge of the ground, and the manœuvre adapted to it, which is very possible.

Meanwhile the combat had finished, and Murat, whose attention was no longer diverted by the enemy, was wholly occupied with the thoughts of his quarrel. Shut up with Belliard, and hiding himself, in a manner, in his tent, as his memory recalled the expressions of the marshal, his blood became more and more inflamed with shame and rage. "He had been set at defiance, and publicly insulted, and Davoust still lived! What did he care for the anger of the emperor, and for his decision? It was his business to revenge his own wrong! What signified his rank? It was his sword alone that had made him a king, and it was to that alone he should appeal!" He was already snatching up his arms to go and attack Davoust, when Belliard stopped him, by urging existing circumstances, the example he ought to set to the army, the enemy to be pursued, and that it would be wrong to distress his friends and delight the foe by so desperate a proceeding.

The general says, that he then saw the king curse his crown, and strive to swallow the affront; but that tears of spite rolled down his cheeks and fell upon his clothes. Whilst he was thus tormenting himself, Davoust, obstinately persisting in his opinion, said that the emperor had been misinformed, and remained quietly in his headquarters.

Napoleon returned to Viazma, where he was obliged to stop to ascertain the advantages that he might derive from his new conquest. The accounts which he received from the interior of Russia, represented the hostile government as appropriating to itself our successes, and inculcating the belief that the loss of so many provinces was the effect of a general plan of retreat, adopted beforehand. Papers seized at Viazma stated that *Te Deum* had been sung at Petersburgh for pretended victories at Witepsk or Smolensk. "What!" he exclaimed in astonishment, "*Te Deum*! Dare they then lie to God as well as to men?"

For the rest, most of the intercepted Russian letters expressed the same astonishment. "While our villages are blazing," said they, "we hear nothing here but the ringing of bells, hymns of thanksgiving, and triumphant reports. It seems as if they would make us thank God for the victories of the French. Thus there is lying in the air, lying on earth, lying in words and in writing, lying to Heaven and earth, lying in every thing. Our great men treat the Russians like children, but there is no small degree of credulity in believing us to be so credulous."

Very just reflections, if means so gross had been employed to deceive those who were capable of writing such letters. At any rate, though these political falsehoods are generally resorted to, it was plain that when carried to such excess, they were a satire either on the governors or the governed, and, perhaps, on both.

During this time the advanced guard pushed the Russians as far as Gjatz, exchanging a few balls with them,—an exchange which was almost always to the disadvantage of the French, the Russians taking care to employ only their long pieces, which carried much farther than ours. Another remark which we made was, that from Smolensk the Russians had neglected to burn the villages and the mansions. As they are of a character which aims at effect, this obscure evil probably appeared to them to be a useless one. They were satisfied with the more conspicuous conflagrations of their cities.

This defect, if that negligence proceeded from it, turned, as is frequently the case with all other defects, to the advantage of their enemies. In these villages, the French army found forage, corn, ovens for baking, and shelter. Others observed, on this point, that all these devastations were allotted to Cossacks, to barbarians; and that these hordes, either from hatred or contempt of civilisation, seemed to take a savage and particular pleasure in the destruction of the towns.

CHAPTER IV

BARCLAY'S PROBLEMS
AND HIS PLAN

ON the 1st of September, about noon, there was only a copse of fir-trees between Murat and Gjatz. The appearance of Cossacks obliged him to deploy his first regiments, but in his impatience, he soon sent for some horse, and having himself driven the Russians from the wood which they occupied, he crossed it and found himself at the gates of Gjatz. This sight animated the French, and they instantly made themselves masters of the town as far as the river which parts it into two, and the bridges of which had been already set on fire.

There, as at Smolensk and Viazma, whether by chance, or from the relic of a Tartar custom, the bazaar was on the Asiatic side, on the bank opposite to us. The Russian rear-guard, secured by the river, had time, therefore, to burn the whole of that quarter. Nothing but the promptitude of Murat saved the other.

The troops crossed the Gjatz as they could, on planks, in a few boats, and by fording. The Russians disappeared behind the flames, whither our foremost riflemen followed them,—when they saw an inhabitant come forth, approach them, and cry out that he was a Frenchman. His joy and his accent confirmed his assertion. They conducted him to Davoust, who interrogated him.

According to the account of this man, a complete change had just been made in the Russian army. A violent clamour had been raised from its ranks against Barclay, which was re-echoed by the nobility, the merchants, and by all Moscow. "That general, that minister, was a traitor; he caused all their divisions to be destroyed piece-meal; he was dishonouring the army by an interminable flight; yet, at the same time, they were labouring under the disgrace of an invasion, and their towns were in flames. If it was necessary to determine upon this ruin, they might as well sacrifice themselves; there would be at least some honour in that, whereas, to suffer themselves to be sacrificed by a stranger, was losing every thing, the honour of the sacrifice not excepted.

"But why employ this stranger? Was not the contemporary, the comrade, the rival of Suwarrow yet living? A Russian was wanted to save Russia!" And they all called for, all were anxious for Kutusoff and a battle. The Frenchman added, that Alexander had yielded; that the insubordination of Bagration, and the universal outcry, had obtained from him that general and his consent to a battle; and that, moreover, after drawing the invading army so far, the Russian emperor had himself judged a general engagement unavoidable.

Finally, he related, that the arrival of Kutusoff on the 29th of August at Tzarewo-zaimizcze, between Viazma and Gjatz, and the announcement of a speedy battle, had intoxicated the enemy with double joy; that all had immediately marched towards Borodino,— not to continue their flight, but to fix themselves on this frontier of the government of Moscow, to root themselves to the soil, and defend it; in short, there to conquer or die.

An incident, otherwise not worthy of notice, seemed to confirm this intelligence; this was the arrival of a Russian officer with a flag of truce. He had so little to say, that it was evident from the first that he came only as an observer. His manner was particularly displeasing to Davoust, who read in it something more than assurance. A French general having inconsiderately asked this stranger what we should find between Viazma and Moscow, the Russian proudly replied, "Pultowa." This answer bespoke a battle; it pleased the French, who are fond of a smart repartee, and delighted to meet with enemies worthy of them.

This officer was conducted back without precaution, as he had been brought. He saw that there was no obstacle to prevent access to our very head-quarters; he traversed our advanced posts without meeting with a single vidette; every where the same negligence was perceptible, and the temerity so natural to Frenchmen and to conquerors. Everyone was asleep; there was no watchword, no patroles; our soldiers seemed to despise these details, as too trivial. Wherefore so many precautions? They were the assailants, they were victorious: it was for the Russians to defend themselves! This officer has since said, that he was tempted to take advantage that very night of our imprudence, but that he did not find any Russian corps within his reach.

The enemy, in his haste to burn the bridges over the Gjatz, left behind some of his Cossacks; they were taken and conducted to the emperor, who was approaching on horseback. Napoleon wished to question them himself. He sent for his interpreter, and caused two of these Scythians, whose strange dress and wild look were remarkable, to be placed by his side. In this manner he entered Gjatz, and passed through the town. The answers of these barbarians corresponded with the account of the Frenchman; and during the night of the 1st of September, all the reports from the advanced posts confirmed their accuracy.

In this manner did Barclay, singly against all, support till the very last moment that plan of retreat, which in 1807 he had vaunted to one of our generals as the only expedient for saving Russia. Among us, he was commended for having persisted in this prudent defensive system, in spite of the clamours of a proud nation irritated by misfortune, and before so aggressive an enemy.

He had, no doubt, failed, in suffering himself to be surprised at Wilna, and for not considering the marshy course of the Berezina as the proper frontier of Lithuania; but it was remarked that, subsequently, at Witepsk and Smolensk, he had anticipated Napoleon; that on the Loutcheza, on the Dnieper, and at Valoutina, his resistance had been proportionate to time and place; that this petty warfare, and the losses occasioned by it, had been but too much in his favour; every retrograde step of his drawing us to a greater distance from our reinforcements, and carrying him nearer to his: in short, all that he had done, he had done judiciously, whether he had hazarded, defended, or abandoned.

And yet he had drawn upon himself general censure! But this was, in our opinion, his highest panegyric. We thought the better of him for despising public opinion, when it had gone astray; for having contented himself with watching all our motions in order to profit by them, and for having proved that, most frequently, nations are saved in spite of themselves.

Barclay's character exhibited itself in still brighter colours during the rest of the campaign. This commander-in-chief and minister at war, who was deprived of the command, that it might be given to Kutusoff, voluntarily served under him, and showed as much zeal in obedience, as he had formerly in the command.

CHAPTER V

SKIRMISHES AND PLANNING

THE Russian army at length halted. Miloradowitch, with sixteen thousand recruits, and a host of peasants, bearing the cross and shouting, "*'Tis the will of God!*" hastened to join its ranks. We were informed that the enemy were turning up the whole plain of Borodino, and covering it with entrenchments, apparently with the determination of rooting themselves there, and not falling back any further.

Napoleon announced a battle to his army; he allowed it two days to rest, to prepare its arms, and to collect subsistence. He merely warned the detachments sent out in quest of provisions, that "if they did not return the following day, they would deprive themselves of the honour of fighting."

The emperor then endeavoured to obtain some information concerning his new adversary. Kutusoff was described to him as an old man, the groundwork of whose reputation had been formerly laid by a single wound. He had since skilfully profited by circumstances. The very defeat of Austerlitz, which he had foreseen, added to his renown, which was further increased by his late campaigns against the Turks. His valour was indisputable, but he was charged with regulating its vehemence according to his private interest; for he calculated every thing. His genius was slow, vindictive, and, above all, crafty—the true Tartar character!—knowing the art of preparing an implacable war with a fawning, supple, and patient policy.

In other respects, he was more an adroit courtier than an able general; but formidable by his renown, by his address in augmenting it, and in making others concur in this object. He had contrived to flatter the whole nation, and every individual of it, from the general to the private soldier.

It was added, that there was in his person, in his language, nay, even in his very dress, his superstitious practices and his age, a remnant of Suwarrow,—the stamp of an ancient Muscovite, an air of nationality, which rendered him dear to the Russians; at Moscow, the joy at his appointment had been carried to intoxication; people embraced one another in the streets, and considered themselves as saved.

When Napoleon had learned these particulars, and given his orders, he awaited the event with that tranquillity of mind peculiar to extraordinary men. He quietly employed himself in exploring the environs of his head-quarters. He remarked the progress of agriculture; but at the sight of the Gjatz, which pours its waters into the Wolga, he, who had conquered so many rivers, felt anew the first emotion of his glory; he was heard to boast of being the master of those waves destined to visit Asia; as if they were proceeding to announce his approach, and to open for him the way to that quarter of the globe.

On the 4th of September, the army, still divided into three columns, departed from Gjatz and its environs. Murat had gone on a few leagues before. Ever since the arrival of Kutusoff, clouds of Cossacks had been incessantly buzzing about the heads of our columns. Murat was exasperated at seeing his cavalry forced to deploy against so feeble an obstacle. It was asserted, that on that day, from one of those sudden impulses worthy of the ages of chivalry, he dashed suddenly and alone towards their line, halted when within a few paces of them, and there, sword in hand, made a sign for them to retire, with an air and gesture so commanding, that these barbarians obeyed, and fell back in amazement.

This circumstance, which was related to us on the spot, was received without incredulity. The martial air of that monarch, the splendour of his chivalrous dress, his reputation, and the novelty of such an action, caused this momentary ascendancy to appear true, in spite of its improbability; for such was Murat, a theatrical monarch by

the splendour of his dress, and a true king by his extraordinary valour
and his inexhaustible activity; bold as the attack, and always armed
with that air of superiority, that threatening boldness, which is the
most dangerous of offensive weapons.

He had not marched long, however, before he was forced to halt.
At Griednewa, between Gjatz and Borodino, the high road suddenly
descends into a deep ravine, whence it again rises as suddenly to
a spacious height, which Kutusoff had ordered Konownitzin to
defend. That general at first made a vigorous resistance against the
foremost troops of Murat; but as the army closely followed the latter,
every moment gave increased energy to the attack, and diminished
that of the defence; presently the advanced-guard of the viceroy
engaged on the right of the Russians, where a charge by the Italian
chasseurs was withstood for a moment by the Cossacks, which
excited astonishment; they became intermixed.

Platoff himself admitted that in this affair an officer was wounded
near him, at which he was by no means surprised; but that he
nevertheless caused the sorcerer who accompanied him to be flogged
before all his Cossacks, loudly charging him with laziness for
neglecting to turn aside the balls by his conjurations, as he had been
expressly directed to do.

Konownitzin was vanquished and retired; on the 5th his blood-
stained track was followed to the vast convent of Kolotskoi; fortified
as these habitations were of old in those too highly vaunted Gothic
ages, when civil wars were so frequent, that every place, not excepting
even these sacred abodes of peace, was transformed into a military
post.

Konownitzin, who was attacked on both right and left, made no
stand either at Kolotskoi or Golowina; but when the advanced-guard
debouched from that village, it beheld the whole plain and the woods
infested with Cossacks, the rye-crops spoiled, the villages sacked; in
short, a general destruction. By these signs it recognised the field of
battle, which Kutusoff was preparing for the grand army. Behind these
clouds of Scythians were perceived three villages; they presented a
line of a league in extent. The intervals between them, intersected by
ravines and woods, were covered with the enemy's riflemen. In a first

moment of ardour, some French horsemen galloped into the midst of these Russians, and were nearly cut off.

Napoleon then appeared on a height, from which he took a survey of the whole country, with that eye of a conqueror which sees every thing at once, and without confusion: which penetrates through obstacles, puts aside accessories, discovers the capital point, and fixes it with the look of an eagle, like prey on which he is about to dart with all his might and all his impetuosity.

He knew that, a league before him, at Borodino, the Kologha, a river running in a ravine, along the margin of which he proceeded a few wersts, turned abruptly to the left, and discharged itself into the Moskwa. He guessed that a chain of considerable heights alone could have opposed its course, and so suddenly changed its direction. These were, no doubt, occupied by the enemy's army, and on this side it could not be easily attacked. But the Kologha, both banks of which he followed, while it covered the right of the position, left their left exposed.

The maps of the country were insufficient; at any rate, as the ground necessarily sloped towards the principal stream, which was the most considerable, merely from being the lowest, it followed, that the ravines which ran into it must rise, become shallower, and be at length lost, as they receded from the Kologha. Besides, the road to Smolensk, which ran on his right, sufficiently marked their commencement; why should it have been formerly carried to a distance from the principal stream of water, and consequently from the most habitable places, if not to avoid the ravine and the hills which bordered them?

The demonstrations of the enemy corresponded with these inductions of his experience,—no precautions, no resistance in front of their right and their centre; but before their left a greater number of troops, a marked solicitude to profit by the slightest accidents of the ground, in order to dispute it, and, finally, a formidable redoubt; this was, of course, their weak side, since they covered it with such care. Nay, more; it was on the flank of the high road, and on that of the grand army, that this redoubt was placed; it was therefore of the utmost importance to carry it, if he would advance: Napoleon gave orders to that effect.

How much the historian is at a loss for words to express the *coup d'œil* of a man of genius!

The villages and the woods were immediately occupied; on the left and in the centre were the army of Italy, Compans's division, and Murat; on the right, Poniatowski. The attack was general; for the army of Italy and the Polish army appeared at once on the two wings of the grand imperial column. These three masses drove back the Russian rear-guards upon Borodino, and the whole war was concentrated on a single point.

This curtain being withdrawn, the first Russian redoubt was discovered; too much detached in advance of their position, which it defended without being defended by it. The nature of the ground had compelled the choice of this insulated situation.

Compans skilfully availed himself of the undulations of the ground; its elevations served as platforms to his guns for battering the redoubt, and screened his infantry while drawing up into columns of attack. The 61st marched foremost; the redoubt was taken by a single effort, and with the bayonet; but Bagration sent reinforcements, by which it was retaken. Three times did the 61st recover it from the Russians, and three times was it driven out again; but at length it maintained itself in it, covered with blood and half destroyed.[1]

Next day, when the emperor reviewed that regiment, he inquired where was its third battalion? "In the redoubt," was the reply of the colonel. But the affair did not stop there; a neighbouring wood still swarmed with Russian light troops, who sallied every moment from this retreat to renew their attacks, which were supported by three divisions: at length the attack of Schewardino by Morand, and of the woods of Elnia by Poniatowski completely disheartened the troops of Bagration, and Murat's cavalry cleared the plain. It was chiefly the firmness of a Spanish regiment that foiled the enemy; they at last gave way, and that redoubt, which had been their advanced post, became ours.

At the same time the emperor assigned its place to each corps, the rest of the army formed in line, and a general discharge of musketry, accompanied at intervals with that of a few cannon, ensued. It continued till each side had fixed its limit, and darkness rendered their fire uncertain.

One of Davoust's regiments then sought to take its rank in the first line. Owing to the darkness, it passed beyond it, and got into the midst of the Russian cuirassiers, who attacked it, threw it into disorder, took from it three pieces of cannon, and killed or took three hundred men. The rest immediately fell into platoons, forming a shapeless mass, but making so formidable a resistance, that the enemy could not again break it; and this regiment, with diminished numbers, finally regained its place in the line of battle.

1. The redoubt was not taken by assault; it was abandoned by the Russians. Of course, no such reply as that which M. Segur mentions, was made to Napoleon by the colonel of the third battalion.—*Ed.*

CHAPTER VI

DISPOSITION OF THE RUSSIANS AT BORODINO

THE emperor encamped behind the army of Italy, on the left of the high road; the old guard formed in squares around his tents. As soon as the fire of small arms had ceased, the fires were kindled. Those of the Russians burned brightly, in an immense semicircle; ours gave a pale, unequal, and irregular light,—the troops arriving late and in haste, on an unknown ground, where nothing was prepared for them, and where there was a want of wood, especially in the centre and on the left.

The emperor slept little. On general Caulaincourt's return from the conquered redoubt, as no prisoners had fallen into our hands, Napoleon, surprised, kept asking him repeatedly, "Had not his cavalry then charged apropos? Were the Russians determined to conquer or die?"—The answer was, that "being fanaticised by their leaders, and accustomed to fight with the Turks, who give no quarter, they suffered themselves to be killed sooner than surrender." The emperor then fell into a deep meditation; and judging that a battle of artillery would be the most certain, he multiplied his orders to bring up, with all speed, the parks which had not yet joined him.

That very night, a cold mizzling rain began to fall, and the autumn set in with a violent wind. This was an additional enemy, which it was necessary to take into account; for this period of the year corresponded with the age on which Napoleon was entering, and every one knows the influence of the seasons of the year on the like seasons of life.

During that night how many different agitations! The soldiers and the officers had to prepare their arms, to repair their clothing, and to combat cold and hunger; for their existence was a continual combat. The generals, and the emperor himself, were uneasy, lest their defeat of the preceding day should have disheartened the Russians, and they should steal off in the dark. Murat had anticipated this; we imagined several times that we saw their fires burn more faintly, and that we heard the noise of their departure; but day alone eclipsed the light of the enemy's bivouacs.

This time there was no need to go far in quest of them. The sun of the 6th found the two armies again, and displayed them to each other, on the same ground where it had left them the evening before. There was a general feeling of exultation. This vague, feeble, moveable warfare, in which our efforts were paralysed, where we were plunging into a fathomless depth, was at last brought to a point! our feet touched the bottom,—we were close to the goal! all was about to be decided.

The emperor took advantage of the first rays of dawn, to advance between the two lines, and to go from height to height along the whole front of the hostile army. He found the Russians crowning all the eminences, in a vast semicircle, two leagues in extent, from the Moskwa to the old Moscow road. Their right bordered the Kologha, from its influx into the Moskwa to Borodino; their centre, from Gorcka to Semenowska, was the salient part of their line. Their right and left receded. The Kologha rendered their right inaccessible.

The emperor perceived this immediately and as, from its distance, this wing was not more threatening than vulnerable, he took no account of it. For him then the Russian army commenced at Gorcka, a village situated on the high road, and at the point of an elevated plain which overlooks Borodino and the Kologha. This sharp projection is surrounded by the Kologha, and by a deep and marshy ravine; its lofty crest, to which the high road ascends on leaving Borodino, was strongly entrenched, and formed a separate work on the right of the Russian centre, of which it was the extremity.

On its left, and within reach of its fire, rose a detached hill, commanding the whole plain; it was crowned by a formidable redoubt, provided with twenty-one pieces of cannon. In front and on its right it was encompassed by the Kologha and by ravines; its left inclined to and supported itself upon a long and wide table-land, the foot of which descended to a muddy ravine, a branch of the Kologha. The crest of this table-land, which was lined by the Russians, declined and receded as it ran towards the left, in front of the grand army; it then kept rising as far as the yet smoking ruins of the village of Semenowska. This salient point terminated Barclay's command and the centre of the enemy: it was armed with a strong battery, covered by an entrenchment.

Here began the left wing of the Russians under Bagration. The less elevated crest which it occupied undulated as it gradually receded to Utitza, a village on the old Moscow road, where the field of battle ended. Two hills, armed with redoubts, and bearing diagonally upon the entrenchment of Semenowska, which flanked them, marked the front of Bagration.

From Semenowska to the wood of Utitza there was an interval of about twelve hundred paces. It was the nature of the ground which had decided Kutusoff thus to refuse this wing; for here the ravine, which was under the table-land in the centre, just commenced. It was scarcely an obstacle; the slopes of its banks were very gentle, and the summits suitable for artillery were at some distance from its margin. This side was evidently the most accessible, since the redoubt of the 61st, which that regiment had taken the preceding day, no longer defended the approach: this was even favoured by a wood of large pines, extending from the redoubt just mentioned to that which appeared to terminate the line of the Russians.

But their left wing did not end there. The emperor knew that behind this wood was the old Moscow road; that it turned round the left wing of the Russians, and passing behind their army, ran again into the new Moscow road in front of Mojaisk. He judged that it must be occupied; and, in fact, Tutchkoff with his *corps d'armée*, had placed himself across it at the entrance of a wood; he had covered himself by two heights, on which he had planted a formidable artillery.

But this was of little consequence, because, between this detached corps and the last Russian redoubt, there was a space of five or six hundred fathoms and a covered ground. If we did not begin with overwhelming Tutchkoff, we might therefore occupy it, pass between him and the last of Bagration's redoubts, and take the left wing of the enemy in flank; but the emperor could not satisfy himself on this point, as the Russian advanced posts and the woods forbade his farther advance, and intercepted his view.

Having finished his reconnoissance, he formed his plan. "Eugene shall be the pivot!" he exclaimed, "it is the right that must commence. As soon as, under cover of the wood, it has taken the redoubt opposite to it, it must make a movement to the left, and march on the Russian flank, sweeping and driving back their whole army upon their right and into the Kologha."

The general plan thus conceived, he applied himself to the details. During the night, three batteries, of sixty guns each, must be opposed to the Russian redoubts; two facing their left, the third before their centre. At daybreak, Poniatowski and his army, reduced to 5000 men, must advance on the old Smolensk road, turning the wood on which the French right wing and the Russian left were supported. He would flank the one and annoy the other; the army would wait for the report of his first shots.

Instantly, the whole of the artillery should commence upon the left of the Russians, its fire would open their ranks and redoubts, and Davoust and Ney should rush into the gaps; they should be supported by Junot and his Westphalians, by Murat and his cavalry, and lastly, by the emperor himself, with 20,000 guards. It was against these two redoubts that the first efforts should be made; it was by them that he would penetrate into the hostile army, thenceforth mutilated, and whose centre and right would then be uncovered, and almost enveloped.

Nevertheless, as the Russians showed themselves in redoubled masses on their centre and their right, threatening the Moscow road, the sole line of operation of the grand army; as in throwing his chief force and himself on their left, Napoleon was about to place the Kologha between him and that road, his only means of retreat, he resolved to strengthen the army of Italy which occupied it, and joined with it two of Davoust's divisions and Grouchy's cavalry. As to his left, he judged that one Italian division, the Bavarian cavalry, and that of Ornano, about 10,000 men, would suffice to cover it. Such were the plans of Napoleon.

CHAPTER VII

PREPARATIONS
OF THE FRENCH

HE was on the heights of Borodino, taking a last survey of the whole field of battle, which confirmed him in his plan, when Davoust made his appearance. This marshal had just been examining the left of the Russians with greater care, because this was the ground on which he was to act, and he distrusted his eyesight.

He begged the emperor "to place at his disposal five divisions, 35,000 strong, and to unite with them Poniatowski, whose force was too weak to turn the enemy by itself. Next day he would set this force in motion; he would cover its march with the last shades of night, and with the wood on which the Russian left wing was supported, and beyond which he would pass by following the old road from Smolensk to Moscow; then, all at once, by a rapid manœuvre, he would deploy 40,000 French and Poles on the flank and in the rear of that wing. There, while the emperor would occupy the front of the Muscovites by a general attack, he would march impetuously from redoubt to redoubt, from reserve to reserve, driving every thing from left to right on the high-road of Mojaisk, where they should put an end at once to the Russian army, the battle, and the war."

The emperor listened attentively to the marshal; but, after meditating in silence for some minutes, he replied, "No! it is too great a movement; it would remove me too far from my object, and make me lose too much time."

The prince of Echmühl, however, from conviction, persisted in his point; he undertook to accomplish his manœuvre before six in the morning; he protested that in another hour the greatest part of its effect would be produced. Napoleon, impatient of contradiction, sharply replied with this exclamation, "Ah! you are always for turning the enemy; it is too dangerous a manœuvre!" The marshal, after this rebuff, said no more: he then returned to his post, murmuring against a prudence which he thought unseasonable, and to which he was not accustomed; and he knew not to what cause to attribute it, unless the looks of so many allies, who were not to be relied on, an army so reduced, a position so remote, and age, had rendered Napoleon less enterprising than he was.

The emperor, having decided, had returned to his camp, when Murat, whom the Russians had so often deceived, induced him to imagine that they were going to run away once more without fighting. In vain did Rapp, who was sent to observe their attitude, return and say, that he had seen them entrenching themselves more and more; that they were numerous, judiciously disposed, and appeared determined much rather to attack, if they were not anticipated, than to retreat: Murat persisted in his opinion, and the emperor, uneasy, returned to the heights of Borodino.

He there perceived long black columns of troops covering the high road and spreading over the plain; then large convoys of wagons, provisions, and ammunition, in short, all the dispositions indicative of a stay and a battle. At that very moment, though he had taken with him but a few attendants, that he might not attract the notice and the fire of the enemy, he was recognised by the Russian batteries, and a cannon-shot suddenly interrupted the silence of that day.

For, as it frequently happens, nothing was so calm as the day preceding that great battle. It was like a thing mutually agreed upon! Wherefore do each other useless injury? Was not the next day to decide every thing? Besides, every one had to prepare himself; the different corps, their arms, their force, their ammunition; they had to resume all their unity, which on a march is always more or less deranged. The generals had to observe their reciprocal dispositions of attack, defence, and retreat, in order to adapt them to each other and the ground, and to leave as little as possible to chance.

Thus these two colossal foes, on the point of commencing their terrible contest, watched each other attentively, measured one another with their eyes, and silently prepared for a tremendous conflict.

The emperor, who could no longer entertain doubts of a battle, returned to his tent to dictate the order of it. There he meditated on his awful situation. He saw that the two armies were equal; about 120,000 men, and 600 pieces of cannon on each side. The Russians had the advantage of ground, of speaking but one language, of one uniform, of being a single nation, fighting for the same cause, but a great number of them being irregular troops and recruits. The French had as many men, but more soldiers; for the state of his corps had just been submitted to him; he had before his eyes an account of the strength of his divisions, and as it was neither a review, nor a distribution, but a battle that was in prospect, this time the statements were not exaggerated. His army was reduced indeed, but sound, supple, nervous—like those manly bodies, which, having just lost the plumpness of youth, display forms more masculine and strongly marked.

Still, during the last few days that he had marched in the midst of it, he had found it silent, from that silence which is imposed by great expectation or great astonishment; like Nature the moment before a violent tempest, or crowds at the instant of an extraordinary danger.

He felt that it wanted rest of some kind or other, but that there was no rest for it but in death or victory; for he had brought it into such a necessity of conquering, that it must triumph at any rate. The temerity of the situation into which he had urged it was evident, but he knew that of all faults that was the one which the French most willingly forgave; that in short they doubted neither of themselves nor of him, nor of the general result, whatever might be their individual hardships.

He reckoned, moreover, on their habit and thirst of glory, and even on their curiosity; no doubt they wished to see Moscow, to be able to say that they had been there, to receive there the promised reward, perhaps to plunder, and, above all, there to find repose. He did not observe in them enthusiasm, but something more firm: an entire confidence in his star, in his genius, the consciousness of their superiority, and the proud assurance of conquerors in the presence of the vanquished.

Full of these sentiments, he dictated a proclamation, simple, grave, and frank, such as befitted the circumstances, and men who were not just commencing their career, and whom, after so many sufferings, it would have been idle to pretend to exalt.

Accordingly, he addressed himself solely to the reason of all, or, what is the same thing, to the real interest of each; he finished with glory, the only passion to which he could appeal in these deserts, the last of the noble motives by which it was possible to act upon soldiers always victorious, enlightened by an advanced civilisation and long experience; in short, of all generous illusions, the only one that could have carried them so far. This harangue will some day be deemed admirable; it was worthy of the commander and of the army; it did honour to both.

"Soldiers!" said he, "here is the battle which you have so ardently desired. Victory will now depend upon yourselves; it is necessary to us; it will give us abundance, good winter quarters, and a speedy return home! Behave as you did at Austerlitz, at Friedland, at Witepsk, and at Smolensk, and afford to remotest posterity occasion to cite your conduct on that day; let it be said of you, 'He was in the great battle under the walls of Moscow!'"

CHAPTER VIII

NAPOLEON'S CONCERNS

IN the middle of the day, Napoleon remarked an extraordinary movement in the enemy's camp; in fact, the whole Russian army was drawn up and under arms, and Kutusoff, surrounded with every species of religious and military pomp, took his station in the midst of it. He had made his popes and his archimandrites dress themselves in those splendid and majestic insignia, which they have inherited from the Greeks. They marched before him, carrying the venerated symbols of their religion, and particularly that holy image, formerly the protectress of Smolensk, which, by their account, had been miraculously saved from the profanation of the sacrilegious French.

When the Russian saw that his soldiers were sufficiently excited by this extraordinary spectacle, he raised his voice, and began by putting them in mind of heaven, the only country which remains to the slave. In the name of the religion of equality, he endeavoured to animate these serfs to defend the property of their masters; but it was principally by exhibiting to them that sacred image which had taken refuge in their ranks, that he appealed to their courage, and raised their indignation.

Napoleon, in his mouth, "was a universal despot! the tyrannical disturber of the world! a poor worm! an arch-rebel, who had overturned their altars, and polluted them with blood; who had exposed the true ark of the Lord, represented by the holy image, to the profanation of men, and the inclemency of the seasons." He then told them of their cities reduced to ashes; reminded them that they were about to fight for their wives and children; added a few words respecting the emperor, and concluded by appealing to their piety and their patriotism. These were the virtues of instinct with this rude and simple people, who had not yet advanced beyond sensations, but who, for that very reason, were so much more formidable as soldiers; less diverted from obedience by reasoning; confined by slavery to a narrow circle, in which they are reduced to a small number of sensations, which are the only sources of their wants, wishes, and ideas.

As to other characteristics, proud for want of comparison, and credulous as they are proud, from ignorance—worshippers of images, idolaters as much as Christians can be; for they had converted that religion of the soul, which is wholly intellectual and moral, into one entirely physical and material, to bring it to the level of their brute and short capacity.

This solemn spectacle, however, their general's address, the exhortations of their officers, and the benedictions of their priests, served to render their courage fanatical. All, even to the meanest soldier, fancied themselves devoted by God himself to the defence of Heaven and their sacred soil.

With the French there was no solemnity, either religious or military, no review, no means of excitation; even the address of the emperor was not distributed till very late, and read the next morning so near the time of action, that several corps were actually engaged before they could hear it read. The Russians, however, whom so many powerful motives should have inflamed, added to their invocations the sword of St. Michael, thus seeking to borrow aid from all the powers of heaven; while the French sought for it only within themselves, persuaded that real strength exists only in the heart, and that *there* is to be found the "celestial host."

Chance so ordered it, that on that very day the emperor received from Paris the portrait of the king of Rome, that infant, whose birth had been hailed by the empire with the same transports of joy and hope as it had been by the emperor. Every day since that happy event, the emperor, in the interior of his palace, had given loose, when near his child, to the expression of the most tender feelings; when, therefore, in the midst of these distant fields, and all these menacing preparations, he saw once more that sweet countenance, how his warlike soul melted! With his own hand he exhibited this picture outside his tent; he then called his officers, and even some of the soldiers of his old guard, desirous of sharing his pleasure with these veteran grenadiers, of showing his private family to his military family, and making this symbol of hope shine in the midst of imminent peril.[1]

In the evening, an aide-de-camp of Marmont, who had been despatched from the field of battle near Salamanca, arrived at that of Moskwa. It was the same Fabvier who has since made such a figure in our civil dissensions. The emperor received graciously the aide-de-camp of the vanquished general. On the eve of a battle, the fate of which was so uncertain, he felt disposed to be indulgent to a defeat; he listened to all that was said to him respecting the scattered state of his forces in Spain, and the number of commanders-in-chief, and admitted the justice of it all; but he explained his reasons, which it enters not into our province to mention here.[2]

Night returned, and with it came the fear that, under cover of its shades, the Russian army might escape from the field of battle. Napoleon's anxiety was so great as to prevent him from sleeping. He kept calling incessantly to know the hour, inquiring if any noise was heard, and sending persons to ascertain if the enemy was still before him. His doubts on this subject were so strong, that he had given orders that his proclamation should not be read to his troops until the next morning, and then only in case of the certainty of a battle.

Tranquillized for a few moments, anxiety of an opposite description again seized him. He became frightened at the destitute state of the soldiers. Weak and famished as they were, how could they support a long and terrible shock? In this danger he looked upon his guard as his sole resource: it seemed to be his security for both armies. He sent for Bessières, the marshal in whom he had the greatest confidence for commanding it; he wished to be certain that this chosen reserve wanted nothing;—he called him back several times, and repeated his pressing questions. He desired that these old soldiers should have three days' biscuit and rice distributed among them from their wagons of reserve; finally, dreading that his orders had not been obeyed, he got up once more, and questioned the grenadiers on guard at the entrance of his tent, if they had received these provisions. Satisfied by their answer, he went in, and soon fell into a doze.

Shortly after, he called once more. His aide-de-camp found him now supporting his head with both hands; he seemed, by what was heard, to be meditating on the vanities of glory. "What is war? A trade of barbarians, the whole art of which consists in being the strongest on a given point!" He then complained of the fickleness of fortune, which he said he began to experience. Seeming to revert to more encouraging ideas, he recollected what had been told him of the tardiness and carelessness of Kutusoff, and expressed his surprise that Beningsen had not been preferred to him. He thought of the critical situation into which he had brought himself, and added, "that a great day was at hand, that the battle would be a terrible one." He asked Rapp if he thought we should gain the victory? "No doubt;" was the reply, "but it will be sanguinary." "I know it," resumed Napoleon, "but I have 80,000 men; I shall lose 20,000, I shall enter Moscow with 60,000: the stragglers will there rejoin us, and afterwards the battalions on the march, and we shall be stronger than we were before the battle." In this estimate he seemed to include neither his guard nor the cavalry.

Again assailed by his first anxiety, he sent once more to examine the attitude of the Russians; he was informed that their fires burned with undiminished brightness, and that by the number of these, and the moving shadows surrounding them, it was supposed that it was not merely a rear-guard, but a whole army that kept feeding them. The certainty of their presence at last quieted the emperor, and he tried to take some rest.

But the marches which he had recently made with the army, the fatigues of the preceding days and nights, so many cares, and his intense and anxious expectation, had worn him out; the chilness of the atmosphere had struck to him: an irritating fever, a dry cough, and excessive thirst, consumed him. During the remainder of the night, he made vain attempts to quench the burning thirst which consumed him. This fresh disorder was complicated with an old complaint; he had been struggling since the day before with a painful attack of that cruel disorder[3] which had been long threatening him.

At last at five o'clock, one of Ney's officers came to inform him that the marshal was still in sight of the Russians, and wished to begin the attack. This news seemed to restore the strength of which the fever had deprived him. He arose, called his officers, and sallied out, exclaiming, "We have them at last! Forward! Let us go and open the gates of Moscow."

1. After having shown the portrait to his officers, Napoleon exclaimed, "Take him away; he sees a field of battle too soon!"
2. Napoleon, on the contrary, expressed extreme dissatisfaction at the conduct of Marshal Marmont.—*Ed.*
3. Dysuria.

CHAPTER IX

THE BATTLE OF BORODINO

IT was half-past five in the morning, when Napoleon arrived near the redoubt which had been conquered on the 5th of September. There he waited for the first dawn of day, and for the first fire of Poniatowski's infantry. The sun rose. The emperor, showing it to his officers, exclaimed, "Behold the sun of Austerlitz!" But it was opposite to us. It rose on the Russian side, made us conspicuous to their fire, and dazzled us. We then first perceived that, owing to the darkness, our batteries had been placed out of reach of the enemy, and it was necessary to push them more forward. The enemy allowed this to be done: he seemed to hesitate in being the first to break the awful silence.

The emperor's attention was directed towards his right, when all at once about seven o'clock, the battle began upon his left. Shortly after, he was informed, that one of the regiments of Prince Eugene, the 106th, had got possession of the village of Borodino, and its bridge, which it should have destroyed; but that, being carried away by the ardour of success, it had crossed that passage in spite of the cries of its general, in order to attack the heights of Gorcki, where it was overwhelmed by the front and flank fires of the Russians. It was added, that the general who commanded that brigade had been killed, and that the 106th regiment would have been entirely destroyed had it not been for the 92d, which voluntarily ran up to its assistance and collected and brought back its survivors.

It was Napoleon himself who had just ordered his left wing to make a violent attack. Probably, he had only reckoned on a partial execution of his orders, and wished to keep the enemy's attention directed to that side. But he multiplied his orders, used the most violent excitations, and engaged a battle in front, the plan of which he had conceived in an oblique order.

During this action, the emperor judging that Poniatowski was closing with the enemy on the old Moscow road, gave him the signal to attack. Suddenly, from that peaceful plain, and the silent hills, volumes of fire and smoke were seen spouting out, followed by a multitude of explosions, and the whistling of bullets, tearing the air in every direction. In the midst of this noise, Davoust, with the divisions of Compans and Dessaix, and thirty pieces of cannon in front, advanced rapidly on the first Russian redoubt.

The enemy's musketry began, and was answered only by the French cannon. The French infantry marched without firing: it was hurrying on to get within reach of and extinguish the fires of the enemy, when Compans, the general of that column, and his bravest soldiers, were wounded and fell: the rest, disconcerted, halted under the shower of balls in order to return it, when Rapp, rushing to replace Compans, again led his soldiers on with fixed bayonets, and at a running pace, against the enemy's redoubt.

He was himself just on the point of reaching it the first, when he was in his turn hit: it was his twenty-second wound. A third general, who succeeded him, also fell. Davoust himself was wounded. Rapp was carried to the emperor, who said to him, "What, Rapp, always hit! But what are they doing above?" The aide-de-camp answered, that it would require the guard to finish. "No!" replied Napoleon, "I shall take good care of that; I have no wish to see it destroyed; I shall gain the battle without it."[1]

Ney, then, with his three divisions reduced to 10,000 men, hastened into the plain to the assistance of Davoust. The enemy divided his fire. Ney rushed forward. The 57th regiment of Compans's division, finding itself supported, took fresh courage; by a last effort it succeeded in reaching the enemy's intrenchments, scaled them, mingled with the Russians, put them to the bayonet, overthrew and killed the most obstinate of them. The rest fled, and the 57th maintained itself in its conquest. At the same time Ney made so furious an attack on the two other redoubts, that he wrested them from the enemy.

It was now mid-day; the left of the Russian line being thus forced, and the plain cleared, the emperor ordered Murat to advance with his cavalry and complete the victory. An instant was sufficient for that prince to show himself on the heights and in the midst of the enemy, who again made his appearance there; for the second Russian line and the reinforcements, led on by Bagawout and sent by Tutchkoff, had come to the assistance of the first line. They all rushed forward, resting upon Semenowska, in order to retake their redoubts. The French, who were still in the disorder of victory, were astonished and fell back.

The Westphalians, whom Napoleon had just sent to the assistance of Poniatowski, were at that moment crossing the wood which separated that prince from the rest of the army; through the dust and smoke they got a glimpse of our troops, who were retreating. By the direction of their march they guessed them to be enemies, and fired upon them. They persisted in their mistake, and thereby increased the disorder.

The enemy's cavalry vigorously followed up their advantage; they surrounded Murat, who had forgot himself in his endeavours to rally his troops; they were already stretching out their arms to lay hold of him, when he threw himself into the redoubt and escaped from them. But there he found only some panic-struck soldiers, running round the parapet in a state of the greatest confusion. They only wanted an outlet to run away.

The presence of the king and his cries first restored confidence to a few. He himself seized a musket: with one hand he fought, with the other he elevated and waved his plume, calling to all his men and restoring them to their first valour by that authority which example gives. At the same time Ney had again formed his divisions. Their fire stopped the enemy's cuirassiers, and threw their ranks into disorder. They let go their hold, Murat was at last disengaged, and the heights were reconquered.

Scarcely had the king emerged from this peril, when he ran into another; with the cavalry of Bruyere and Nansouty, he rushed upon the enemy, and by obstinate and repeated charges overthrew the Russian lines, pushed and drove them back on their centre, and, within an hour, completed the total defeat of their left wing.

But the heights of the ruined village of Semenowska, where the left of the enemy's centre commenced, were still untouched; the reinforcements which Kutusoff incessantly drew from his right, were supported by them. Their commanding fire was poured down upon Ney and Murat's troops, and stopped their victory; it was indispensable to acquire that position. Maubourg, with his cavalry, first cleared the front; Friant, one of Davoust's generals, followed him with his infantry. Dufour and the 15th light were the first to climb the steep; they dislodged the Russians from the village, the ruins of which were badly entrenched. Friant, although wounded, followed up and secured this advantage.

1. The guard was never brought into action but to decide or complete the victory. In this instance, the battle had not long been begun.—*Ed.*

CHAPTER X

THE STRUGGLE
FOR DOMINANCE

THIS vigorous action opened to us the road to victory; it was necessary to rush into it; but Murat and Ney were exhausted; they halted, and, while they were rallying their troops, they sent to Napoleon to ask for reinforcements. Napoleon was then seized with a hesitation which he never before displayed; he deliberated long with himself, and at last, after repeated orders and counter-orders to his young guard, he expressed his belief that the appearance of Friant, and Maubourg's troops on the heights would be sufficient, the decisive moment not appearing to him to be yet arrived.

But Kutusoff took advantage of this respite, which he had no reason to expect; he summoned the whole of his reserve, even to the Russian guards, to the support of his uncovered left wing. Bagration, with all these reinforcements, re-formed his line, his right resting on the great battery which Prince Eugene was attacking, his left on the wood which bounded the field of battle towards Psarewo. His fire cut our ranks to pieces; his attack was violent, impetuous, and simultaneous; infantry, artillery, and cavalry, all made a grand effort. Ney and Murat stood firm against this tempest; the question with them was no longer about following up the victory, but about retaining it.

The soldiers of Friant, drawn up in front of Semenowska, repelled the first charges, but when they were assailed with a shower of balls and grape shot, they began to give way; one of their leaders got tired, and gave orders to retreat. At that critical moment, Murat ran up to him, and, seizing him by the collar, exclaimed, "What are you about?" The colonel, pointing to the ground, covered with half his troops, answered, "You see well enough that it is impossible for us to stand here."—"Very well, I will remain!" exclaimed the king. These words stopped the officer: he looked Murat steadily in the face, and, turning round, coolly said, "You are right! Soldiers, face to the enemy! Let us go and be killed!"[1]

Meanwhile, Murat had just sent back Borelli to the emperor to ask for assistance; that officer pointed to the clouds of dust which the charges of the cavalry were raising upon the heights, which had hitherto remained tranquil since they had been taken. Some cannon-balls also for the first time fell close to where Napoleon was stationed; the enemy seemed to be approaching; Borelli insisted, and the emperor promised his young guard. But, scarcely had it advanced a few paces, when he himself called out to it to halt. The count de Lobau, however, made it advance by degrees, under pretence of dressing the line. Napoleon perceiving this, repeated his order.

Fortunately, the artillery of the reserve advanced at that moment, to take a position on the conquered heights; Lauriston had obtained the emperor's consent to that manœuvre, but it was at first rather a permission than an order. Shortly after however, he thought it so important, that he urged its execution with the only movement of impatience he exhibited during the whole of that day.

It is not known whether his doubts as to the results of Prince Poniatowski and Prince Eugene's engagement on the right and left kept him in uncertainty; what is certain is, that he seemed to be apprehensive lest the extreme left of the Russians should escape from the Poles, and return to take possession of the field of battle near the rear of Ney and Murat. This at least was one of the causes of his retaining his guard in observation upon that point. To such as pressed him, his answer was, "that he wished to have a clearer view; that his battle was not yet begun; that it would be a long one; that they must learn to wait; that time entered into every thing; that it was the element of which all things are composed; that nothing was yet sufficiently unravelled." He then inquired the hour, and added, "that the hour of his battle was not yet come; that it would begin in two hours."

But it never began: the whole of that day he was sitting down, or walking about leisurely, in front and a little to the left of the redoubt which had been conquered on the 5th, on the borders of a ravine, at a great distance from the battle, of which he could scarcely see any thing after it got beyond the heights; not at all uneasy when he saw it return nearer to him, nor impatient with his own troops, or the enemy. He merely made some gestures of melancholy resignation, on every occasion, when they came to inform him of the loss of his best generals. He rose several times to take a few turns, but immediately sat down again.[2]

Every one around him looked at him with astonishment. Hitherto, during these great shocks, he had displayed an active coolness; but here it was a dead calm, a nerveless and sluggish inactivity. Some fancied they traced in it that dejection which is generally the follower of violent sensations: others, that he had already become indifferent to every thing, even to the emotion of battles. Several remarked, that the calm constancy and *sang froid* which great men display on these great occasions, turn, in the course of time, to phlegm and heaviness, when age has worn out their springs. Those who were most devoted to him, accounted for his immobility by the necessity of not changing his place too much, when he was commanding over such an extent, in order that the bearers of intelligence might know where to find him. Finally, there were others who, on much better grounds, attributed it to the shock which his health had sustained, to a secret malady, and to the commencement of a violent indisposition.

The generals of artillery, who were also surprised at their stagnation, quickly availed themselves of the permission to fight which was just given them. They very soon reached the summit of the heights. Eighty pieces of cannon were discharged at once. The Russian cavalry was first broken by that brazen line, and obliged to take refuge behind its infantry.

The latter advanced in dense masses, in which our balls at first made wide and deep holes; they still, however, continued to advance, when the French batteries crushed them by a second discharge of grape-shot. Whole platoons fell at once; their soldiers were seen trying to keep together under this terrible fire. Every instant, separated by the dead bodies, they closed together over them, treading them under foot.

At last they halted, not daring to advance farther, and yet unwilling to retreat; either because they were struck, and, as it were, petrified with horror, in the midst of this great destruction, or because Bagration was wounded at that moment; or, perhaps, because their generals, after the failure of their first disposition, knew not how to change it, from not possessing, like Napoleon, the great art of putting such immense bodies into motion at once, in unison, and without confusion. In short, these listless masses allowed themselves to be mowed down for two hours, making no other movement than their fall. It was a most horrible massacre; and our brave and intelligent artillerymen could not help admiring the motionless, blind, and resigned courage of their enemies.

The victors were the first to tire out. They became impatient at the tardiness of this battle of artillery. Their ammunition being nearly exhausted; they came to a decision in consequence of which Ney moved forward, extending his right, which he made to advance rapidly, and again turn the left of the new front which had been opposed to him. Davoust and Murat seconded him, and the remnants of Ney's corps became the conqueror over the remains of Bagration's.

The battle then ceased in the plain, and became concentrated on the rest of the enemy's heights, and near the great redoubt, which Barclay, with the centre and the right, continued to defend obstinately against Eugene.

In this manner, about mid-day, the whole of the French right wing, Ney, Davoust, and Murat, after annihilating Bagration and the half of the Russian line, presented itself on the half-opened flank of the remainder of the hostile army, of which they could see the whole interior, the reserves, the abandoned rears, and even the commencement of the retreat.

But as they felt themselves too weak to throw themselves into that gap, behind a line still formidable, they called aloud for the guard. "The young guard! only let it follow them at a distance! Let it show itself, and take their place upon the heights! They themselves will then be sufficient to finish!"

General Belliard was sent by them to the emperor. He declared, "that, from their position, the eye could penetrate, without impediment, as far as the road to Mojaisk, in the rear of the Russian army; that they could there see a confused crowd of flying and wounded soldiers, and carriages retreating; that it was true there was still a ravine and a thin copse between them, but that the Russian generals were so confounded, that they had no thought of turning these to any advantage; that, in short, only a single effort was required to arrive in the middle of that disorder, to seal the enemy's discomfiture, and terminate the war!"

The emperor, however, still hesitated, doubted, and ordered that general to go and look again, and to return and bring him word. Belliard, surprised, went and returned with all speed; he reported, "that the enemy began to think better of it; that the copse was already lined with his sharp-shooters; that the opportunity was about to escape; that there was not a moment to be lost, otherwise it would require a second battle to terminate the first!"

But Bessières, who had just returned from the heights, to which Napoleon had sent him to examine the attitude of the Russians, asserted, that, "far from being in disorder, they had retreated to a second position, where they seemed to be preparing for a fresh attack." The emperor then said to Belliard, "That nothing was yet sufficiently unravelled; that to make him bring his reserves into play, he wanted to see more clearly upon his chessboard." This was his expression—which he repeated several times, at the same time pointing on one side to the old Moscow road, of which Poniatowski had not yet made himself master; on the other to an attack of the enemy's cavalry in the rear of our left wing; and, finally, to the great redoubt, against which the efforts of Prince Eugene had yet been ineffectual.

Belliard, in consternation, returned to the King of Naples, and informed him of the impossibility of obtaining the reserve from the emperor; he said, "he had found him still seated in the same place, with a suffering and dejected air, his features sunk, and a dull look; giving his orders languishingly, in the midst of these dreadful warlike noises, to which he seemed completely a stranger!" At this account, which was communicated to Ney, the latter, furious and hurried away by his ardent and impetuous character, exclaimed, "Are we then come so far, to be satisfied with a field of battle? What business has the emperor in the rear of the army? There, he is only within reach of reverses, and not of victory. Since he will no longer make war himself; since he is no longer the general, as he wishes to be the emperor everywhere, let him return to the Tuileries, and leave us to be generals for him!"

Murat was more calm; he recollected having seen the emperor the day before, as he was riding along observing that part of the enemy's line, halt several times, dismount, and with his head resting upon the cannon remain there some time in the attitude of suffering. He knew what a restless night he had passed, and that a violent and incessant cough cut short his breathing. The king guessed that fatigue, and the first attacks of the equinox, had shaken his weakened frame, and that in short, at that critical moment, the action of his genius was in a manner chained down by his body; which had sunk under the triple load of fatigue, of fever, and of a malady, which, probably, more than any other, prostrates the moral and physical strength of its victims.

Still, farther incitements were not wanting; for shortly after Belliard, Daru, urged by Dumas, and particularly by Berthier, said in a low voice to the emperor, "that from all sides it was the cry that the moment for sending the guard was now come." To which Napoleon replied, "And if there should be another battle to-morrow, where is my army to fight with?" The minister urged no farther, surprised to see, for the first time, the emperor putting off till the morrow, and adjourning his victory.

1. The guard was never brought into action but to decide or complete the victory. In this instance, the battle had not long been begun.—*Ed.*

2. Napoleon remained at the redoubt because it was a central point, whence he could best direct the movements of his army. The assertion that, during the battle, he was in a state of torpor appears, from evidence, to be erroneous.—*Ed.*

CHAPTER XI

A COSTLY VICTORY

BARCLAY, meanwhile, with the right, kept up a most obstinate struggle with Prince Eugene. The latter, immediately after the capture of Borodino, passed the Kologha in the face of the enemy's great redoubt. There, particularly, the Russians had calculated upon their steep heights, encompassed by deep and muddy ravines, upon our exhaustion, upon their entrenchments defended by heavy artillery, in short, upon 80 pieces of cannon, planted on the borders of these heights, bristling with iron and flames! But these elements, art and nature, all failed them at once; assailed by a first burst of that *French fury*, which has been so celebrated, they saw Morand's soldiers appear suddenly in the midst of them, and fled in disorder.

Eighteen hundred men of the 30th regiment, with General Bonnamy at their head, had just made this great effort.

It was there that Fabvier, the aide-de-camp of Marmont, who had arrived but the day before from the heart of Spain, made himself conspicuous; he had thrown himself as a volunteer, and on foot, at the head of the most advanced light soldiers, as if he had come there to represent the army of Spain, in the midst of the grand army; and, inspired with that rivalry of glory which makes heroes, wished to exhibit it in front, and be the first in every danger.

He fell wounded in that too famous redoubt; for the triumph was short-lived; the attack wanted concert, either from precipitation in the first assailant, or tardiness in those who followed. There was a ravine to pass, the depth of which afforded a protection from the enemy's fire; it is affirmed that many of our troops halted there. Morand, therefore, was left alone in the face of several Russian lines. It was yet only ten o'clock. Friant, who was on his right, had hot yet commenced the attack of Semenowska; and, on his left, the divisions of Gerard, Broussier, and the Italian guard, were not yet in line.

This attack, besides, should not have been made so precipitately; the intention had been only to keep Barclay in check, and occupied on that side, the battle having been arranged to begin by the right wing, and pivot on the left. This was the emperor's plan, and we know not why he himself altered it at the moment of his execution; for it was he who, on the first discharge of the artillery, sent different officers in succession to Prince Eugene, to urge his attack.

The Russians, recovering from their first surprise, rushed forward in all directions. Kutusoff and Yermoloff advanced at their head with a resolution worthy of so great an occasion. The 30th regiment, single against a whole army, ventured to attack it with the bayonet; it was enveloped, crushed, and driven out of the redoubt, where it left a third of its men, and its intrepid general pierced through with twenty wounds. Encouraged by their success, the Russians were no longer satisfied with defending themselves, but attacked in their turn. Then were seen united, on that single point, all the skill, strength, and fury, which war can bring forth. The French stood firm for four hours on the declivity of that volcano, under the shower of iron and lead which it vomited forth. But to do this, required all the skill and determination of Prince Eugene, and the idea, so insupportable to long-victorious soldiers, of confessing themselves vanquished.

Each division changed its general several times. The viceroy went from one to the other, mingling entreaties and reproaches, and, above all, reminding them of their former victories. He sent to apprise the emperor of his critical situation; but Napoleon replied, "That he could not assist him; that he must conquer; that he had only to make a greater effort; that the heat of the battle was there."[1] The prince was rallying all his forces to make a general assault, when suddenly his attention was diverted by furious cries proceeding from his left.

Ouwaroff, with two regiments of cavalry, and some thousand cossacks, had attacked his reserve, and thrown it into disorder. He ran thither instantly, and, seconded by Generals Delzons and Ornano, soon drove away that troop, which was more noisy than formidable; after which he returned to put himself at the head of a decisive attack.

It was about that time that Murat, forced to remain inactive on the plain where he commanded, had sent, for the fourth time, to his brother-in-law, to complain of the losses which his cavalry were sustaining from the Russian troops, protected by the redoubts which were opposed to Prince Eugene. "He only requested the cavalry of guard, with whose assistance he could turn the entrenched heights, and overthrow them along with the army which defended them."

The emperor seemed to give his consent, and sent in search of Bessières, who commanded these horse-guards. Unfortunately they could not find the marshal, who, by his orders, had gone to look at the battle somewhat nearer. The emperor waited nearly an hour without the least impatience, or repeating his order; and, when the marshal returned, he received him with a pleasant look, heard his report calmly, and allowed him to advance as far as he might judge it advisable.

But it was too late; he could no longer flatter himself with the idea of making the whole Russian army prisoners, or perhaps of taking entire possession of Russia; the field of battle was all he was likely to gain. He had allowed Kutusoff leisure to recollect himself, and that general had fortified all the points of difficult approach which remained to him, and his cavalry covered the plain.

The Russians had thus, for the third time, renewed their left wing, in the face of Ney and Murat. The latter summoned the cavalry of Montbrun, who had been killed. General Caulaincourt succeeded him; he found the aides-de-camp of the unfortunate Montbrun in tears for the loss of their commander. "Follow me," said he to them, "weep not for him, but come and avenge his death!"

The king pointed out to him the enemy's fresh wing; he must break through it, and push on as far as the gorge of their great battery; when there, during the time that the light cavalry is following up its advantage, he, Caulaincourt, must turn suddenly on the left with his cuirassiers, in order to take in the rear that terrible redoubt whose front fire is still mowing down the ranks of the viceroy.

Caulaincourt's reply was, "You shall see me there soon, alive or dead." He immediately set off, overthrew all before him, and turning suddenly round on the left with his cuirassiers, was the first to enter the bloody redoubt, when he was struck dead by a musket-ball. His conquest was his tomb.

They ran immediately to acquaint the emperor with this victory, and the loss which it had occasioned. The grand equerry, brother of the unfortunate general, listened, and was at first petrified; but he soon summoned courage against this misfortune, and, but for the tears which silently coursed down his cheeks, you might have thought that he felt nothing. The emperor, uttering an exclamation of sorrow, said to him, "You have heard the news, do you wish to retire?" But, as at that moment we were advancing against the enemy, the grand equerry made no reply; he did not retire; he only half uncovered himself to thank the emperor and to refuse.

While this decisive charge of cavalry was executing, the viceroy, with his infantry, was on the point of reaching the mouth of this volcano, when suddenly he saw with fires extinguished, its smoke disappear, and its summit glittering with the moving and resplendent armour of our cuirassiers. These heights, hitherto Russian, had at last become French; he hastened forward to share and terminate the victory, and to strengthen himself in this position.

But the Russians had not yet abandoned it; they returned with greater obstinacy and fury to the attack; successively as they were beat back by our troops, they were again rallied by their generals, and, finally, the greater part perished at the foot of the works which they had themselves raised.

Fortunately, their last attacking column presented itself towards Semenowska and the great redoubt without its artillery, the progress of which had no doubt been retarded by the ravines. Belliard had barely time to collect thirty cannon against this infantry. They came almost close to the mouths of our pieces, which overwhelmed them so apropos, that they wheeled round and retreated without being able even to deploy. Murat and Belliard then said, that if they could have had at that moment 10,000 infantry of the reserve, their victory would have been decisive; but that, being reduced to their cavalry, they considered themselves fortunate in being able to keep possession of the field of battle.

On his side, Grouchy, by sanguinary and repeated charges on the left of the great redoubt, secured the victory and scoured the plain. But it was impossible to pursue the fugitive Russians; fresh ravines, with armed redoubts behind them, protected their retreat. There they defended themselves with fury until the approach of night, covering in this manner the great road to Moscow, their holy city, their magazine, their depôt, their place of refuge.

From this second range of heights, their artillery overwhelmed the first which they had abandoned to us. The viceroy was obliged to conceal his panting, exhausted, and thinned lines, in the hollows of the ground, and behind the half-destroyed entrenchments. The soldiers were obliged to get upon their knees, and crouch themselves up behind these shapeless parapets. In that painful posture they remained for several hours, kept in check by the enemy, who stood in check of them.

It was about half-past three o'clock when this last victory was achieved; there had been several such during the day; each corps successively beat that which was opposed to it, without being able to take advantage of its success to decide the battle; as, not being supported in proper time by the reserve, each halted exhausted. But at last all the first obstacles were overcome; the firing gradually slackened, and got to a greater distance from the emperor. Officers were coming in to him from all parts. Poniatowski and Sebastiani, after an obstinate contest, were also victorious. The enemy halted and entrenched himself in a new position. It was getting late, our ammunition was exhausted, and the battle ended.

Belliard then returned for the third time to the emperor, whose sufferings appeared to have increased; he mounted his horse with difficulty, and rode slowly along the heights of Semenowska. He found a field of battle imperfectly gained, as the enemy's bullets, and even their musket-balls, still disputed the possession of it with us.

In the midst of these warlike noises, and the still burning ardour of Ney and Murat, he continued always in the same state, his gait desponding, and his voice languid. The sight of the Russians, however, and the noise of their continued firing, seemed again to inspire him; he went to take a nearer view of their last position, and even wished to drive them from it. But Murat, pointing to the scanty remains of our own troops, declared that it would require the guard to finish; on which, Bessières, continuing to insist, as he had always done, on the importance of this *corps d'élite*, objected "the distance the emperor was from his reinforcements; that Europe was between him and France; that it was indispensable to preserve, at least, that handful of soldiers, which was all that remained to answer for his safety." And as it was then nearly five o'clock, Berthier added, "that it was too late; that the enemy was strengthening himself, in his last position; and that it would require a sacrifice of several more thousands, without any adequate result." Napoleon then thought of nothing but to recommend the victors to be prudent. Afterwards he returned, still at the same slow pace, to his tent, that had been erected behind the battery which was carried two days before, and in front of which he had remained ever since the morning, an almost motionless spectator of all the vicissitudes of that terrible day.

As he was thus returning, he called Mortier to him, and ordered him "to make the young guard now advance, but on no account to pass the new ravine which separated us from the enemy." He added, "that he gave him in charge to guard the field of battle; that that was all he required of him; that he was at liberty to do whatever he thought necessary for that purpose, and nothing more." He recalled him shortly after to ask "if he had properly understood him; recommended him to make no attack; but merely to guard the field of battle." An hour afterwards he sent to him to reiterate the order, "neither to advance nor retreat whatever might happen."

1. Napoleon sent the legion of the Vistula to succour Prince Eugene.—*Ed.*

CHAPTER X

RESULTS OF THE BATTLE

AFTER he had retired to his tent, great mental anguish was added to his previous physical dejection. He had seen the field of battle; the places had spoken still more loudly than men; the victory which he had so eagerly pursued, and so dearly bought, was incomplete. Was this he who had always pushed his successes to the furthest possible limits, whom fortune had just found cold and inactive at a time when she was offering him her last favours?

The losses were certainly immense, and out of all proportion to the advantages gained. Every one around him had to lament the loss of a friend, a relation, or a brother; for the fate of battles had fallen on the most distinguished. Forty-three generals had been killed or wounded. What a mourning for Paris! what a triumph for its enemies! what a dangerous subject for the reflections of Germany! In his army, even in his very tent, his victory was silent, gloomy, isolated, even without flatterers!

The persons whom he had summoned, Dumas and Daru, listened to him and said nothing; but their attitude, their downcast eyes, and their silence, spoke more eloquently than words.

It was now ten o'clock. Murat, whom twelve hours' fighting had not exhausted, again came to ask him for the cavalry of his guard. "The enemy's army," said he, "is passing the Moskwa in haste and disorder;[1] I wish to surprise and finish it." The emperor repelled this sally of immoderate ardour; afterwards he dictated the bulletin of the day.

He seemed pleased at announcing to Europe, that neither he nor his guard had been at all exposed. By some this care was regarded as a refinement of self-love; but those who were better informed thought very differently. They had never seen him display any vain or gratuitous passion, and their idea was, that at that distance, and at the head of an army of foreigners, who had no other bond of union but victory, he had judged it indispensable to preserve a select and devoted body.

His enemies, in fact, would have no longer any thing to hope from fields of battle; neither his death, as he had no need to expose his person in order to insure success, nor a victory, as his genius was sufficient at a distance, even without bringing forward his reserve. As long, therefore, as this guard remained untouched, his real power and that which he derived from opinion would remain entire. It seemed to be a sort of security to him, against his allies, as well as against his enemies: on that account he took so much pains to inform Europe of the preservation of that formidable reserve; and yet it scarcely amounted to 20,000 men, of whom more than a third were new recruits.

These were powerful motives, but they did not at all satisfy men who knew that excellent reasons may be found for committing the greatest faults. They all agreed, "that they had seen the battle which had been won in the morning on the right, halt where it was favourable to us, and continue successively in front, a contest of mere strength, as in the infancy of the art! it was a battle without any plan, a mere victory of soldiers, rather than of a general! Why so much precipitation to overtake the enemy, with an army panting, exhausted, and weakened? and when we had come up with him, why neglect to complete his discomfiture, and remain bleeding and mutilated, in the midst of an enraged nation, in immense deserts, and at 800 leagues' distance from our resources?"

Murat then exclaimed, "that in this great day he had not recognized the genius of Napoleon!" The viceroy confessed "that he had no conception what could be the reason of the indecision which his adopted father had shown." Ney, when he was called on for his opinion, was singularly obstinate in advising him to retreat.[2]

Those alone who had never quitted his person, observed, that the conqueror of so many nations had been overcome by a burning fever, and above all by a fatal return of that painful malady which every violent movement, and all long and strong emotions, excited in him. They then quoted the words which he himself had written in Italy fifteen years before: "Health is indispensable in war, and nothing can replace its loss;" and the exclamation, unfortunately prophetic, which he had uttered on the plains of Austerlitz: "Ordener is worn out. One is not always fit for war; I shall be good for six years longer, after which I must lie by."

During the night, the Russians made us sensible of their vicinity by their tiresome clamours. Next morning there was an alert close to the emperor's tent. The old guard was actually obliged to run to arms; a circumstance which, after a victory, seemed insulting. The army remained motionless until noon, or, rather, it might be said, that there was no longer an army, but a single vanguard. The rest of the troops were dispersed over the field of battle, to carry off the wounded, of whom there were 20,000. They were taken to the great abbey of Kolotskoi, two leagues in the rear.

Larrey, the surgeon-in-chief, had just taken assistants from all the regiments; the *ambulances* had rejoined, but all was insufficient. He has since complained, in a printed narrative, that no troop had been left him to procure the most necessary articles in the surrounding villages.

The emperor then rode over the field of battle; never did one present so horrible an appearance. Every thing concurred to make it so; a gloomy sky, a cold rain, a violent wind, houses burnt to ashes, a plain turned topsy-turvy, covered with ruins and rubbish, in the distance the sad and sombre verdure of the trees of the north; soldiers roaming about in all directions, and hunting for provisions, even in the haversacks of their dead companions; horrible wounds, for the Russian musket-balls are larger than ours; silent bivouacs, no singing or story telling—a gloomy taciturnity.

Round the eagles were seen the remaining officers and subalterns, and a few soldiers, scarcely enough to protect the colours. Their clothes had been torn in the fury of the combat, were blackened with powder, and spotted with blood; and yet, in the midst of their rags, their misery, and disasters, they had a proud look, and at the sight of the emperor uttered some shouts of triumph, but they were rare and excited; for in this army, capable at once of analysis and enthusiasm, every one was sensible of the position of all.

French soldiers are not easily deceived; they were astonished to find so many of the enemy killed, so great a number wounded, and so few prisoners, there being not 800 of the latter. By the number of these, the extent of a victory had been formerly calculated. The dead bodies were rather a proof of the courage of the vanquished, than the evidence of a victory. If the rest retreated in such good order, proud, and so little discouraged, what signified the gain of a field of battle? In such extensive countries, would there ever be any want of ground for the Russians to fight on?

As for us, we had already too much, and a great deal more than we were able to retain. Could that be called conquering it? The long and straight furrow which we had traced with so much difficulty from Kowno, across sands and ashes; would it not close behind us, like that of a vessel on an immense ocean! A few peasants, badly armed, might easily efface all traces of it.

In fact they were about to carry off, in the rear of the army, our wounded and our marauders. Five hundred stragglers soon fell into their hands. It is true that some French soldiers, arrested in this manner, affected to join these Cossacks; they assisted them in making fresh captures, until finding themselves sufficiently numerous, with their new prisoners, they collected together suddenly and got rid of their unsuspecting enemies.

The emperor could not value his victory otherwise than by the dead. The ground was strewed to such a degree with Frenchmen, extended prostrate on the redoubts, that they appeared to belong more to them than to those who remained standing. There seemed to be more victors killed there than there were still living.

Amidst the crowd of corpses which we were obliged to march over in following Napoleon, the foot of a horse encountered a wounded man, and extorted from him a last sign of life or of suffering.

The emperor, hitherto equally silent with his victory, and whose heart felt oppressed by the sight of so many victims, gave an exclamation; he felt relieved by uttering cries of indignation, and lavishing the attentions of humanity on this unfortunate creature. To pacify him, somebody remarked that it was only a Russian, but he retorted warmly, "that after victory there are no enemies, but only men!" He then dispersed the officers of his suite, in order to succour the wounded, who were heard groaning in every direction.

Great numbers were found at the bottom of the ravines, into which the greater part of our men had been precipitated, and where many had dragged themselves, in order to be better protected from the enemy, and the violence of the storm. Some groaningly pronounced the name of their country or their mother; these were the youngest: the elder ones waited the approach of death, some with a tranquil, and others with a sardonic air, without deigning to implore for mercy, or to complain; others besought us to kill them outright: these unfortunate men were quickly passed by, having neither the useless pity to assist them, nor the cruel pity to put an end to their sufferings.

One of these, the most mutilated (one arm and his trunk being all that remained to him), appeared so animated, so full of hope, and even of gaiety, that an attempt was made to save him. In bearing him along, it was remarked that he complained of suffering in the limbs which he no longer possessed; this is a common case with mutilated persons, and seems to afford additional evidence that the soul remains entire, and that feeling belongs to it alone, and not to the body, which can no more feel than it can think.

The Russians were seen dragging themselves along to places where dead bodies were heaped together, and offered them a horrible retreat. It has been affirmed by several persons; that one of these poor fellows lived for several days in the carcase of a horse, which had been gutted by a shell, and the inside of which he gnawed.[3] Some were seen straightening their broken leg by tying the branch of a tree tightly against it, then supporting themselves with another branch, and walking in this manner to the next village. Not one of them uttered a groan. Perhaps, when far from their own homes, they looked less for compassion. But certainly they appeared to support pain with greater fortitude than the French; not that they suffered more courageously, but that they suffered less; for they have less feeling in body and mind, which arises from their being less civilized, and from their organs being hardened by the climate.

During this melancholy review, the emperor in vain sought to console himself with a cheering illusion, by having a second enumeration made of the few prisoners who remained, and collecting together some dismounted cannon; from seven to eight hundred prisoners, and twenty broken cannon, were all the trophies of this imperfect victory.

1. This is an error. The defeated Russians had no occasion to pass the Moskwa; it was not in their line of retreat.—*Ed.*

2. M. de Segur is said to have copied these assertions from the Petersburgh Gazette—*Ed.*

3. "M. de Seger," sarcastically remarks General Gorgaud, "ought to have told us what was the stature of the man or of the horse."—*Ed.*

CHAPTER XIII

ADVANCE TO MOJAISK

AT the same time, Murat kept pushing the Russian rear-guard as far as Mojaisk: the road which it uncovered on its retreat was perfectly clear, and without a single fragment of men, carriage, or dress. All their dead had been buried, for they have a religious respect for the dead.

At the sight of Mojaisk, Murat fancied himself already in possession of it, and sent to inform the emperor that he might sleep there. But the Russian rear-guard had taken a position outside the walls of the town, and the remains of their army were placed on a height beyond it. In this way they covered the Moscow and the Kalouga roads.

Perhaps Kutusoff hesitated which of these two roads to take, or was desirous of leaving us in uncertainty as to the one he had taken, as actually happened. Besides, the Russians felt it a point of honour to bivouac at only four leagues from the scene of our victory. That also allowed them time to disencumber the road behind them and clear away their fragments.

Their attitude was equally firm and imposing as before the battle, which we could not help admiring; but something of this was also attributable to the length of time we had taken to quit the field of Borodino, and to a deep ravine which was between them and our cavalry. Murat did not perceive this obstacle; but general Dery, one of his officers, guessed it. He went and reconnoitred the ground, close to the gates of the town, under the Russian bayonets.

But the king of Naples, quite as fiery as at the beginning of the campaign, or of his military life, made nothing of the obstacle; he summoned his cavalry, called to them furiously to advance, to charge and break through these battalions, gates, and walls! In vain did his aide-de-camp urge the impossibility of effecting his orders; he pointed out to him the army on the opposite heights, which commanded Mojaisk, and the ravine where the remains of our cavalry were about to be swallowed up. Murat, in greater fury than ever, insisted "that they must march, and if there was any obstacle, they would see it." He then made use of insulting phrases to urge them on, and his orders were about to be carried,—with some delay, nevertheless, for there was generally an understanding to retard their execution, in order to give him time to reflect, and to allow time for a counter-order, which had been anticipated, to arrive before any misfortune happened, which was not always the case, but was so this time. Murat was satisfied with wasting his cannon and powder on some drunken and straggling Cossacks by whom he was almost surrounded, and who attacked him with frightful howls.

This skirmish, however, was sufficiently serious to add to the losses of the preceding day, as general Belliard was wounded in it. This officer, who was a great loss to Murat, was employed in reconnoitring the left of the enemy's position. As it was approachable, the attack should have been made on that side, but Murat never thought of any thing but striking what was immediately before him.

The emperor arrived on the field of battle only at night-fall, escorted by a very feeble detachment. He advanced towards Mojaisk, at a still slower pace than the day before, and so completely absent, that he neither seemed to hear the noise of the engagement, nor that of the bullets which were whistling around him.

Some one stopped him, and pointed out to him the enemy's rear-guard between him and the town; and, on the heights behind, the fires of an army of 50,000 men. This sight was a proof of the incompleteness of his victory, and how little the enemy were discouraged; but he seemed quite insensible of it; he listened to the reports with a dejected and listless air, and returned to sleep at a village some little distance off, which was within reach of the enemy's fire.

The Russian autumn had triumphed over him; had it not been for that, perhaps the whole of Russia would have yielded to our arms on the plains of the Moskwa: its premature inclemency was a most seasonable assistance to their empire. It was on the 6th of September, the very day before the great battle! that a hurricane announced its fatal commencement. It struck Napoleon. Ever since the night of that day, it has been seen that a wearying fever had dried up his blood, and oppressed his spirits, and that he was quite overcome by it during the battle; the suffering he endured from this, added to another still more severe, for the five following days arrested his march, and bound up his genius.[1] This it was which preserved Kutusoff from total ruin at Borodino, and allowed him time to rally the remainder of his army, and withdraw it from our pursuit.

On the 9th of September we found Mojaisk still standing and open to us: but beyond it the enemy's rear-guard was on the heights which command it, and which their army had occupied the day before. Some of our troops entered the town for the purpose of passing through it in pursuit of the enemy, and others to plunder and find lodgings for themselves. They found neither inhabitants nor provisions, but merely dead bodies, which they were obliged to throw out of the windows, in order to get themselves under cover, and a number of dying soldiers, who were all collected into one spot. These last were so numerous, and had been so scattered about, that the Russians had not dared to set fire to the habitations; but their humanity, which was not always so scrupulous, gave way to the desire of firing on the first French they saw enter, which they did with shells: the consequence was, that this wooden town was soon set fire to, and a part of the unfortunate wounded whom they had abandoned were consumed in the flames.

While we were making attempts to save them, fifty voltigeurs of the 33d climbed the heights, of which the enemy's cavalry and artillery still occupied the summit.[2] The French army, which had halted under the walls of Mojaisk, was surprised at seeing this handful of men, scattered about on this uncovered declivity, teasing with their fire thousands of the enemy's cavalry. All at once what had been foreseen, happened; several of the enemy's squadrons put themselves in motion, and in an instant surrounded these bold fellows, who immediately formed, and kept facing and firing at them in all directions; but they were so few in the midst of a large plain, and the number of cavalry about them was so great, that they soon disappeared from our eyes. A general exclamation of sorrow burst from the whole of our lines. Every one of the soldiers with his neck stretched, and his eye fixed, followed the enemy's movements, and endeavoured to distinguish the fate of his companions in arms. Some were lamenting the distance they were at, and wishing to march; others mechanically loaded their muskets or crossed their bayonets with a threatening air, as if they had been near enough to assist them. Their looks were sometimes as animated as if they were fighting, and at other times as much distressed as if they had been beat. Others advised and encouraged them, forgetting that they were out of reach of hearing.

Several volleys of smoke, ascending from amidst the black mass of horses, prolonged the uncertainty. Some cried out, that it was our men firing, and still defending themselves, and that they were not yet beaten. In fact, a Russian commanding officer had just been killed by the officer commanding these *tirailleurs*. This was the way in which he replied to the summons to surrender. Our anxiety lasted some minutes longer, when all at once the army set up a cry of joy and admiration at seeing the Russian cavalry, intimidated at this bold resistance, separate in order to avoid their well-directed fire, disperse, and at last allow us to see once more this handful of brave fellows master of this extensive field of battle, of which it only occupied a few feet.

When the Russians saw that we were manœuvring seriously to attack them, they disappeared without leaving us any traces to follow them. This was the same they had done at Witepsk and Smolensk, and what was still more remarkable, the second day after their great disaster. At first there was some uncertainty whether to follow the road to Moscow or that to Kalouga, after which Murat and Mortier proceeded, at all hazards, towards Moscow.

They marched for two days, with no other food than horse-flesh and bruised wheat, without finding a single person or thing by which to discover the Russian army. That army, although its infantry only formed one confused mass, did not leave behind it a single fragment;

such was the national spirit and habit of obedience in it, collectively and singly, and so thoroughly unprovided were we with every kind of information, as well as resources, in this deserted and thoroughly hostile country.

The army of Italy was advancing at some leagues' distance on the left of the great road, and surprised some of the armed peasantry, who were not accustomed to fighting; but their master, with a dagger in his hand, rushed upon our soldiers like a mad man: he exclaimed that he had no longer a religion, empire, or country to defend, and that life was odious to him; they were willing, however, to leave him that, but as he attempted to kill the soldiers who surrounded him, pity yielded to anger, and his wish was gratified.

Near Krymskoié, on the 11th of September, the hostile army again made its appearance, firmly established in a strong position. It had returned to its plan of looking more to the ground, in its retreat, than to the enemy. The duke of Treviso at first satisfied Murat of the impossibility of attacking it; but the smell of powder soon intoxicated that monarch. He committed himself, and obliged Dufour, Mortier, and their infantry, to advance to his support. They formed the remains of Friant's division, and the young guard. On that occasion, 2000 men of that reserve which had been so unseasonably spared on the day of battle, were sacrificed without the least utility; and Mortier was so enraged, that he wrote to the emperor, that he would no longer obey Murat's orders. For it was by letter that the generals of the vanguard communicated with Napoleon. He remained for three days at Mojaisk, confined to his apartment, still consumed by a burning fever, overwhelmed with business, and worn out with anxiety. A violent cold had deprived him of his voice. Compelled to dictate to seven persons at once, and unable to make himself heard, he wrote on different papers the heads of his despatches. When any difficulty arose, he explained himself by signs.

There was a moment when Bessières enumerated to him all the generals who were wounded on the day of the battle. This fatal list affected him so poignantly, that by a violent effort he recovered his voice, and interrupted the marshal by the sudden exclamation, "Eight days at Moscow, and there will be an end to it!"

Meantime, although he had hitherto placed all his futurity in that capital, a victory so sanguinary and so little decisive lowered his hopes. His instructions to Berthier of the 11th of September, for marshal Victor, exhibited his distress: "The enemy attacked at the heart, no longer trifles with us at the extremities. Write to the duke of Belluno to direct all, infantry, cavalry, artillery, and isolated soldiers, to Smolensk, in order to proceed from thence to Moscow."

In the midst of these bodily and mental sufferings, which he carefully concealed from his army, Davoust obtained access to him; his object was to offer himself again, notwithstanding his wound, to take the command of the vanguard, promising that he would contrive to march night and day, reach the enemy, and compel him to fight, without squandering, as Murat did, the strength and lives of the soldiers. Napoleon only answered him by extolling in high terms the audacious and inexhaustible ardour of his brother-in-law.

He had just before heard, that the enemy's army had again been found: that it had not retired upon his right flank, towards Kalouga, as he had feared it would; that it was still retreating, and that his vanguard was already within two day's march of Moscow. That great name, and the great hopes which he attached to it, revived his strength, and on the 12th of September, he was sufficiently recovered to set out in a carriage, in order to join his vanguard.

1. In answer to this, general Gorgaud says, "When a great number of persons, such as his secretaries, physicians, and officers, are still alive; when these individuals know perfectly well that Napoleon was in his habitual state of health, and that he laboured with his wonted ardour, and tired several horses; when they can testify that it was not till the night of the 7th that, in consequence of the activity which he had displayed on the eve of and during the battle, he lost his voice how can M. de Segur venture to state things which so many witnesses are able to contradict?"—*Ed*.

2. The number of voltigeurs was about an hundred, and their gallant officer was a captain, of the name of Callier.—*Ed*.

ALSO AVAILABLE FROM NONSUCH PUBLISHING

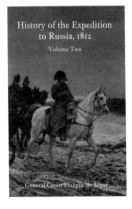

The second volume of de Segur's epic account of Napoleon's Russian campaign, this book starts with the triumphant entry into Moscow and ends with the ignominious return to France of the remnants of the Grand Army. This eye-witness account of the horrors of the French retreat provides a unique perspective on one of history's most famous military setbacks.

1 84588 022 6
£10
384 pages

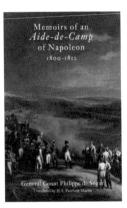

Memoirs traces the author's remarkable rise throught the ranks of the French army and records the key moments in Napoleon's campaign to gain mastery over Europe. As a staff officer he is able to provide a unique perspective on the military campaign, as well as more personal details of Napoleon's rule. Detailed and authoritative, this is a rivetting account of the events which tore Europe apart.

1 84588 005 6
£12
384 pages

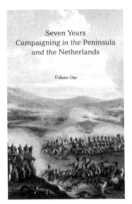

In August 1808 Richard D. Henegan landed in Portugal as part of the British army sent to repel the French invasion of the Iberian Peninsula. His account follows his own experiences as Military Commissary from his arrival in Portugal to the dramatic events of the Battle of Waterloo. This is a fascinating and vivid account of the highs and lows of life in Wellington's army. In two volumes.

1 84588 039 0/1 84588 040 4
£10
192 pages

For further information please see: www.nonsuch-publishing.com